Keywords in Composition Studies

Edited by

Paul Heilker
Virginia Tech

Peter Vandenberg
DePaul University, Chicago

Boynton/Cook Publishers
HEINEMANN
Portsmouth, NH

Boynton/Cook Publishers, Inc.
A subsidiary of Reed Elsevier Inc.
361 Hanover Street
Portsmouth, NH 03801-3912

Offices and agents throughout the world

Copyright © 1996 by Boynton/Cook Publishers

Library of Congress Cataloging-in-Publication Data

Keywords in composition studies / edited by Paul Heilker, Peter
  Vandenberg.
     p.   cm.
  Includes bibliographical references.
    1. English language—Rhetoric—Study and teaching—Terminology.
  2. English language—Composition and exercises—Terminology.
I. Heilker, Paul, 1962–   II. Vandenberg, Peter.
PE1404.K49 1996
808′ .042′014—dc20

                                                 96-20318
                                                  CIP

Editor: Peter Stillman
Cover design: Darci Mehall
Manufacturing: Louise Richardson

Printed in the United States of America on acid-free paper
99 98 97 96 DA 1 2 3 4 5 6

Keywords in
Composition Studies

for Gary Tate

Contents

Contents

Acknowledgments

The editors would like to thank those who helped support this project: the Faculty Research and Development Committee of the College of Liberal Arts and Sciences at DePaul University, who provided a Summer Research Grant, and the Loyola University of Chicago College of Arts and Sciences Endowment for the Humanities, which provided a Summer Research Stipend.

Early versions of two of the essays herein were published in *English Journal*, "deconstruction" (84.2, February 1995: 122–23) and "audience" (84.4, April 1995: 79–80).

Introduction

I don't know a subject in which study of the resourcefulness of its key terms doesn't amount to the subject, properly studied, itself.

—I. A. Richards, *Speculative Instruments*

This book represents the first systematic inquiry into composition studies' critical terms. In brief yet heavily researched essays, its contributors explore the development of and interconnections among more than fifty of the most consequential words in the field. In this sense, *Keywords in Composition Studies* is an introduction to the principal ideas and ideals of compositionists —a useful resource, a supplement to the field's books, essay collections, and journals.

Yet this book is not a dictionary or an encyclopedia; it does not attempt to capture the established knowledge of a unified discipline through its vocabulary, but explores the multiple layers of meaning inhabiting the words writing teachers and theorists have and continue to depend upon most. Each essay begins with the presumption that its central term is important precisely *because* its meaning is open, overdetermined. In this sense, *Keywords in Composition Studies* is something of an anti-resource; not a trustworthy expedient to conventional study, but a practical model for reading disciplinary discourse by attending to its dominant trope, definition.

* * *

In the Phaedrus, Socrates elevates to the divine the matter of definition—what he calls "perceiving and bringing together in one idea the scattered particulars": "[I]f I think any other man is able to see things that can naturally be collected into one[,] . . . him I follow after and walk in his footsteps as if he were a god" (135). According to Plato, the virtues of "clearness and consistency" are achieved by any discourse that begins with definition, the dialectician's first order of business.

At least since Nietzsche, however, what we call the "Modern Rhetorical Tradition" has been marked by a series of reminders that "clearness and consistency" are secured not by a sacred illumination, but through a process of forgetting, neglecting, denying. "[A] word becomes a concept," Nietzsche suggests,

> insofar as it simultaneously has to fit countless more or less similar cases[,] . . . cases which are never equal and [are] thus altogether unequal. . . . Just as it is certain that one leaf is never totally the same as another, so it is certain that the concept "leaf" is formed by arbitrarily discarding these individual differences and by forgetting the distinguishing aspects. (891)

Chaim Perelman suggests, moreover, that definitions are "mostly abbreviations," tropes that "aim, not at clarifying the meaning of an idea, but at stressing aspects that will produce [a] persuasive effect" (1090). And Derrida's deconstruction of the "metaphysics of presence," among other things, makes a casualty of definition. We might achieve confidence in "clarity and consistency" by blinding ourselves, by deferring the chain of differences or traces marked by every term. "[E]ach word," Julia Kristeva claims, "is an intersection of words where at least one other word can be read" (66). Or as Mikhail Bakhtin puts it, each "word is shaped in dialogic interaction with an alien word that is already in the object . . . [and by] the profound influence of the answering word that it anticipates" (279–280).

By the time I. A. Richards wrote *How to Read a Page* in 1942, more than twenty years of studying interpretation had brought him to the conclusion that "the more important a word is, and the more central and necessary its meanings are in our pictures of ourselves and the world, the more ambiguous and possibly deceiving the word will be" (23). Richards proposed that our most important words are always characterized by a "systematic ambiguity," the capability to "say very different, sometimes even contradictory, things to different readers" (22). Such words, Richards declared, "are the servants of too many interests to keep to single, clearly defined jobs" (23). To de-fine, then, is to con-fine, to prevent a word from reverberating.

In the academy, according to Foucault, disciplines act to restrict and constrain the context for meaning: "[t]he discipline is a principle of control over the production of discourse" (1161). Knowledge is produced within a discipline through determinate relationships among "a domain of objects, a set of methods, a corpus of propositions considered to be true, a play of rules and definitions" (1160). The reverberation of meaning is not halted by these principles, but adherents are "disciplined" not to attend to it. A primary receiver for rhetorical theory, composition studies maintains some of the "hard structures" of disciplinarity—editors, reviewers, and conference planners certainly function as principles of constraint—though it hardly requires the "complex and heavy requirements" for propositions that Foucault describes (1160). With relatively few disciplinary limitations in place to hinder its reach, a continuous acquisition of methods, theories, and agendas over the past twenty years has made composition studies the university's most dynamic, prolific, and fragmented post-disciplinary project.

While there is consensus about little else, there is a good deal of recognition that compositionists are identified by a "voraciously eclectic" borrowing (Schilb 1992, 34). Composition studies may not be a discipline in Foucault's sense of that term, but it is something of a "magnetic field," an institutional site delimited by its pull on and alteration of what originates elsewhere. Following Edward Said, John Schilb has used the phrase "traveling theory" to describe this process of acquisition and alteration. Yet as Schilb implies, theories are nothing if not rhetorical; theories don't "travel" so much as they are articulated and interpreted differently by folks standing in different contexts with different needs and desires. And as Schilb makes clear, theories cannot be independent from the words that constitute them. The composition and recomposition of "imported" theory is in large measure what goes on "in" composition studies as the field endlessly redefines itself, a process Patricia Harkin and Schilb have called *contending with words*.

It may well be that the field's most important accomplishment has been to determine that no single orientation, no single epistemology or methodology, is capable of answering all the questions that must be asked about writing and how it might be taught. Yet while many have valorized the post-disciplinary nature of composition studies, one recognizable result of fewer constraints has been a decreasing confidence in our ability to understand each other. A sampling of those who frequently publish in composition studies' professional journals revealed that 33 respondents claimed use of 48 different research methodologies and thirteen discrete pedagogical approaches (Fontaine). Our vocabulary lacks (a) discipline.

As the essays throughout this book demonstrate, our professional debates often turn on the use of specialized terms in conversations about writing that were developed in other contexts for other purposes. Yet what is perhaps more problematic is the vocabulary that we *do* have in common, a vocabulary largely made up of "imported" claims that have lost their accents yet are heavily infused with divergent significations. The terms we *do* share mark the contested intersections, the points of conflict among competing epistemological and methodological orientations "within" composition studies. These words are being hotly debated; they are claimed in differing ways and are thus charged with a variety of subtle (yet powerful), idiosyncratic, and often contradictory meanings. The struggle to establish control over which issues we will address and the manner(s) in which we will carry out our research is embodied in the rich, dense, unsettled meanings of the most important terms in the field.

Like Janice Lauer, who advocates "multimodality, a dialogic interaction among modes of inquiry" (421), we are hardly interested in constraining composition studies or its heavily contested vocabularies. What has been called the "shopping cart approach to scholarship," the practice of picking and choosing ingredients from every aisle of the academic supermarket, has resulted in a very rich and rewarding lexical stew. Like Richards, who considered his rhetorical cup half full, we too prefer to see the contested and unsettled nature of composition's terminology positively: " 'ambiguity' is a sinister-looking word and it is better to say 'resourcefulness' " (22).

In compiling his list of 103 overdetermined words, Richards decided that the most "resourceful" terms are those that "cover the ideas we can least avoid using" and those "we are forced to use in explaining other words" (22–23). While we reject the implication that ideas can be comfortably separated from the words that constitute them, the terms in this book certainly do become foregrounded when composition scholars debate what is most important to the field. And quite frequently these terms are used to define each other, sometimes masking and sometimes accentuating their shifting dispositions.

It is in this second sense that Richards anticipates Raymond Williams's widely influential *Keywords: A Vocabulary of Society and Culture.* In the introduction to that book, Williams writes that each term he includes "forced itself on my attention because the problems of its meanings seemed to me inextricably bound up with the problems it was being used to discuss" (15). Williams came to the realization that in order to analyze the issues and problems of culture and society he would have to analyze the problems and issues *inside the vocabulary*:

> new ways of seeing existing relationships appear in language in a variety of ways: in the invention of new terms[,] . . . in the adaptation and alteration (indeed at times reversal) of older terms[,] . . . in extension . . . or transfer. . . . [S]uch changes are not always simple or final. Earlier and later senses coexist, or become actual alternatives in which problems of contemporary belief and affiliation are contested. (22)

Unlike Richards's terms, all of which could be found in a single Sunday newspaper, or Williams's, which he proposes can be explained for a "general availability," the terms herein—and our approach to them—are consistently more specialized. While words like *reading, revision, authority*, and *error* all appear in general usage, the instability of their meanings in the professional discourse about writing instruction is far greater than in general discussion. And although the published research of composition scholars is decidedly eclectic in its borrowing, we have narrowed the scope of our inquiry to journals, books, monographs, dissertations, and conference papers that make rhetoric, composition, and writing pedagogy their foci.

While our goal is not to provide fixed, unitary meanings, but rather to elucidate the layers of contesting voices that co-inhabit the field's central terms, we and our contributors share the concern that our means and our ends in this endeavor may be inherently, irrevocably contradictory. The non-agonistic rhetorical stance we have tried to maintain in our efforts to "accurately" and "fairly" compose these essays can be seen as a self-deluding fiction. In the very process of rendering the fluid, actively contested meanings of these terms we risk reifying them. We hazard valorizing the meanings we include and devaluing those we did not discover (yet which exist "out there" nonetheless).

Moreover, we find ourselves bound up in composition studies' post-disciplinary dilemma: While we intend to represent the discourse of composition studies as ragged and unfinished, the book as a whole risks mapping the field as a flat and domesticated landscape. In declaring "composition studies" our domain of inquiry and the locus of our readership, we inevitably reinforce disciplinary boundaries in the process of showing how they are perforated. By attending to "important" books and articles, we contribute to their possible canonization, while those we do not cite may be further marginalized. In short, by exploring the tangles of our disciplinary discourse, we untangle them to some degree; by attempting to demonstrate the impossibility of containing the meanings of our keywords, we may contain them.

In this book we have nonetheless attempted to model—to embody and enact—a way of reading our professional discourse. Each essay is a contextualized exploration, an inquiry into ways its keyword has been deployed in the institutional arrangement of composition studies. The contributors to this volume have not presumed to define these terms to deaden debate, much less to diminish their complexity. Each essay attempts to demonstrate the shifting and conflicted relationship between meaning and cultural/disciplinary values, to trace the assimilation and omission of different strands of meaning in the historical evolution of a term (however discontinuous and jarring that evolution may be) through an examination of the texts that constitute our field.

The roster of keywords included here is, of course, highly selective, but not capriciously so. As we did, readers will think of countless other terms that might have been included given more space. Yet each essay considers a term that is both in common use in composition studies—a part of the field's general parlance—yet highly contested—a focal point or nexus of several significant debates. We have attempted here to select terms which are both "fundamental" to the field's vocabulary (like *essay*, *invention*, and *students*) and of current interest (like *academic discourse*, *epistemology*, and *intertextuality*).

Take, as an extended example, the word *theory*, a keyword of the first order. Sometimes writers overtly trace alternatives as they stipulate a definition. John Warnock, for instance, notes that

> the word theory . . . may carry a pejorative sense—"mere theory"—or a restricted sense, something like "empirically verified predictive explanation of the behavior of phenomena". . . . The word theory comes from the Greek *thea*, meaning "a viewing". . . . Etymologically, then, the word implies a frame, a text, and a context, a completed act of relating parts to parts and parts to wholes. . . . By theory, I mean something like "structure of meaningful relationships" or "that abstract conception of the whole by which the relation of part to part and part to whole may be well understood." (17)

In like manner, noting that he had previously "used the terms theory and philosophy . . . interchangeably to refer to any general propositions about writing and its teaching," Richard Fulkerson stipulates that

> a *full* "theory" of composition would include . . . a commitment about what constitutes good writing . . . a conception of how writers go about creating texts . . . some perspective about classroom procedures and curricular designs . . . [and] an epistemology. (410–411, emphasis ours).

As Fulkerson demonstrates, the instability of a keyword is often established by declaring it an umbrella term for a number of related concepts. In such cases, definition is yoked to division, the process of "dividing things by classes, . . . not trying to break any part after the manner of a bad carver" (Plato 135). Joseph Harris, for example, considers theory as "constative statement" (theory as knowledge) and "performative act" (theory as persuasion). "We can ask," Harris suggests, "not only what a theory has to say about the nature of composing or interpreting but also what changes it would have us make in our work as teachers and intellectuals" (142–143). Lester Faigley separates "postmodern theory" from "critical theory" and proposes that the division can be mediated by "nonessentialist feminism, which draws from both bodies of theory" (213). John Clifford and Schilb however, while declaring themselves less than "secure" with *critical theory*, suggest that the term encompasses "postmodernism" and imply a distinction between it and "writing theory" (1).

Sometimes a keyword's contested meanings are explicitly critiqued. Schilb (1991), for instance, writes that theory "bears contradictory meanings and thus proves unstable" (91). "In one sense of the word," he says, " 'theory' provides us with firm, objective, universal, bedrock principles for our 'practice.' In another sense, though, 'theory' relentlessly unsettles our claims to absolute knowledge." Likewise, he says, while scholars "invoke 'theory' as they seek to provide [our] discipline with a stronger, clearer intellectual framework . . . [which] will enable us to coalesce as a field," they do so by citing "theory" which "challenges the notion of disciplinary borders . . . [and] expose[s] the arbitrariness of topological divisions in the first place" (92). Sometimes keywords are consciously compared and contrasted with other terms in an attempt to understand their meanings. Charles I. Schuster, for instance, notes that "[t]he opposite of 'theory' is not 'practice' but 'thoughtlessness' or even 'mindlessness.' Theory is not opposed to practice; it is opposed to muddled thought, to confusion. . . . [T]heory and practice are inseparable, indivisible" (42).

But far more often, the meanings of a keyword are implicit and must be "read" from the contexts surrounding its usages, particularly when it functions tropologically, as a metaphor or a metonym for much larger issues. *Meaning*, then, quickly takes on an expansive sense—what the keyword *means* to our field's disciplinary and institutional past, present, and future; what it *means* to our professional, intellectual, and emotional lives; what it *means* to our (changing) values. In these ways, the contestations over meaning can become more complex, more political, and more personal. Steven Mailloux, for instance, describes theory positively, as "a growing empirical and rhetorical body of knowledge that all serious teachers of composition must master," as the means by which "composition teachers are becoming specialists within the English Department (not just second-class citizens)" (271). Howard B. Tinberg suggests, however, that "[t]he rush toward theory in the field might just as well be described as a rush to get out of the classroom" (37). Stanley Fish discusses "theory hope—the promise that theory seems to offer" composition instructors (342), the promise of "a better set of methods for operating in the world" (346), while Schuster notes that since "practice" seems to be "a foundational principle of our discipline, . . . theory is suspect—and conceivably dangerous. . . . [I]t invites confusion, possibly paralysis" (35). Whereas Patricia Bizzell contends that "an overarching theory" could heal the long-standing and often bitter rift between literature and composition (175), Sandra Stotsky argues that "borrowed" theories "may pose unresolvable problems . . . and serve as unintended conceptual barriers to important new research in the field" (37).

As the expression goes, "We're just getting started here." The impossibility of "covering" the range of meanings related to a keyword will be apparent in every essay in the same way that our limited list of terms represents the impossibility of gathering *all* of composition's keywords together in a single book. The essays in this volume are meant to be suggestive, indicative of a range of terms and meanings too expansive to be corralled into our very small discursive pens. The study of our field's evolving vocabulary must be a fluid project, one carried out not within this book but with it as we continue composing composition studies.

Paul Heilker

Peter Vandenberg

Works Cited

Bakhtin, Mikhail. 1981. "Discourse in the Novel." *The Dialogic Imagination.* Edited by Michael Holquist. Translated by Caryl Emerson and Michael Holquist. Austin: University of Texas Press. 259–422.

Bizzell, Patricia. 1986. "On the Possibility of a Unified Theory of Composition and Literature." *Rhetoric Review* 4: 174–179.

Bizzell, Patricia, and Bruce Herzberg, eds. 1990. *The Rhetorical Tradition: Readings from Classical Times to the Present.* Boston: Bedford.

Clifford, John, and John Schilb, eds. 1994. *Writing Theory and Critical Theory.* New York: MLA.

Faigley, Lester. 1994. "Street Fights over the Impossibility of Theory: A Report of a Seminar." Clifford and Schilb, 212–235.

Fish, Stanley. 1989. "Anti-Foundationalism, Theory Hope, and the Teaching of Composition." *Doing What Comes Naturally: Change, Rhetoric, and the Practice of Theory in Literary and Legal Studies.* Durham: Duke University Press. 342–355.

Fontaine, Sheryl I. 1992. "The Phenomenology of Editorial Review: The Writer's Perspective." Conference Paper. Conference on College Composition and Communication. Cincinnati, OH.

Foucault, Michel. 1990. "The Order of Discourse." Trans. Ian McLeod. In Bizzell and Herzberg, 1154–1164.

Fulkerson, Richard. 1990. "Composition Theory in the Eighties: Axiological Consensus and Paradigmatic Diversity." *College Composition and Communication* 41: 409–429.

Harkin, Patricia, and John Schilb, eds. 1991. *Contending with Words: Composition and Rhetoric in a Postmodern Age.* New York: MLA.

Harris, Joseph. 1994. "The Rhetoric of Theory." Clifford and Schilb, 141–147.

Kristeva, Julia. 1980. *Desire in Language: A Semiotic Approach to Literature and Art.* Ed. Leon S. Roudiez. Trans. Thomas Gora, Alice Jardine, and Leon S. Roudiez. New York: Columbia University Press.

Lauer, Janice M. 1992. "A Note to *JAC* Readers." *Journal of Advanced Composition* 12: 421–422.

Mailloux, Steven. 1978. "Literary Criticism and Composition Theory." *College Composition and Communication* 29: 267–271.

Nietzsche, Friedrich. 1990. "On Truth and Lies in a Nonmoral Sense." Trans. Daniel Breazeale. In Bizzell and Herzberg, 888–896.

Perelman, Chaim. 1990. "The New Rhetoric: A Theory of Practical Reasoning." Trans. E. Griffin-Collart and O. Bird. In Bizzell and Herzberg, 1077–1103.

Plato. 1990. *Phaedrus.* Trans. H. N. Fowler. In Bizzell and Herzberg, 113–143.

Schilb, John. 1991. "What's at Stake in the Conflict between 'Theory' and 'Practice' in Composition." *Rhetoric Review* 10: 91–97.

———. 1992. " 'Traveling Theory' and the Defining of New Rhetorics." *Rhetoric Review* 11: 34–48.

Richards, I. A. 1994. "From *How to Read A Page.*" *Professing the New Rhetorics.* Ed. Theresa Enos and Stuart C. Brown. Englewood Cliffs, NJ: Blair. 16–37.

———. 1994. "From *Speculative Instruments.*" *Professing the New Rhetorics.* Ed. Theresa Enos and Stuart C. Brown. Englewood Cliffs, NJ: Blair. 38–39.

Schuster, Charles I. 1991. "Theory and Practice." *An Introduction to Composition Studies.* Ed. Erika Lindemann and Gary Tate. New York: Oxford University Press. 33–48.

Stotsky, Sandra. 1990. "On Planning and Writing Plans—Or Beware of Borrowed Theories!" *College Composition and Communication* 41: 37–57.

Tinberg, Howard B. 1991. " 'An Enlargement of Observation': More on Theory Building in the Composition Classroom." *College Composition and Communication* 42: 36–44.

Warnock, John. 1976. "Who's Afraid of Theory?" *College Composition and Communication* 27: 16–20.

Williams, Raymond. 1983. *Keywords: A Vocabulary of Culture and Society.* Revised Edition. New York: Oxford.

academic discourse

The evolution of the term *academic discourse* in composition studies reflects the field's deepening awareness of variation in language use in professional communities and society generally. In the mid-to-late 1970s, usage of the term expanded, mainly through the work of Mina Shaughnessy, who used it to explicate cultural and linguistic conventions implicit in college teachers' expectations for student writing. Shaughnessy also employed the term to explain the difficulties underprepared student writers faced in their efforts "to approximate the high or formal style of academia" (1977a, 197) and to show how college writing often demanded tactics of disputation that posed special difficulties for students with non-mainstream cultural backgrounds. Her appreciation of these difficulties helped inscribe the term in controversies about the cultural relativity of language standards, such as those sparked by sociolinguistic work showing the "logic of non-standard English" (Labov) and NCTE's 1974 declaration endorsing "students' right to their own language."

In the late 1970s, Shaughnessy's goal of providing "a precise taxonomy of . . . academic vocabulary" for students was pursued by some compositionists who took a "close look at academic discourse" (Shaughnessy 1977b, 320). Patricia Bizzell argued that Shaughnessy's sense of academic discourse includes not merely surface features of language, but also "such ethical qualities as 'formal courtesy' and 'shrewd assessments of what constitutes adequate proof' " (1978, 355). Bizzell identified "the ethos of academic discourse" by considering the relationship between knowledge, language, and community (1978, 354–355; 1979). She defined academic discourse first and foremost by its rational qualities, contrasting "the 'rituals' of academic discourse" with students' "rhetorical postures" such as "the bald assertion of an opinion" and the assumption that "rational debate cannot resolve controversial problems," and suggested that such discourse comprises a shared "compendium of [cultural] knowledge that anyone should possess" (1978, 353–354). In short, academic discourse is the language of "a particular cultural group who shares this 'common stock' of knowledge" and a language

9

that offers the academic community "better opportunities for rational criticism of the here and now that we share with the larger community" (1978, 354; 1979, 770–771).

Expanding usage of the term was fueled by the writing-across-the-curriculum movement and the research on disciplinary language practices WAC has enabled. Indeed, since the early 1980s, the term has become a scene of increasing conflict over both what academic discourse *is* and what role specialized disciplinary languages should play in writing instruction. Bizzell argued that "academic discourse *constitutes* the academic community" (1982, 197). In making this case, she supported Elaine Maimon's view that academic genres "are defined by various scholarly communities to embody conventions particular to their disciplines" and constitute the academic discourse community (1983, 118; see also 111–113). Bizzell used the term to fault the "individualistic" biases of "authentic voice" pedagogies (such as Elbow's and Macrorie's) and of the then "current emphasis on writing as a cognitive process" (1982, 194–195). While Bizzell commended Maimon's conception of academic discourse, particularly as it is embodied in her influential textbook *Writing in the Arts and Sciences* (1982, passim), Bizzell's sense of academic discourse entailed a self-reflective critical component not evident in Maimon's representation of academic genres. For instance, Bizzell cautioned that "we need to reexamine the knowledge the academy disestablishes as well as that which it endorses" (1982, 206). However, despite their differences, Maimon and Bizzell perceived academic discourse as the requisite for becoming a member of the academic community, and therefore shared the goal of making the composition course "an introduction to composing academic discourse in the arts and sciences" (Maimon 1983, 117, 120–121; see also 1981; Bizzell 1982, 197). In contrast to this perspective, some compositionists by the late 1980s used this term pejoratively. Donald C. Stewart called academic discourse a "disgrace . . . whose purpose is to impede genuine communication with every resource the writer can muster" (68). Other critics used the term to describe professional elitism implicit in the unnecessary use of specialized language (Elbow 145–147) or the fragmented, alienating quality of much specialized knowledge (Spellmeyer 111, 115, 274).

As the 1980s progressed, a number of compositionists articulated a more heterogeneous, mutable conception of academic discourse and a more problematic sense of whatever "community" it might constitute. For instance, in his influential essay "Inventing the University," David Bartholomae argued that

> [e]very time a student sits down to write for us, he has to invent the university for the occasion. . . . The student has to learn to speak our language, . . . to try on the peculiar ways of knowing, . . . reporting, . . . and arguing that define the discourse of our community. Or perhaps I should say the *various* discourses of our community. (134)

Learning the " 'distinctive register' of academic discourse," the student must "mimic" or "appropriate (or be appropriated by) a specialized discourse" (162, 135). The shifts between singular and plural nouns in Bartholomae's essay—from "our language" to "peculiar ways" to "the discourse" to "the *various* discourses of our community"—are revealing. Bartholomae suggests the possibility of conflict within and between the "specialized codes" (156) of disciplines, but also invokes the unanalyzed unity of "our language" and "our community." Indeed, in a 1989 critique of representations of the "academic discourse community," Joseph Harris consolidates an emerging awareness that many influential "social" views of writing in the 1980s tended to "invoke the idea of community in ways at once sweeping and vague: positing discursive utopias . . . yet failing to state the operating rules or boundaries," consequently suggesting a "'normal discourse' in the university" free from "conflict or change" (12). In opposition to social perspectives that present "academic discourse as coherent and well-defined," Harris contends that we should consider "it as polyglot, as a sort of space in which competing beliefs intersect with and confront one another" (20). In 1990, Bizzell offered a similar sense of heterogeneity, contention, and mutability in her revised thinking on the "academic discourse problem," which she argued cannot be addressed simply by "let[ting] the freshman writing class inculcate the requisite knowledge . . . to participate in the academic discursive community," because that community "is not such a stable entity . . . is more unstable than this—more fraught with contradiction, more polyvocal" (258; see also 1992, 235).

Perhaps because of such skepticism about the unity and stability of academic discourse in general, competing terms such as "disciplinary discourse" (Bazerman 62, 66, 68), "discipline-specific discourse conventions" (Jones and Comprone 66) and "disciplinary style" (Linton *et al.* 64, 65, 73) have become more common in commentary concerning the role of specialized language in writing instruction. Some researchers follow older arguments in claiming that composition programs in English should explicitly teach "disciplinary genres" and "disciplinary style" even if all that is possible is to "introduce students to formal differences in the writing characteristic of different disciplines" or "[n]oticing the surface features of a disciplinary genre" (Linton *et al.* 64–65). By contrast, other researchers eschew attempts to "establish boundaries around [the] knowledge bases and discourse conventions [of disciplines]," instead emphasizing how "overlapping spheres of academic discourse" interact with the multiple literacies students bring with them to the university (Chiseri-Strater 164–165). In a similar vein, Cinthia Gannett has argued that it is inadequate simply to dichotomize between the "language habits and conventions of . . . marginal students and those of the university community." Rather, "a central task of social constructionist work is to explore the convergences, coalitions, and tensions . . . of discursive networks (some deriving from disciplines, others from particular methodologies, such as deconstruction, or from interdisciplinary enterprises, such as

feminism) which collectively compose the academic discourse 'community.' "
Such work, Gannett contends, cannot afford to neglect the "critical connections" between such discursive networks and "the host of other discursive
communities to which people belong" (8).

Obviously, the "academic discourse problem" remains far from resolved.
Indeed, it seems likely that political differences over the basic purposes of
language teaching and research will continue to unsettle both normative and
descriptive definitions of academic discourse for the foreseeable future.

Daniel Mahala
University of Missouri-Kansas City
Jody Swilky
Drake University

Works Cited

Bazerman, Charles. 1992. "From Cultural Criticism to Disciplinary Participation:
Living with Powerful Words." *Writing, Teaching and Learning in the Disciplines.*
Ed. Anne Herrington and Charles Moran. New York: MLA. 61–68.

Bartholomae, David. 1985. "Inventing the University." *When a Writer Can't Write:
Studies in Writer's Block and Other Composing Process Problems.* Ed. Mike
Rose. New York: Guilford. 134–165.

Bizzell, Patricia. 1978. "The Ethos of Academic Discourse." *College Composition
and Communication* 29: 351–355.

———. 1979. "Thomas Kuhn, Scientism, and English Studies." *College English* 40:
764–771.

———. 1982. "College Composition: Initiation into the Academic Discourse Community." *Curriculum Inquiry* 12: 191–207.

———. 1990. "Beyond Anti-Foundationalism to Rhetorical Authority: Problems
Defining 'Cultural Literacy.' " *College English* 52: 661–675.

———. 1992. *Academic Discourse and Critical Consciousness.* Pittsburgh: University of Pittsburgh Press.

Chiseri-Strater, Elizabeth. 1991. *Academic Literacies: The Public and Private Discourse of University Students.* Portsmouth: Boynton/Cook.

Elbow, Peter. 1991. "Reflections on Academic Discourse: How It Relates to Freshmen
and Colleagues." *College English* 53: 135–155.

Gannett, Cinthia. 1992. *Gender and the Journal: Diaries and Academic Discourse.*
Albany: State University of New York Press.

Harris, Joseph. 1989. "The Idea of Community in the Study of Writing." *College
Composition and Communication* 40: 11–22.

Jones, Robert, and Joseph J. Comprone. 1993. "Where Do We Go Next in Writing
across the Curriculum?" *College Composition and Communication* 44: 59–67.

Labov, William. 1972. "The Logic of Nonstandard English." *Language in the Inner
City.* Philadelphia, University of Pennsylvania Press: 201–240.

Linton, Patricia, Robert Madigan, and Susan Johnson. 1994. "Introducing Students to Disciplinary Genres: The Role of the General Composition Course." *Language and Learning across the Disciplines* 1.2: 63–78.

Maimon, Elaine. 1981. *Instructor's Manual: Writing in the Arts and Sciences.* Cambridge, MA: Winthrop.

———. 1983. "Maps and Genres." *Composition and Literature: Bridging the Gap.* Ed. Winifred Bryan Horner. Chicago: University of Chicago Press. 110–125.

Shaughnessy, Mina. 1977a. *Errors and Expectations: A Guide for the Teacher of Basic Writing.* New York: Oxford University Press.

———. 1977b. "Some Needed Research on Writing." *College Composition and Communication* 28: 317–320.

Spellmeyer, Kurt. 1993. *Common Ground: Dialogue, Understanding, and the Teaching of Composition.* Englewood Cliffs: Prentice Hall.

Stewart, Donald C. 1988. "Collaborative Learning and Composition: Boon or Bane?" *Rhetoric Review* 7: 58–83.

"Students' Right to Their Own Language." 1974. *College Composition and Communication* 25: 1–32.

argument

While many terms in the lexicon of composition studies are clearly meta-phors, *argument* functions as a metonym. Traditionally, what has been packed into this term are the rational, logical, non-emotional reasoning processes involved in persuasive writing.

Both the traditional definition of argument and contentions over its meaning tend to emerge from its classical sources. Achieving a kind of intellectual cache from its roots in Western philosophy, particularly in Aris-totle, argument is often associated with an essentially agonistic strategy of persuasion. In this view, an argument is seen as something that involves a proponent, armed with a thesis, and an opponent. The argument is, thus, an intellectual skirmish that can be "won" when the arguer foresees objections and counters them with evidence or proofs that are deemed more logical than the opponent's. A typical example of the traditional treatment of argument is Richard A. Katula and Richard W. Roth's 1980 article, "A Stock Issues Approach to Writing Arguments." Citing Aristotle as their theoretical forbear, Katula and Roth define argument as "not simply that emotionally based, contentious rhetoric . . . but that mode of communication which is intended to change attitudes and provide acceptable, logical bases for belief and action" (183).

Finding an Aristotelian definition of *argument* requires considerable synthesis, since there is no single primary source for his theory. Aristotle deals with argument in all six treatises in the *Organon*. Most compositionists working with argument draw on two works: the *Prior Analytics*, where Aristotle works out his theory of perfect inference via the syllogism and initially defines an *enthymeme* as "a syllogism from probabilities and signs" (2.27); and the *Rhetoric*, which extends the theory of the enthymeme and the example, the rhetorical tools of logical deduction and induction introduced in the *Analytics*. The second sentence of the *Rhetoric* links it to the dialectic of the *Analytics* and establishes the agonistic nature of Aristotelian argument: All people, Aristotle writes, use both dialectic and rhetoric, the former "to test and maintain an argument," and the latter "to defend themselves and attack" (1.1; 1354a). It is interesting to note how composition scholars have tried to distance themselves from this agonistic stance. For example, John Gage, in an argument writing textbook that relies heavily on Aristotelian theory, tells students that "I have treated argument here as a matter of finding and presenting the best possible reasons you can for your reader's understanding and assent, and not as a matter of trying to 'win' your case by overpowering the 'opposition' " (vii–viii).

It is not only the agonistic nature of Aristotelian argument that has caused composition scholars to bristle. If they consult the *Analytics*, they find argument as a complicated system of syllogizing that seems difficult to teach and disconnected from actual arguments in real situations. In his 1964 book, *The Uses of Argument*, Stephen Toulmin questions the Aristotelian "micro-structure of arguments" (96) and develops a new pattern for analyzing arguments based on jurisprudence. In lieu of the Aristotelian method of beginning with premises and syllogizing about the conclusions that must follow from them, Toulmin begins by examining the assertion, the claim, an arguer makes. Confronted with a claim, he writes, "we can challenge the assertion, and demand to have our attention drawn to the grounds (backing, data, facts, evidence, considerations, features) on which the merits of the assertion are to depend. We can, that is, demand an argument" (11). Though some teachers have simplified it for pedagogy (see Kneupper), Toulmin's model does not really alter the complexity of syllogizing: It is essentially an enthymeme that moves from conclusion to premises, rather than vice versa, and, according to James Stratman, composition teachers report that students have difficulties plugging the material from "real world" arguments into the model.

It almost seems as though compositionists could overlook the complexity of Aristotelian (or Toulminian) argument if it didn't appear so focused on shutting off dialogue. That feature, however, has motivated two schools of contention over argument. Richard Young, Alton Becker, and Kenneth Pike initiated the first of these in their 1970 textbook, *Rhetoric: Discovery and Change*, introducing "Rogerian argument" to composition studies. Young, Becker, and Pike see "traditional argument" as most commonly "dyadic": "the writer . . . addresses his message directly to the audience he seeks to change" (273). Young, Becker, and Pike find traditional argument "ineffective in those dyadic situations that involve strong values and beliefs," and propose "an effective alternative to traditional argument" (274) suggested by the psychotherapist Carl Rogers. According to Young, Becker, and Pike, "[t]he writer who uses the Rogerian strategy attempts to do three things: (1) to convey to the reader that he is understood, (2) to delineate the area within which he believes the reader's position to be valid, and (3) to induce him to believe that he and the writer share similar moral qualities (honesty, integrity, and good will) and aspirations (the desire to discover a mutually acceptable situation)" (275). Doug Brent writes in a retrospective on Rogerian argument that Young, Becker, and Pike's non-agonistic strategy was one of several attempts, coming at the height of the Cold War, redefining argument as negotiation, not simply change: "conflict resolution [was] not just an ideal but a matter of human survival" (453).

Rogerian argument has not proved an unobjectionable alternative to Aristotelianism. In 1990, Phyllis Lassner reported that women students were angered by the presumption, inherent in Rogerianism, that the arguer must remain self-effacing and tentative with her audience. Lassner's concerns fit within a body of feminist composition theory that critiques the agonistic, monologic nature of argument, either traditional or Rogerian. In 1978, Sheila Ortiz Taylor contended that, given the inherent "politeness" of "women's language, . . . the aims and tactics of the argumentative edge constitute a double-bind" (385–387) for women being taught argumentative writing. Taylor sees traditional argument embodied in Sheridan Baker's directive in the third edition of *The Practical Stylist*: "The best thesis is a kind of affront to somebody" (3). Taylor writes, "[t]aught by society to defer and to qualify or avoid criticism, women are required by an institution, an agent of society at large, to assert, to oppose, compete, persist, and finally to compel agreement" (387). The most thorough feminist critique of argument theory and a suggestion of a feminist alternative to Aristotelianism are in Catherine Lamb's 1991 essay, "Beyond Argument in Feminist Composition." Detailing strategies of "mediation" and "negotiation," Lamb offers "several features of a feminist alternative to monologic argument": "Knowledge is cooperatively and collaboratively constructed"; "[t]he 'attentive love' of maternal thinking is present to at least some degree"; "[t]he writing which results is likely to emphasize process"; and "power is experienced as mutually enabling" (21).

David A. Jolliffe
DePaul University, Chicago

Works Cited

Aristotle. 1989. *Prior Analytics.* Trans. Robin Smith. Indianapolis: Hackett.

——. 1991. *On Rhetoric: A Theory of Civic Discourse.* Trans. George A. Kennedy. New York: Oxford University Press.

Baker, Sheridan. 1973. *The Practical Stylist.* 3rd edition. New York: Crowell.

Brent, Doug. 1991. "Young, Becker, and Pike's 'Rogerian' Rhetoric: A Twenty-Year Reassessment." *College English* 53: 452–466.

Gage, John T. 1991. *The Shape of Reason: Argumentative Writing in College.* 2nd edition. New York: Macmillan.

Katula, Richard A., and Richard W. Roth. 1980. "A Stock Issues Approach to Writing Arguments." *College Composition and Communication* 31: 183–196.

Kneupper, Charles. 1978. "Teaching Argument: The Toulmin Model." *College Composition and Communication* 29: 237–241.

Lamb, Catherine E. 1991. "Beyond Argument in Feminist Composition." *College Composition and Communication* 42: 11–24.

Lassner, Phyllis. 1990. "Feminist Responses to Rogerian Argument." *Rhetoric Review* 8: 220–232.

Stratman, James F. 1982. "Teaching Written Argument: The Significance of Toulmin's Layout for Sentence-Combining." *College English* 44: 718–733.

Taylor, Sheila Ortiz. 1978. "Women in a Double-Bind: Hazards of the Argumentative Edge." *College Composition and Communication* 29: 385–389.

Toulmin, Stephen E. 1964. *The Uses of Argument.* Cambridge: Cambridge University Press.

Young, Richard E., Alton L. Becker, and Kenneth L. Pike. 1970. *Rhetoric: Discovery and Change.* New York: Harcourt, Brace, and World.

audience

In a 1990 article published in *College Composition and Communication*, Richard Fulkerson declares that composition studies has achieved something of a "consensus on what constitutes good writing" (414). According to Fulkerson, the disciplinary attention given over to audience and audience analysis in writing textbooks and books about the teaching of writing is one reflection of the field's tacit agreement with "a rhetorical approach in which readers and their responses are the final criteria of effectiveness" (415). Yet as Fulkerson allows, consensus on the importance of audience to effective composing does not constitute agreement of any sort about what the term might mean. James Porter argues that *audience* is "especially problematic when we assume that it has a fixed meaning or if we ourselves fix the meaning in the way we teach or write about audience" (6).

Concern with audience can be connected to the recovery of classical rhetoric and its contemporary application to writing instruction (see Ede). In Book II of the *Rhetoric*, Aristotle declares that knowledge of the character of an audience can be understood by analysis of its wealth, power, and relative youth. Armed with an "account of types of character," a speaker can choose persuasive strategies that will correspond with "emotions and moral qualities of each character type" (121–122). Lisa Ede and Andrea Lunsford have used the term "audience addressed" to refer to such positions that "emphasize the concrete reality of the writer's audience" and assume that "knowledge of this audience's attitudes, beliefs, and expectations is . . . essential" (156). Russell Long concludes that such positions reduce students' conceptualizing of audience to "noxious stereotyping" that teachers of composition "in any other context . . . fight diligently against" (223).

The usefulness of conceptions of "real" audience has been a matter of question in the field of Speech Communication for several decades. As early as 1966, Otto Clevenger asserted that every audience is distinguished by plurality, that "each individual behaves as he does because of his prior experience coupled with the stimuli operating upon him at the moment, including the context as he perceives it. . . . [E]xperiences, contexts, and stimuli . . . are infinitely variable" (9–10). Refiguring audience as an active plurality necessitates a shift from audience analysis to audience construction. Edwin Black asserts that any given discourse exerts "the pull of an ideology"; those who attend it "look to the discourse . . . for cues that tell them how they are to view the world" (113).

Whether one conceives of "a real audience (not a teacher), who actually needs to know something" (Flower and Hayes 45) or imagines audience to be a "characterized reader" (Ross), audience is often framed as "an essential part of the writing process" (Berkenkotter 396). Just the same, some scholars have figured audience as a "force" that is "powerfully inhibiting" and ought to be ignored in the earliest stages of process (Elbow 51). According to Cherryl Armstrong, "writers may not disregard their audience as much as be tyrannized by it" (86). Armstrong proposes that a student writer develop a dual "audience awareness" in which "the writer conceives of the audience as a teacher in the role of examiner" and "herself in the role of reader" (87).

Refusing the importance of a "real" audience in most writing situations, Long argues that audience belongs more properly under the purview of rhetorical invention:

> a writer's choice of alternatives determines his audience; that is, his decisions create a very specific reader who exists only for the duration of the reading experience. Rather than beginning with the traditional question, "who is my audience?", we now begin with, "who do I want my audience to be?". . . . What attitudes, ideas, actions are to be encouraged? (225)

Noting that texts are often valued because they violate expectations and thereby create change, Peter Vandenberg argues that to confine student writers to the production of "transactional" texts denies students a conception of audience as heuristic.

In composition studies, this conception of "audience created"—what Ede and Lunsford call "audience invoked"—often references Walter Ong. He contends that a successful writer develops the ability to "fictionalize in his imagination an audience he has learned to know not from daily life but from earlier writers who were fictionalizing in their imagination audiences they had learned . . . and so on" (11). For Ong, a writer must first "construct in his imagination, clearly or vaguely, an audience cast in some sort of role—entertainment seekers, reflective sharers of experience and so on" (12). Barry Kroll argues that such a conception of audience may be "intimately connected with (and perhaps even indistinguishable from) a sense of genre and convention . . . gained not from social interaction but from broad exposure to various forms of written discourse" (182).

Few, if any, in composition appear to equate audience entirely with textuality, however. Laurie J. Anderson, for example, suggests that "audience" is an incomplete concept, dependent on an understanding of "conventional register . . . an accepted, imposed, or expected way of writing that is shared by both writer and reader" (112). Following the work of Douglas Park—"[t]o identify an audience means identifying a situation" (486)—recent work on audience appears to detail a symbiotic construction of writer, audience, and text. For Park, the basic issue of audience is one of "student writers learning to see themselves as social beings in a social situation" (488). Suggesting that audience is "a vital force of beliefs, attitudes, knowledge, existing in writing, in pre-texts that the willing writer can consult," Porter argues for a "sophistic notion of audience" in which a "writer does not 'analyze' an audience so much as become one with it" (114–115).

The sheer bulk of research on audience in composition studies appears to have a dual effect; it has widened the range of meanings that the term can be said to cover as it necessitates continued reference to the term. Like literacy or feminism, one cannot usefully deploy the term *audience* without qualification, illustration, or elaboration, nor can one introduce related or oppositional terms without reference to it. As Porter suggests, "[a]s soon as we claim decisively and univocally that 'Audience is such and such,' we are lost" (8).

Peter Vandenberg
DePaul University, Chicago

Works Cited

Anderson, Laurie J. 1987. "A Sense of Audience or Conventional Wisdom?" *Journal of Advanced Composition* 7: 112–120.

Aristotle. 1954. *Rhetoric.* Trans. W. Rhys Roberts. New York: Random.

Armstrong, Cherryl. 1986. "Reader-Based and Writer-Based Perspectives in Composition Instruction." *Rhetoric Review* 5: 84–89.

Berkenkotter, Carol. 1981. "Understanding a Writer's Awareness of Audience." *College Composition and Communication* 32: 388–399.

Black, Edwin. 1970. "The Second Persona." *Quarterly Journal of Speech* 56: 109–119.

Clevenger, Otto. 1966. *Audience Analysis.* New York: Bobbs-Merrill.

Ede, Lisa. 1984. "Audience: An Introduction to Research." *College Composition and Communication* 35: 140–155.

Ede, Lisa, and Andrea Lunsford. 1984. "Audience Addressed/Audience Invoked: The Role of Audience in Composition Theory and Pedagogy." *College Composition and Communication* 35: 155–171.

Elbow, Peter. 1987. "Closing My Eyes as I Speak: An Argument for Ignoring Audience." *College English* 49: 50–69.

Flower, Linda, and John Hayes. 1980. "The Dynamics of Composing: Making Plans and Juggling Constraints." *Cognitive Processes in Writing.* Ed. Lee W. Gregg and Erwin R. Steinberg. Hillsdale, NJ: Erlbaum.

Fulkerson, Richard. 1990. "Composition Theory in the Eighties: Axiological Consensus and Paradigmatic Diversity." *College Composition and Communication* 41: 409–429.

Kroll, Barry. 1984. "Writing for Readers: Three Perspectives on Audience." *College Composition and Communication* 35: 172–185.

Long, Russell. 1980. "Writer-Audience Relationships." *College Composition and Communication* 31: 221–226.

Ong, Walter. 1975. "The Writer's Audience Is Always a Fiction." *PMLA* 90: 9–21.

Park, Douglas B. 1986. "Analyzing Audiences." *College Composition and Communication* 37: 478–488.

Porter, James E. 1992. *Audience and Rhetoric: An Archaeological Composition of the Discourse Community.* Englewood Cliffs, NJ: Prentice Hall.

Ross, William T. 1984. "Self and Audience in Composition." *Freshman English News* 13: 14–16.

Vandenberg, Peter. 1992. "Pick Up This Cross and Follow: (Ir)Responsibility and the Teaching of 'Writing for Audience' " *Composition Studies* 20: 84–97.

authority

The term authority finds mention in virtually every segment of composition studies. Its variations in meaning derive in part from its several shades of dictionary definition. As "the power to enforce laws, exact obedience, command, determine, or judge," authority pertains to classroom dynamics and student agency; as "justification or grounds," authority alludes to teacher response and evaluation; as "the power to influence or persuade resulting from knowledge or experience," authority relates to student voice in papers. According to Henry Giroux, authority represents "a historical construction shaped by diverse, competing traditions" whose conditional nature renders it incapable of possessing a "universal meaning" (qtd. in Mortensen and Kirsch 557). As Peter Mortensen and Gesa Kirsch note, the presence of multiple, contingent meanings suggests that it is misleading to discuss the "concept" of authority, suggesting instead a discussion of "concepts of authority" (556).

The issue of power is often embedded in such discussions. Mortensen and Kirsch contend that, in the academy, "authority is the legitimate force that attenuates raw power: authority conditions the power to persuade, the power to coerce, the power to initiate or mandate action" (560). Accordingly, many composition instructors attempt to empower students by teaching them to write with authority. Mortensen and Kirsch claim that despite their differences, current composition theories suffer limitations in their interpretation of authority. Both theories that privilege assimilation and those that favor resistance tend to "objectify authority, to cast it as something fixed and autonomous that writers or writing can possess" (557), ignoring asymmetrical power relations. In current-traditional theory, according to Mortensen and Kirsch, authority resides within the work itself and "even the most effective challenges to current-traditional rhetoric . . . still tend to align authority with technique" (562). In cognitive theory, authority lies, ready to be tapped, within the writer's mind, positioning every writer with the inherent ability to write. Authority, then, is seen as an independent entity waiting to be learned or used, making the instructor's job that of teaching students how to find and use this skill (Mortensen and Kirsch 563).

According to Lester Faigley, in expressivism, authority resides within the author, requiring students to find and present their "authentic voice" (121–122; see also Elbow). Recently, Ann M. Penrose and Cheryl Geisler complicated this concept of student voice, contending that to write from authority, students need to feel a sense of expertise about their subject, confident to walk the fine line between writing within conventions while simultaneously resisting those conventions (506–507). Students who write without this comfort of an inside stance "transfer" information (507), attempting to gain authority in their writing by citing other authors. In order to claim the "right to speak" (506) in a community, Penrose and Geisler assert, "writers must value their own experiences and responses" (515), evaluate claims of others against their own understanding instead of accepting those claims as facts, and see themselves as "creators" rather than "reporters" of knowledge (512).

Social constructionists, according to Mortensen and Kirsch, situate authority not in "texts or minds, but rather [as] negotiated and constructed in discourse by individuals who observe conventions for the representation of knowledge" (563). Although they credit social construction theory for its rejection of a "model of authority grounded in absolute, transcendent truth," they highlight its continued dependence on authority as an autonomous entity to be garnered by "those who before their apprenticeship lacked any relevant cognitive or social abilities" (563). When students enter the university, they set out to master the institutional conventions in order to "gain discursive authority" (556–557; see also Bartholomae). In this sense, authority becomes a quality students must acquire, a goal toward which each student must strive.

Implicit in the discussion of authority lies the assumption that "[o]bedience and containment are crucial to keeping order in the discursive universe of institutions" (Mortensen and Kirsch 560). In their discussion of authority in academy, Mortensen and Kirsch present two "functional" categories: the "authority of office" and the "authority of expertise" (559). When teachers respond to student papers, by virtue of their position as teacher (office) and their place in their field (expertise), they risk appropriating the text as they direct the student's revision strategy. According to Lil Brannon and C. H. Knoblauch, teacher comments can carry this authority and send the message to students that "the teacher's agenda is more important than their own" (158), causing them to obediently sublimate their own authority to their instructors'. Basing his discussion of authority on the work of Hans-Georg Gadamer, Peter Sotiriou advocates a shift in the emphasis in authority from one based on obedience to one grounded in knowledge (7–8). Gadamer asserts that authority is granted when "the individual, group, or text has something to teach" (qtd. in Sotiriou 8). Sotiriou contends that allowing students a chance to let their own knowledge instruct others may help them assume more confidence in that knowledge, allowing them more control over their writing (18).

While the question of classroom structure may seem superficial, students' perception of their authority (power) in the classroom can alter their perception of their authority (control) over their writing and their confidence. Cheryl L. Johnson argues that the politics of the classroom work to "authorize and to deauthorize speech" (409), thus affecting student's voices in class discussions, which carries over into their papers. Reports of classroom experiments, which reached their height in the early 1970s, reveal that many composition classrooms attempted trials of the "student-directed" course (see Jones). Kenneth A. Bruffee challenged these popular experiments in student control, asserting that much of the "innovative" curricula perpetuates the traditional authoritarian individualist mode of education "under a new guise" (458). Bruffee questioned the underlying concept of authority that many courses share: "[T]hose who assert themselves forcefully and can handle their 'new found freedom' are the better students" (464). As Mortensen and Kirsch suggest, this model "presupposes[s] that discourse communities function largely as egalitarian forums" (557; see also Jarratt 113). When teachers pass their authority (control) to the most vocal student or other authority figure, the classroom does not lose its authoritarian stance; transferring authority (control) from teacher to students does not guarantee a transformation of the classroom from authoritarian to democratic. For Bruffee, instilling authority in students means teaching them responsibility and self-control (Bruffee 465; see also Shor 101–103). For both Bruffee and Ira Shor, allowing students, under the guidance of a teacher, to gradually usurp greater authority (power) over the class dynamics can lead to greater authority (self-control) over their writing.

Mortensen and Kirsch contend that feminist critiques of authority move beyond a notion of authority based on "autonomy, individual rights, and abstract rules" and toward "a model based on dialogue, connectedness, and contextual rules" (557). In a study of women's writing in the academy, Kirsch found that women entering the academy struggled with the sometimes conflicting goals of building their authority within their field while "simultaneously questioning and challenging the academic system in which they find themselves" (3). If authority coincides with the writer's mastery of the discourse community's conventions, a writer attempting to break away from convention and create her own voice may jeopardize her perceived authority within the institution.

Clearly, authority escapes singular definition. As composition studies strives to balance the acceptance of less traditional voices with the demands of conformity to academic conventions, the conflicted, multiple concepts of authority will no doubt remain foregrounded in the field's debates.

Jennifer A. Clough
DePaul University

Works Cited

Bartholomae, David. 1985. "Inventing the University." *When a Writer Can't Write: Studies in Writer's Block and Other Composing Process Problems.* Ed. Mike Rose. New York: Guilford. 134–165.

Brannon, Lil, and C.H. Knoblauch. 1982. "On Students' Right to Their Own Texts: A Model of Teacher Response." *College Composition and Communication* 33: 157–167.

Bruffee, Kenneth A. 1972. "The Way Out: A Critical Survey Innovations in College Teaching." *College English* 33: 457–470.

Elbow, Peter. 1981. *Writing with Power: Techniques for Mastering the Writing Process.* New York: Oxford University Press.

Faigley, Lester. 1994. *Fragments of Rationality: Postmodernity and the Subject of Composition.* Pittsburgh: University of Pittsburgh Press.

Jarratt, Susan C. 1991. "Feminism and Composition: The Case for Conflict." *Contending with Words: Composition and Rhetoric in a Postmodern Age.* Ed. Patricia Harkin and John Schilb. New York: The Modern Language Association of America. 105–123.

Johnson, Cheryl L. 1994. "Participatory Rhetoric and the Teacher as Racial/Gendered Subject." *College English* 56: 409–419.

Jones, Granville H. 1971. "Postmortem: Student-Directed Courses I and II." *College English* 33: 284–293.

Kirsch, Gesa E. 1993. *Women Writing the Academy: Audience, Authority, and Transformation.* Carbondale, IL: Southern Illinois University Press.

Mortensen, Peter, and Gesa E. Kirsch. 1993. "On Authority in the Study of Writing." *College Composition and Communication* 44: 556–572.

Penrose, Ann M., and Cheryl Geisler. 1994. "Reading and Writing without Authority." *College Composition and Communication* 45: 505–520.

Shor, Ira. 1987. *Critical Teaching and Everyday Life.* Chicago: The University of Chicago Press.

Sotiriou, Peter. 1993. "The Question of Authority in the Composition Classroom: A Gadamerian Perspective." *The Writing Instructor* 1: 7–20.

basic writing/writers

Although there are a number of terms used to describe underprepared undergraduate writers and the courses that define them, the inception of the *Journal of Basic Writing* in 1975 appears to have established *basic writing* as the general description of pedagogy geared toward students who do not typically utilize conventional academic discourse (Gray 3; see also Kasden 4). According to Mina Shaughnessy (1976), "Basic writing, alias remedial, developmental, pre-baccalaureate, or even handicapped English, is commonly thought of as a writing course for young men and women who have many things wrong with them" (234). In a footnote a dozen years later, Mike Rose qualifies his remarks thus: "I will use the adjective 'remedial' and occasionally the adjective 'basic' . . . with some reservation, for they are often more pejorative than accurately descriptive" (353). And by 1987, Theresa Enos writes, "*Basic writing* is a troublesome and diverse term, having become so inclusive that it seems to defy formal definition" (v).

Noting that the "teaching of writing to severely underprepared" students is "the frontier of a profession," Shaughnessy (1987) elaborates on the pejorative nature of the terms associated with these students. *Remedial, English for the disadvantaged, compensatory, developmental*, and *basic* all suggest, to varying degrees, that the shortcoming is within the student more so than within the student's educational experience (177; see also 1979, 4). Moreover, she points to the relativeness of such labels: "One school's remedial student may be another's regular or even advanced freshman" (177–178). The tenor of Shaughnessy's essay here is sympathetic to the students who, through open admissions, have been given an opportunity to experience higher education. In fact, at times she calls them "new students," certainly a more respectful label than the conventional, widely used ones that intrinsically suggest fault. Shaughnessy (1976) notes, for instance, that "medical metaphors dominate the pedagogy (*remedial, clinic, lab, diagnosis*, and so on)" and that "teachers and administrators tend to discuss basic writing students much as doctors tend to discuss their patients" (234). Andrea

Lunsford (1987) echoes Shaughnessy's convictions that such medical terminology should be abandoned and that basic writing should be moved "from the fringes of concern into the full academic community where it becomes . . . an opener of long-closed doors to academic discourse, to intellectual rigor, to the way writing helps create ourselves and our worlds" (226). The nature of defining differences in writing ability, however, presupposes the language of "deficit theory" (Hull *et al.* 324) because one is forced to show how a particular concept is different from, and inferior to, the prototype. Hence, the primary metaphors for basic writing betray a reliance on the notion of deficit. The inside/outside metaphor has been most prevalent in the discipline (Wall and Coles 244; Foster 161–162), allowing for a mainstream/margins metaphor (Wall and Coles 232) and a boundary/passport metaphor (DiPardo 5; 169).

Basic writing students are generally constructed as those who find academic writing tasks especially challenging, and *basic writing* is often defined by certain artifactual evidence. Shaughnessy (1987) describes basic writing students as those who "produce . . . small numbers of words with large numbers of errors" and who seem to "be restricted as writers, but not necessarily as speakers, to a very narrow range of syntactic, semantic, and rhetorical options" (179). Similarly, basic writing is "clearly" identified as "relatively brief and unelaborated, with little subordination[,] . . . many intrusions from oral language that are less appropriate to written language[,] . . . [and] punctuation, capitalization, [and] spelling [which] are erratic" (Kutz *et al.* 39). Basic writers have also been portrayed as those students who use consistently inadequate prewriting strategies (Perl 22), who "lack the skills needed to write at all" and who would benefit from the lessons on writing from classical rhetoric (Tiner 374). Gail Stygall (1988) notes yet another facet of the basic writer—marked tenacity in the face of unusual adversity: "Like two boxers who are bleeding and winded but not yet ready to quit, basic writers reel into the freshman classroom each year" (28).

Definitions of *basic writing* and *basic writers*, however, are also based on characteristics not readily observed (see, e.g., Kutz *et al.* 40). Lunsford (1978) adds a dimension by noticing in basic writing students "a consistent egocentricity" which prevents their adopting a distanced voice as generally desired in academic writing (3). And in contrast to the scholarship that defines *basic writing* primarily on the basis of semantics or syntax, E. D. Hirsch, Jr. sees a culturally situated cause: a lack of "that whole system of unspoken, tacit knowledge that is shared between speaker and writer" (29). A somewhat different perception of cultural causes is based on economic and social factors which might inhibit success in academic settings because such success is neither prevalent nor outwardly esteemed in one's home culture; hence, those from working-class backgrounds or crime-ridden neighborhoods must make a deliberate, calculated choice to succeed in academia (Rondinone 884–885). Min-zhan Lu similarly points to the investment of culture in language, taking exception with what she terms Shaughnessy's essentialist view of linguistic codes as if those codes can exist separately from "the dynamic power struggle within and among diverse discourses" (329).

George H. Jensen spotlights the contestation between definitions of *basic writing* as symptom and as social interaction when he observes that many researchers tend to ignore Shaughnessy's thesis that basic writers are diverse and complicated. He worries that the individual characteristics—such as insecurity, preoccupation with "errors," holistic thinking, and gregarious-ness—that these researchers identified will combine to form an inaccurate, negative generalization of *the* basic writer (53–54).

The term *basic*, however, has not always pointed to deficiency. In a 1937 handbook described as "the kind of book which can be used by all freshman regardless of their ultimate intentions" (Moffett and Johnson vii), *basic writing* represents the essential knowledge about composing required at the college level. "For those who are seeking merely a competence in English composition, the sections on the word, sentence, paragraph, exposition, and letter writing constitute a complete course" (Moffett and Johnson viii).

Since the mid-seventies, however, *basic writing* has been consistently, if not exclusively, connected with remediation, marking it as a stop-gap measure for a temporary problem (Stygall 1994, 339) and encouraging administrators to define the field a particular way by staffing it with temporary adjunct faculty and teaching assistants (Stygall 1994, 339; DiPardo 170). Such a deficit-oriented use of the term leads to a great irony: unlike students who enroll in technical writing or creative writing classes to work toward identi-fication as technical or creative writers, students enrolled in basic writing classes begin with identification as basic writers and work to distance themselves from it.

Bill Bolin
East Texas State University

Works Cited

DiPardo, Anne. 1993. *A Kind of Passport: A Basic Writing Adjunct Program and the Challenge of Student Diversity.* NCTE Research Report No. 24. Urbana, IL: National Council of Teachers of English.

Enos, Theresa, ed. 1987. *A Sourcebook for Basic Writing Teachers.* New York: Random House.

Foster, David. 1992. *A Primer for Writing Teachers: Theories, Theorists, Issues, Problems.* Portsmouth, NH: Boynton/Cook Heinemann.

Gray, Barbara Quint. 1979. "Introduction." *Journal of Basic Writing* 2: 3–5.

Hirsch, E. D., Jr. 1980. "Culture and Literacy." *Journal of Basic Writing* 3: 27–47.

Hull, Glynda, Mike Rose, Kay Losey Fraser, and Marisa Castellano. 1991. "Reme-diation as Social Construct: Perspectives from an Analysis of Classroom Dis-course." *College Composition and Communication* 42: 299–329.

Jensen, George H. 1986. "The Reification of the Basic Writer." *Journal of Basic Writing* 5: 52–64.

Kasden, Lawrence N. 1980. "An Introduction to Basic Writing." *Basic Writing: Essays for Teachers, Researchers, Administrators.* Ed. Lawrence N. Kasden and Daniel R. Hoeber. Urbana, IL: National Council of Teachers of English. 1–9.

Kutz, Eleanor, Suzy Q. Groden, and Vivian Zamel. 1993. *The Discovery of Competence: Teaching and Learning with Diverse Student Writers.* Portsmouth, NH: Boynton/Cook Heinemann.

Lu, Min-zhan. 1994. "Redefining the Legacy of Mina Shaughnessy: A Critique of the Politics of Linguistic Innocence." *The Writing Teacher's Sourcebook.* 3rd ed. Ed. Gary Tate, Edward P. J. Corbett, and Nancy Myers. New York: Oxford University Press. 327–337.

Lunsford, Andrea A. 1978. "Aristotelian Rhetoric: Let's Get Back to the Classics." *Journal of Basic Writing* 2: 2–12.

———. 1987. "An Update of the Bibliography on Basic Writing." *Teaching Composition: Twelve Bibliographic Essays.* Ed. Gary Tate. Fort Worth: Texas Christian University Press. 207–226.

Moffett, Harold Y., and Willoughby H. Johnson. 1937. *Basic Writing: A Textbook for College Freshman.* New York: Harper and Brothers.

Perl, Sondra. 1980. "A Look at Basic Writers in the Process of Composing." *Basic Writing: Essays for Teachers, Researchers, Administrators.* Ed. Lawrence N. Kasden and Daniel R. Hoeber. Urbana, IL: National Council of Teachers of English. 13–32.

Rondinone, Peter. 1993. In "Symposium on Basic Writing, Conflict and Struggle, and the Legacy of Mina Shaughnessy." *College English* 55: 879–903.

Rose, Mike. 1994. "Remedial Writing Courses: A Critique and a Proposal." *The Writing Teacher's Sourcebook.* Ed. Gary Tate, Edward P. J. Corbett, and Nancy Myers. New York: Oxford University Press. 353–370.

Shaughnessy, Mina P. 1976. "Diving In: An Introduction to Basic Writing." *College Composition and Communication* 27: 234–239.

———. 1979. *Errors and Expectations: A Guide for the Teacher of Basic Writing.* New York: Oxford.

———. 1987. "Basic Writing." *Teaching Composition: Twelve Bibliographic Essays.* Ed. Gary Tate. Fort Worth: Texas Christian University Press. 177–206.

Stygall, Gail. 1988. "Politics and Proof in Basic Writing." *Journal of Basic Writing* 7: 28–41.

———. 1994. "Resisting Privilege: Basic Writing and Foucault's Author Function." *College Composition and Communication* 45: 320–341.

Tiner, Elza C. 1994. "Elements of Classical and Medieval Rhetoric in the Teaching of Basic Composition." *The Writing Teacher's Sourcebook.* Ed. Gary Tate, Edward P. J. Corbett, and Nancy Myers. New York: Oxford University Press. 371–377.

Wall, Susan, and Nicholas Coles. 1991. "Reading Basic Writing: Alternatives to a Pedagogy of Accommodation." *The Politics of Writing Instruction: Postsecondary.* Ed. Richard Bullock, John Trimbur, and Charles Schuster. Portsmouth, NH: Boynton/Cook Heinemann: 227–246.

coherence

Coherence is a mysterious term, one of those "I know it when I see it" things that's difficult to explain, measure, or teach. Attempts to categorically define coherence have typically resorted to definition by analogical reasoning, evident in a sampling of older and recent handbooks. Coherence has been equated with cement, the "mortar" keeping the "bricks" of the text from collapsing (Lorch). Or it relates to textiles: the "verbal stitching" holding textual "fabric" together (Halverson and Cooley), the "verbal thread that binds" sentences (Heffernan and Lincoln)—the result of premeditated "weaving" and "proper" assemblage (Cargill *et al.*). It can be a bonding agent, the "sticking" together of text to make logical sequences (Watt), the "fitting" of information into a textual puzzle (Cooley), or the stacking of "blocks of thought" (Davidson). Sometimes, though, it is assumed to be an organic, inherent property of texts, the composition seen as a fluid and coherence the current that keeps it moving in an uninterrupted "natural flow" of sentences and ideas (Wyrick), and in a logical flow of thoughts (Marius and Wiener). Some portrayals appeal to our sense of texture: coherence described as "smoothness" (Hammond), a "blending" of information into a meaningful whole (Hall). Or the text is envisioned as something like a mobile, coherence being the structure's ability to "hang together" (Hartwell and Bentley). One representation says that coherence entails "signaling," an active communication between text and reader (Eastman). Others define coherence simply as proximity itself, "the clear and close connection of sentences within a paragraph" (Hyde and Brown 9).

Coherence appeared after the Civil War as one of the "abstract rhetorical desiderata" (Connors) of current-traditional rhetoric. Most attempts to define coherence went little beyond categorizing transitional elements and differentiating between coherence and unity, distinct concepts described by some as "independent variables" (Lybbert and Cummings): unity defined on a local level (multiple pieces of related evidence throughout an argument can be said to have unity), coherence as a global issue (the balanced orchestration of such evidence within a complete document). But during the 1970s and 80s a series of studies attempted to more comprehensively articulate the distinction between cohesion (the term replacing "unity") and its more elusive counterpart, coherence (a more thorough overview of which can be found in Larson 65–72).

Many of these studies implicitly define coherence as the quintessential characteristic of text. For W. Ross Winterowd coherence *is* form, the two virtually synonymous, each referring to the "internal set of consistent relationships in any stretch of discourse" (828). M. A. K. Haliday and Ruqaiya Hasan argue that what gives text its essence is its internal network of "cohesive ties"; thus, cohesion equals textuality. Research by these and others (van Dijk; De Beaugrande) introduced new taxonomic vocabularies to composition, and some of these schema were to prove fairly complex (Haliday and Hasan's five major classes of cohesive ties are divided into nineteen subclasses, which are in turn split into dozens of sub-subclasses). Eventually others introduced alternative conceptual frameworks (Fahnestock; Stotsky), but all of these schema imply a fundamentally structuralist construction of coherence, where texts are machines "containing" coherence, the presence of which can be measured through examination of all its connective hardware (transitional features joining semantic relations and so forth). A logical result of all of this interest in codifying the features of coherence is that new definitions for incoherence appear: in one case it is described as the juxtaposition of unrelated ideas (Brostoff); elsewhere as "conceptual and lexical redundancy" (Witte and Faigley).

Joseph M. Williams and Gregory G. Colomb add to the task of defining cohesion vs. coherence by identifying the former as local knots (which, if the writer is graceful enough, will appear invisible), "strings" of topics and sentence themes tied together, whereas the latter refers to "how it all adds up" and how central ideas surface from those ganglia of strings. Although admitting "coherence is abstract," the authors nevertheless characterize it as the perceived "point" of the text at any given time (an idea similar to Betty Bamberg's observation that coherence implies a reader's sustained awareness of topic). Williams and Colomb's distinction between cohesion and coherence gets a little fuzzy as it is not altogether clear where cohesion turns into coherence during the course of its evolution, but both are defined as the "management of information flow," a cycling of material similar to what Herbert H. Clark and Susan E. Haviland call the "given-new contract." Here coherence is the recursive process where the reader encounters familiar information early on in the sentence, followed by newer information, which subsequently forms the familiar information for the next sentence. This conception of coherence as a conversion process is supported by George Goodin and Kyle Perkins.

A difference in thinking occurs around the mid-1980s as theorists like Rochelle Smith begin defining cohesion ("the quality of connected sentences") as text-centered, but coherence ("the global quality of text structure") as a reader-centered phenomenon. Louise Wetherbee Phelps extends this idea, labeling cohesion a stylistic "cuing system" but insisting that coherence is not a property within text but an experience. Coherence is now a collaborative synthesis "belonging to both writer and reader as their joint product through complementary actions" (21). Phelps observes that common definitions of coherence typically emphasize either "flow," a reflection of the dynamic, real time sense of coherence readers experience during the act of reading, or "design," which is a static, retrospective contemplation of the text's overall balance. Since these constructions are incompatible, one grounded in an attention to process and the other to product, Phelps introduces an integrative theory of cohesion where the text's "point" or "purpose" is not embedded within the text, but is rather a construction of the reader who is invited (but not determined) by that text (19).

The implications of this new attention to coherence as "the axis of readers and texts" (Phelps 28) instead of textual property have been played out to some degree in recent attention to the literacy of hypertext. With the advent of newer interactive technologies, coherence seems almost entirely in the hands of the reader who can now navigate her own readerly map by selecting, deleting, and bypassing textual information instead of being relegated to a linear path charted by an absent author. In essence, those working in this area (Barrett; Bolter; Delany and Landow) are defining coherence as an activity initiated, invented, and sustained by the reader within a topographical "writing space" (Bolter) ever open and always permeable. Coherence thus becomes an inherently constructivist enterprise. Jay David Bolter's claim that coherence does indeed exist in those "open texts" which reject closure contrasts sharply with a portrayal like E. D. Hirsch's which assumes that incoherence is the absence of closure. The degree to which the concept of coherence continues to evolve in composition studies would seem to depend in no small way on how closely the discipline keeps pace with such technological and experimental advancements that radically affect the ways we write and read.

Derek Owens
St. John's University

Works Cited

Bamberg, Betty. 1983. "What Makes a Text Coherent?" *College Composition and Communication* 34: 417–429.

Barrett, Edward, ed. 1988. *Text, ConText, and HyperText: Writing with and for the Computer.* Cambridge: MIT Press.

Bolter, Jay David. 1991. *Writing Space: The Computer, Hypertext, and the History of Writing.* Hillsdale: Lawrence Erlbaum Associates.

Brostoff, Anita. 1981. "Coherence: 'Next to' Is Not 'Connected to.' " *College Composition and Communication* 32: 278–294.

Cargill, Oscar, Reginald Call, Homer A. Watt, and William Charvat. 1955. *New Highways in College Composition.* 2nd ed. NY: Prentice-Hall.

Clark, Herbert H., and Susan E. Haviland. 1977. "Comprehension and the Given-New Contract." *Discourse Production and Comprehension.* Roy O. Freedle, ed. Norwood, NJ: ABLEX Publishing. 1–40.

Connors, Robert J. 1986. "Textbooks and the Evolution of the Discipline." *College Composition and Communication* 37: 178–194.

Cooley, Thomas. 1992. *The Norton Guide to Writing.* NY: W.W. Norton.

Davidson, Donald. 1964. *Concise American Composition and Rhetoric.* NY: Charles Scribner's Sons.

De Beaugrande, Robert. 1980. *Text, Discourse, and Process.* Norwood, NJ: ABLEX Publishing.

Delany, Paul, and George P. Landow, ed. 1991. *Hypermedia and Literary Studies.* Cambridge: MIT Press.

Eastman, Richard M. 1978. *Style: Writing and Reading as the Discovery of Outlook.* 2nd ed. NY: Oxford University Press.

Fahnestock, Jeanne. 1983. "Semantic and Lexical Coherence." *College Composition and Communication* 34: 400–16.

Goodin, George, and Kyle Perkins. 1982. "Discourse Analysis and the Art of Coherence." *College English* 44: 57–63.

Halliday, M.A.K., and Ruqaiya Hasan. 1976. *Cohesion in English.* London: Longman.

Hall, Donald. 1976. *Writing Well.* 2nd ed. Boston: Little, Brown & Co.

Halverson, John, and Mason Cooley. 1965. *Principles of Writing.* NY: Macmillan Co.

Hammond, Eugene R. 1989. *Critical Thinking, Thoughtful Writing.* NY: McGraw-Hill.

Hartwell, Patrick, and Robert H. Bentley. 1982. *Open to Language: A New College Rhetoric.* NY: Oxford University Press.

Heffernan, James A. W., and John E. Lincoln. 1990. *Writing: A College Handbook.* 3rd ed. NY: W. W. Norton.

Hirsch, E. D. 1977. *The Philosophy of Composition.* Chicago: University of Chicago Press.

Hyde, Jr., Simeon, and William H. Brown. 1967. *Composition of the Essay.* Reading, MA: Addison-Wesley.

Larson, Richard 1987. "Structure and Form in Non-Narrative Prose." *Teaching Composition: Twelve Bibliographical Essays.* Ed. Gary Tate. Fort Worth: Texas Christian University Press: 39–82.

Lorch, Sue. 1984. *Basic Writing: A Practical Approach.* 2nd ed. Boston: Little, Brown & Co.

Lybbert, E. K., and D. W. Cummings. 1969. "On Repetition and Coherence." *College Composition and Communication* 20: 35–38.

Marius, Richard, and Harvey S. Wiener. 1990. *The McGraw-Hill College Handbook.* 2nd ed. NY: McGraw-Hill.

Phelps, Louise Wetherbee. 1985. "Dialectics of Coherence: Toward an Integrative Theory." *College English* 47: 12–29.

Smith, Rochelle. 1984. "Paragraphing for Coherence: Writing as Implied Dialogue." *College English* 46: 8–21.

Stotsky, Sandra. 1983. "Types of Lexical Cohesion in Expository Writing: Implications for Developing the Vocabulary of Academic Discourse." *College Composition and Communication* 34: 430–446.

van Dijk, Teun. 1977. *Text and Context.* London: Longman.

Watt, William W. 1980. *An American Rhetoric.* 5th ed. NY: Holt, Rinehart, and Winston.

Williams, Joseph M. 1990. *Style: Toward Clarity and Grace.* With two chapters coauthored by Gregory G. Colomb. Chicago: The University of Chicago Press.

Winterowd, W. Ross. 1970. "The Grammar of Coherence." *College English* 31: 828–835.

Witte, Stephen P., and Lester Faigley. 1981. "Coherence, Cohesion, and Writing Quality." *College Composition and Communication* 32: 189–204.

Wyrick, Jean. 1990. *Steps to Writing Well: A Concise Guide to Composition.* 4th ed. Chicago: Holt, Rinehart & Winston.

collaboration

Collaboration refers not to a unified object but rather to a variety of pedagogies and practices, each grounded in somewhat different, and often conflicting, epistemological and ontological assumptions. Under the umbrella term of *collaborative learning* lies a range of pedagogical techniques, which most often involve small groups of two or more working together and which include, but are not limited to, peer planning, review, critique, tutoring, and conferences. As praxis, collaboration signifies not only the phenomenon of two or more authors working on a single project but also extends to the view that all writing is collaborative. As a theory, it is invoked to support bipolar concepts of discourse as both individual acts of cognition and as social acts.

Although collaboration as practice and pedagogy has a long history in the United States, dating back some two hundred years (Gere), collaboration entered our professional literature as a pedagogical tool. In the late 1940s and early 1950s, small peer groups were advocated as a way to manage the post-WW II swelling tides of student enrollments (Maize), to handle the increased paper load (Bernardette), to develop audience awareness (Drake; Hausdorff), and to shift the responsibility for learning to write off of the teacher and onto the student (Hayakawa). However, the assumptions driving the use of collaboration in the classroom varied widely, being grounded in and moving between two competing epistemologies—a Cartesian epistemology that defines writing as an individual act and a postmodern one that sees it as a social act. Anne Ruggles Gere explicates these two opposing views and their implications for writing groups, locating the roots of the former in Piaget and the latter in Vygotsky:

> In Piagetian terms, writing groups provide a means to the end of individual performance in writing, but they are finally peripheral because the essence of writing lies in the individual effort of opening the mind's locked lid. Vygotsky's insistence on the dialectic between the individual and society, however, puts peer response at the center of writing because it makes language integral to thinking and knowing. (83–84)

The tension between these two views, which continues to play itself out in our literature, is evident in our post-WW II professional discussions.

In the late 1960s, Leonard A. Greenbaum and Rudolf B. Schmerl reported on a first-year writing course they had developed to promote learning how to write multi-authored documents. In small groups, students worked together to plan, draft, revise, and edit sections that eventually were compiled into a single monograph. This project entailed two important strands of meaning: collaboration as a method of composing multi-authored documents and collaborative writing as an epistemic process whereby "writing is a means by which you learn something about a subject" (146). Two years later, H. R. Wolf described a collaborative learning classroom in which he acted as a "synthesizer, not authority figure" (443), orchestrating students in small group discussions. But the assumptions driving this method were far different from those driving Greenbaum and Schmerl's approach. For Wolf, collaborative pedagogy was not a social process so much as a tool of the individual: "the papers that students wrote had that unmistakable imprint of the individual asserting his own-being-in-the-world, his own special sense of the world as it meets *his* eye and courses in *his* blood" (443). These two competing views—writing as a social process and writing as an individual journey—and two competing practices—collaboration as a means to produce a single, multi-authored product and to produce multiple single-authored products—are reconfigured in complex ways and appear repeatedly in our literature.

By the 1970s changes in material conditions within academia prompted a vigorous interest in collaboration as a pedagogical tool. With the advent of open enrollment, writing teachers were confronted with the inadequacies of traditional composition pedagogies (Shaughnessy). Collaborative learning was invoked as a method for teaching non-traditional students. For some it continued to provide a way to manage the drudgery of teaching writing (Brosnahan; Hardaway), for others it was a new means for individualizing instruction (Clark; Murray), and for still others it was a recognition of and a way to support learning and writing as social activities (Bruffee 1973).

Although collaborative pedagogical techniques were at times invoked to support traditional teacher-centered classes, most often they were advocated as a way of disrupting the traditional hierarchical power relationships between teacher and student—a goal epitomized in the title of Peter Elbow's *Writing Without Teachers.* Bruffee described this end as one of "establishing a 'poly-centralized' collaborative learning community in which the teacher moves to the perimeter of the action, once the scene is set" (1973, 637). Lou Kelly similarly spoke of seeking to develop "a community of learners" (650), and Jean Pumphrey argued for a "shift in emphasis from teacher-student to student-peer evaluation" (667). This thread appeared throughout the next two decades (e.g., Trimbur; Bruffee 1993) though at times with a twist. For example, for George Held and Warren Rosenberg, "alter[ing] the traditional power structure" (819) of the classroom meant more than creating peer groups; it meant bringing in an undergraduate student as a team teacher. (For a comprehensive review of the research literature on collaboration in the composition classroom, see Anne DiPardo and Sarah Warshauer Freedman.)

While interest in collaboration as a pedagogical tool continued to mount throughout the 1980s, it also significantly expanded as an object of study to include examination of collaboration as a practice both inside and outside of academia. Studies of collaborative practices in the workplace (Odell and Goswami) and in academia (McNenny and Roen) began to appear along with historical studies (Gere) and philosophical and theoretical examinations (Bruffee 1984; LeFevre). (See Bosley, Morgan and Allen for a comprehensive bibliography of research and scholarship on collaborative writing as a practice.) Studies of this practice reveal that there are many models of collaboration, which Lisa Ede and Andrea Lunsford usefully classify under two headings. One they term hierarchical, a product-oriented model "with power and authority distributed vertically within the hierarchy" (67); the other they term dialogic, "a more loose, fluid mode of collaborative writing, one that focused more on the process of collaboration rather than the end products, one that emphasized dialogue and exploration rather than efficiency and closure" (67).

The dialogic model supports the concept that all writing is collaborative, a view that gained currency in the 1980s. Yet this social view of discourse is not a univocal one. Drawing on Bakhtin's theory of "communication chain," Charlotte Thralls, for example, argues "all writing is inherently collaborative" (64). James Reither and Douglas Vipond assert, "writing is collaboration. It cannot be otherwise" (866). Marilyn Cooper and Michael Holzman define writing as social action, and Karen Burke LeFevre argues that invention is a social (i.e., collaborative) act even when undertaken by a single author. These views represent points along a continuum. At one end, collaboration may be understood, though Donald Stewart argues, mistakenly understood, as influence, "mean[ing] the effects of absorbed learning" (67), and at the other end, as the contingent and dynamic effects of social contexts.

Trimbur and Lundy A. Braun best summed up the impact of collaboration on composition studies when they pointed out that "the notion of collaboration has not only generated an important body of research and pedagogical innovation, but the term 'collaboration' has now entered into the discourse of studies of writing as part of the conventional wisdom" (31). Yet the term remains slippery. Byron Stay's use exemplifies this slipperiness when he warns that "the complexity of collaboration allows it to support as well as subvert authority within the group, give voice to students and silence them, improve final products and destroy them" (44; cf. Yin). Similarly, Melanie Sperling's research found collaboration to be "a shifting process shaped not only by conference participants but by the rhetorical circumstances of their talk" (279). Multiple social contexts (e.g., writing classrooms, disciplines, professions), innovations in technology (Selfe) and competing philosophies and rhetorical ends of discourse challenge attempts to pin down one meaning for the term.

Maureen Daly Goggin
Arizona State University

Works Cited

Bernadette, Doris. 1947. "A Practical Proposal to Take the Drudgery out of the Teaching of Freshman Composition and to Restore to the Teacher His Pristine Measure in Teaching." *College English* 8: 383.

Bosley, Deborah S., Meg Morgan, and Nancy Allen. 1990. "An Essential Bibliography on Collaborative Writing." *The Bulletin of the Association for Business Communication* 53: 27–33.

Brosnahan, Leger. 1976. "Getting Freshman Comp All Together." *College English* 37: 657–660.

Bruffee, Kenneth A. 1973. "Collaborative Learning: Some Practical Models." *College English* 34: 634–643.

———. 1984. "Collaborative Learning and the 'Conversation of Mankind'." *College English* 46: 635–652.

———. 1993. *Collaborative Learning: Higher Education, Interdependence, and the Authority of Knowledge.* Baltimore: Johns Hopkins.

Clark, William. 1975. "How to Completely Individualize a Writing Program." *English Journal* 64: 66–69.

Cooper, Marilyn, and Michael Holzman. 1989. *Writing as Social Action.* Portsmouth, NH: Boynton/Cook.

DiPardo, Anne, and Sarah Warshauer Freedman. 1988. "Peer Response Groups in the Writing Classroom: Theoretical Foundations and New Directions." *Review of Educational Research* 58: 119–149.

Drake, Francis. 1950. "Developmental Writing." *College Composition and Communication* 1: 3–6.

Ede, Lisa, and Andrea Lunsford. 1990. *Singular Texts/Plural Authors: Perspectives on Collaborative Writing.* Carbondale, IL: Southern Illinois University Press.

Elbow, Peter. 1973. *Writing without Teachers.* New York: Oxford.

Gere, Anne Ruggles. 1987. *Writing Groups: History, Theory, and Implications.* Carbondale, IL: Southern Illinois University Press.

Greenbaum, Leonard A., and Rudolf B. Schmerl. 1967. "A Team Learning Approach to Freshman English." *College English* 29: 135–152.

Hardaway, Francine. 1974. "What Students Can Do to Take the Burden off You." *College English* 36: 577–580.

Hausdorff, Don. 1959. "An Experiment in Communication as Problem Solving." *College Composition and Communication* 10: 27–32.

Hayakawa, S. I. 1950. "Linguistic Science and the Teaching of Composition." *ETC: A Review of General Semantics* 7: 97–103.

Held, George, and Warren Rosenberg. 1983. "Student-Faculty Collaboration in Teaching College Writing." *College English* 45: 817–823.

Kelly, Lou. 1973. "Toward Competence and Creativity in an Open Class." *College English* 34: 644–660.

LeFevre, Karen Burke. 1987. *Invention as a Social Act.* Carbondale: Southern Illinois University Press.

Maize, Ray. 1951. "The Partner Method of Review at the Air Command and Staff School." *College English* 12: 396–399.

McNenny, Geraldine, and Duane H. Roen. 1992. "The Case for Collaborative Scholarship in Rhetoric and Composition." *Rhetoric Review* 10: 291–310.

Murray, Donald. *A Writer Teaches Writing.* Boston: Houghton Mifflin, 1968.

Odell, Lee, and Dixie Goswami, ed. 1985. *Writing in Non-Academic Settings.* New York: Guilford.

Pumphrey, Jean. 1973. "Teaching English Composition as a Creative Art." *College English* 34: 666–673.

Reither, James A., and Douglas Vipond. 1989. "Writing as Collaboration." *College English* 51: 855–867.

Selfe, Cynthia L. 1992. "Computer-Based Conversations and the Changing Nature of Collaboration." *New Visions of Collaborative Writing.* Ed. Janis Forman. Portsmouth, NH: Boynton/Cook. 147–169.

Shaughnessy, Mina P. 1977. *Errors & Expectations: A Guide for the Teacher of Basic Writing.* New York: Oxford University Press.

Sperling, Melanie. 1990. "I Want to Talk to Each of You: Collaboration and the Teacher-Student Writing Conference." *Research in the Teaching of English* 24: 279–321.

Stay, Byron L. 1994. "When Interests Collide: Collaboration and Demolition." *Composition Studies/Freshman English News* 22: 30–46.

Stewart, Donald C. 1988. "Collaborative Learning and Composition: Boon or Bane?" *Rhetoric Review* 7: 58–83.

Thralls, Charlotte. 1992. "Bakhtin, Collaborative Partners, and Published Discourse: A Collaborative View of Composing." *New Visions of Collaborative Writing.* Ed. Janis Forman. Portsmouth, NH: Boynton/Cook. 63–81.

Trimbur, John. 1985. "Collaborative Learning and Teaching Writing." *Perspectives on Research and Scholarship in Composition.* Ed. Ben W. McClelland and Timothy R. Donovan. New York: Modern Language Association. 87–109.

Trimbur, John, and Lundy A. Braun. 1992. "Laboratory Life and the Determination of Authorship." *New Visions of Collaborative Writing.* Ed. Janis Forman. Portsmouth, NH: Boynton/Cook. 19–36.

Wolf, H. R. 1969. "Composition and Group Dynamics: The Paradox of Freedom." *College English* 30: 441–444.

Yin, Hum Sue. 1992. "Collaboration: Proceed with Caution." *The Writing Instructor* 12: 27–37.

composing/writing

The range of meanings within *composing* and *writing* (referring here to the activity rather than the artifact) speaks volumes about where composition studies comes from and what it has done as a field. Any examination of *composing* and *writing*, which have been used as interchangeable synonyms for at least thirty years, must contend with some basic metaphors that have long shaped the field's discourse around these terms. In general academic discussions, writing has been represented as punishment, frozen speech, a tool of communication, a testable item, and a way to self-commune and get in touch with one's feelings. Composing has been construed as a basic skill or set of skills, a craft, an art, a science, as the transcribing of pre-existing thought or ideas for transmission, and as the mystical ability to select and order just the right items from one's "word horde" to achieve a desired effect. There is also a long record of attempts to equate composing with—or subsume it within—the act of reading. For instance, as J. Hillis Miller has said, "writing is a trope for the act of reading. Every act of writing is an act of reading, an interpretation of some part of the totality of what is" (41).

Nonetheless, scholars in composition studies have long noted that, etymologically, composing means "placing with." In other words, composing literally means putting words together. In a slightly larger sense, many have noted that composing means fashioning wholes by creating relationships among the parts, that composing means synthesizing information and/or values. For instance, in 1970, Robert B. Heilman wrote that composing is "an achieving of oneness: a finding of such unities, small and contingent as they may be, as are possible[,] . . . a resolution of discords, a removal of what doesn't belong, and a discovery of how to belong." This sense of composing slides easily into another common strain: that composing means composing oneself, or as Heilman puts it, "being put together by the process of putting together" (232), a sentiment expressed emblematically in the title to William E. Coles Jr.'s influential book: *Composing: Writing as a Self-Creating Process.*

The representation of writing as a process (as a series of linear and/or recursive steps or stages) is, of course, now commonplace. But the historical development of meanings within this construction is important to note. Thirty years ago, a romantic version of composing can be seen coming to the fore, as in D. Gordon Rohman's assertion that "[w]riting is usefully described as a process, something which shows continuous change in time like growth in organic nature" (106). This romantic portrayal of composing has had a long life and finds expression in the work of scholars like Ann E. Berthoff, who has argued that composing is a process of meaning making, is the activity of abstraction, is *forming*, which proceeds, in great part, by means of imagination or the symbolizing of insight (66–67).

Conversely, composing has also been represented as an arithmetic, automatic, mindless, and biomechanical process. Writing in 1969, Leon A. Jakobovits represented composing as a mathematical operation, as the sequencing of linguistic elements in time-space by means of computational devices, that is, by means of known (mechanical) and unknown (creative) algorithms (325). In like manner, Barrett J. Mandel argued for an understanding of "writing per se as an automatic act," as the "recording and trusting" of "dictation which emanates from some point other than the conscious ego" (364). Mandel focused on composing as a scribal act, on writing as the process by which words "appear on the page through a massive coordination of a tremendous number of motor processes, including the contracting and dilating of muscles in the fingers, hand, arm, neck, shoulder, back, and eyes—indeed in the entire organism," to underscore his contention that writing is a process which "occurs independently of the conscious mind's control" (365).

Yet while Berthoff's and Mandel's constructions of composing may at first seem antithetical, they are, nonetheless, quite similar. Ultimately, for Mandel, "Writing is a human process whereby intuition (or illumination) . . . can disclose itself. Writing doesn't lay out the notions that are lying dormant in the mind waiting to be displayed. Writing is the 'seeing into' process itself" (366). This idea, that writing is not the transcribing of thought but rather the process of creating insight itself, sets the stage for the next major construction of writing and composing in composition studies, the one epitomized in the 1981 work of Linda Flower and John R. Hayes: writing as thinking, as a recursive cognitive activity, as problem-solving; composing as the goal-directed orchestration of a set of distinctive, hierarchical, highly embedded thinking processes.

Writing as thinking is closely related to the portrayal of writing as a process of learning. As Janet Emig said in 1977, "Writing represents a unique mode of learning—not merely valuable, not merely special, but unique" (122). Two years later, William F. Irmscher argued for a similar but somewhat more expansive view of writing as "an action and a way of knowing[,] . . . as investigation, as probing, . . . as a way of learning about anything and everything[,] . . . as a process of growing and maturing[,] . . . as a way of promoting the higher intellectual development of the individual" (241–242). It should be noted that writing as learning is the strand of meaning from which the often-invoked images of writing as exploration and discovery arise. The chief spokesman for this perspective is Donald M. Murray, who has long contended that writing is a process "of discovery through language" (79), an "exploration of what we know and what we feel about what we know" (80). Twenty-five years ago, Walker Gibson argued that these familiar metaphors construe composing as the process of "map-making," as the act of observing, recording, and accurately "reflecting the actual landscape" one is discovering and exploring (255). It would be better, he suggests "to think of composing as pot-making rather than as map-making." In this way, he says, we would understand composing as "forming a man-made structure" rather than as "copying down the solid shorelines of the universe," and thus better appreciate composing as joyful play and pleasure (258).

The most recent evolution in the construction of composing as a process can be generally described as an emphasis on writing as a social process. In 1986, Marilyn M. Cooper argued that writing is an activity through which writers engage with and locate themselves within a mesh of socially constituted systems of ideas, purposes, interpersonal interactions, cultural norms, and textual forms. Two years later, Geoffrey Chase first commended the field's increasing understanding of writing as a social activity, "as a form of cultural production linked to the processes of self and social empowerment" (13), and then elaborated his understanding of composing as the political act of accommodating, opposing, or resisting the dominant verbal-ideological scheme. An understanding of writing as a sociopolitical act undergirds Min-zhan Lu's portrayal of writing as a struggle—a struggle to move from silence to words, a struggle to re-position oneself among verbal-ideological worlds. Furthermore, writing as a social process is the basis for the common trope of composing as conversation (writing as the entering into and engaging in a given disciplinary conversation) as well as the springboard for a variety of poststructuralist views of writing as the social (de)construction of reality, truth, and knowledge, or as James S. Baumlin and Jim W. Corder put it, writing as "the always unstable, always unfinished, always contingent . . . active construction of self and world" (18).

Oddly enough, almost no one has examined students' constructions of composing. Thankfully, however, Lad Tobin has carefully explicated how his own image of composing as "always a voluntary and purposeful journey" (445) clashed with his students' portrayals. His students represented writing as a dissatisfying, frustrating, aimless activity, as wasted motion without intention or intensity, as a journey without purpose and without end, "as an impossible puzzle they must solve, a maze or imprisonment from which they must escape" (448), as a force over which they have no control, as something separate from them which they need to fight off, and "as superficial, cosmetic, and ultimately external" (449). These students portrayed "writing as doing something they hated . . . because it is good for them," writing "as an activity that parents and teachers force on students for their physical, psychological, and spiritual health" (450), "writing as a trip to the dentist" (446).

In sum, the tremendous range of definitions within these keywords gives some indication of just how complex composing/writing is and, moreover, emphasizes just how central the contests over the meanings of these terms are to the debates that animate the field.

Paul Heilker
Virginia Tech

Works Cited

Baumlin, James S., and Jim W. Corder. 1990. "Jackleg Carpentry and the Fall from Freedom to Authority in Writing." *Freshman English News* 18: 18–20.

Berthoff, Ann E. 1981. *Making Meaning: Metaphors, Models, and Maxims for Writing Teachers.* Upper Montclair, NJ: Boynton/Cook.

Chase, Geoffrey. 1988. "Accommodation, Resistance and the Politics of Student Writing." *College Composition and Communication* 39: 13–22.

Coles, William E., Jr. 1974. *Composing: Writing as a Self-Creating Process.* Rochelle Park, NJ: Hayden.

Cooper, Marilyn M. 1986. "The Ecology of Writing." *College English* 48: 364–375.

Emig, Janet. 1977. "Writing as a Mode of Learning." *College Composition and Communication* 28: 122–128.

Flower, Linda, and John R. Hayes, 1981. "A Cognitive Process Theory of Writing." *College Composition and Communication* 32: 365–387.

Gibson, Walker. 1970. "Composing the World: The Writer as Map-Maker." *College Composition and Communication* 21: 255–260.

Heilman, Robert B. 1970. "Except He Come to Composition." *College Composition and Communication* 21: 230–238.

Irmscher, William F. 1979. "Writing as a Way of Learning and Developing." *College Composition and Communication* 30: 240–244.

Jakobovits, Leon A. 1969. "Rhetoric and Stylistics: Some Basic Issues in the Analysis of Discourse." *College Composition and Communication* 20: 314–328.

Lu, Min-zhan. 1987. "From Silence to Words: Writing as Struggle." *College English* 49: 437–448.

Mandel, Barrett J. 1978. "Losing One's Mind: Learning to Write and Edit." *College Composition and Communication* 29: 362–368.

Miller, J. Hillis. 1983. "Composition and Decomposition: Deconstruction and the Teaching of Writing." In *Composition and Literature: Bridging the Gap*, edited by Winifred B. Horner, 38–56. Chicago: University of Chicago Press.

Murray, Donald M. 1972. "Teach Writing as Process not Product." Reprint. In *Rhetoric and Composition: A Sourcebook for Teachers*, edited by Richard L. Graves, 79–82. Rochelle Park, NJ: Hayden, 1976.

Rohman, D. Gordon. 1965. "Pre-Writing: The Stage of Discovery in the Writing Process." *College Composition and Communication* 16: 106–112.

Tobin, Lad. 1989. "Bridging Gaps: Analyzing Our Students' Metaphors for Composing." *College English* 40: 444–458.

composition studies

Composition studies is sometimes described as a field, sometimes as a sub-field, sometimes as a pre-paradigmatic field, and sometimes as a discipline. Composition studies has important connections to both literary studies and rhetoric, but the boundaries of the domains it shares with these adjacent fields are contested. John Schilb says that one conception of composition studies is "that it exists only to serve the 'real' disciplines" (178). Stephen North says that it has sometimes seemed to him as though composition studies "didn't have a core or a center" (Preface). Donna Burns Phillips, Ruth Greenberg, and Sharon Gibson observe that "as yet, composition studies is not universally accepted as a field of study, and it has no research method-ology of its own." Phillips and her co-authors add that "with the growth of rhetoric as a theoretical foundation for scholarship and the emergence of composition specialists, through professional choice or formal graduate pro-grams, the meaning of *composition* has been shifting from a course title to a conceptual paradigm for an emerging discipline" (461).

Janice Lauer has observed that it is necessary for any developing field to define itself and that it typically does so by identifying "its origins, its domain of investigation, its modes of inquiry and methods of evaluation" (20). Lauer contends that the distinct "territory for investigation" in compo-sition studies includes "the nature of the writing process," the "interaction among writer, reader, subject matter, and text," and "the epistemic potential of writing" (21). Erika Lindemann and Gary Tate argue that "Composition studies distinguishes itself from other disciplines, whose focus is invariably on a body of knowledge or a set of texts, by its central concern with an *activity*, the act of writing" (v). Louise Wetherbee Phelps (1986) says that "the primary object of inquiry in composition studies is written discourse in its most comprehensive interpretation," and she adds that composition differs "from other language-related academic fields by making the teaching act itself a primary topic of scholarly inquiries" (183; 187).

Despite this identification of composition's domain of inquiry, Phelps (1988) says the field "has no intrinsic methodology." Instead, she says, it "draws on approaches from across the range of disciplines falling within the natural, critical, and hermeneutical sciences" (77). It is the interplay of its competing methodologies, she contends, that defines composition studies as a field (4). Lauer describes composition studies as a "dappled discipline" and observes that "its scholarship has a highly multidisciplinary cast" (20). She suggests that this "multimodality" helps composition researchers "to avoid a nearsightedness that overlooks many and sometimes even the most significant problems in a field because they exist outside the walls of a particular mode of inquiry." She considers it a virtue that composition studies has "maintained from the beginning what a number of disciplines are just starting to admit— that many of their most important problems can be properly investigated only with multiple research methods" (25–26).

North identifies practitioners, scholars, and researchers as the three major methodological sub-communities within what he calls Composition with a capital "C." North connects the emergence of Composition to the academic reform movement of the late 1950s, to the Basic Issues conferences of 1958, and to the 1963 publication of Richard Braddock, Richard Lloyd-Jones, and Lowell Schoer's *Research in Written Composition* (9–10; 15). The central question facing the Basic Issues conferences was "What is English?" The answer that emerged from the conferences was that English was a "tripod" consisting of language, literature, and composition. According to North, the academic reform movement "demanded the existence of a post-secondary, English department-based expertise in all three legs of the tripod" (13). He adds that those who taught composition tended to be the "lowliest members of the English academic community" and that departmental needs for expertise in the composition leg of the tripod "stood to provide these second-class academic citizens with a way out of their academic 'ghetto' " (14). First, however, they needed to define a mode of "acceptable, formal, academic inquiry" (15). The Braddock, Lloyd-Jones, and Schoer volume promoted research in composition "modeled in method and rigor on research in the sciences" (17). As North describes it, *Research in Written Composition* represents Composition as "a sort of ur-discipline blindly groping its way out of the darkness toward the bright light of a 'scientific' certainty" and "sets the stage" for what he characterizes as a "methodological land rush" (2, 17).

The term *composition studies* appears to have been in common use at least since 1979 (see Park). Robert Connors chose to use the term because, as he explained in a 1983 article, " 'composition' and 'rhetoric' are both misleading in different ways" (1). Connors' purpose in "Composition Studies and Science" was to examine the claim that composition studies was a scientific field, guided like a scientific field by a paradigm. He explained that this claim was grounded in the ideas of Thomas Kuhn and that it had been put forward most significantly by Richard Young and Maxine Hairston

(1–5). Connors went on to consider whether, if composition studies were
found to lack a paradigm, it could be said to be a pre-paradigmatic field
(5, 10). He concluded that composition studies is neither "a mature scientific
field with a paradigm of its own" nor "one whose first paradigm is anywhere
in sight" (17).

Connors suggests that the attempt to define composition studies as a
scientific field is motivated by a "yearning toward the power and success of
the natural sciences" (4). In another context, he has observed that for three
or four decades, those teaching composition "have had an institutional
inferiority complex, and we looked beyond our own discipline for something
that would validate what we do" (Murphy *et al.* 30). Victor Vitanza, however,
argues that composition studies requires no such validation:

> We are twenty-five-hundred years old. We are not a discipline. We are a
> meta-discipline. If we teach writing across the curriculum, doesn't that tell us,
> isn't that a self-evident experience, that we are a meta-discipline. We inform
> all the other disciplines. They don't inform us. (Murphy *et al.* 31)

Susan Jarratt likewise suggests that professionals in composition studies recast
themselves and declare, "We're in control, we're the master discipline over
these other disciplines" (Murphy *et al.* 31).

There is no consensus, however, regarding the nature of the relation
between composition studies and rhetoric. Elizabeth Flynn says that "[r]hetoric
is the parent discipline of composition studies, but the latter is an identifiable
field with its own institutional structure and purposes." She argues that
"[s]erious problems arise if we conflate the two," and she criticizes James
Berlin for having done so (138–139). Andrea Lunsford, like Flynn, draws a
careful distinction between composition studies and rhetoric, but she also
builds on what the two fields have in common. Both fields, according to
Lunsford, "are of necessity strongly cross-disciplinary," but while they are
"closely allied, often overlapping," they are "not synonymous." Rhetoric,
according to Lunsford, "is interested in building and testing theories of
persuasion primarily through the symbol system of language," and "composition is concerned with the way written texts come to be and the way they
are used in the home, school, workplace, and public worlds we all inhabit"
(80). Lunsford argues, however, that both rhetoric and composition "desta-
bilize the concept of text, opening it up and hence bringing into view the
many kinds of discourse formally excluded from examination" (87).

An underlying purpose of Lunsford's article, which was written primarily
for an audience of literary scholars, is to strengthen the position of composition studies within English studies. Lunsford observes that it is only during
"the twenty years or so since I began the PhD program" that "rhetoric and
composition, as areas of inquiry and research, have claimed a place in English
studies, though that place is by no means uncontested" (77). Lunsford's
implication is that rhetoric and composition are engaged in a territorial
struggle with literary studies. Susan Miller, who agrees with this premise,

observes that "composition" and "literature" represent "communities who are imagined to be operating in the same institutional settings, but not in the same ways or at the same levels of power." The two communities, she adds, "look at and act on each other across a boundary that most on either side see dividing 'high' from 'low.' " She argues that the two communities are nevertheless mutually dependent and that "the position of one is actually required by the socially constructed status and larger cultural implications of the other" (2). After noting that all definitions are fictive constructions, Miller explains that her own objective is to substitute a "new narrative" for the established "denigrating tale" and thereby to give writing teachers and students a chance to improve their status (1).

Schilb participates in the same enterprise when he argues that because composition studies "currently comprises diverse topics and methods and has ties to numerous disciplines, it can analyze broad social questions better than literary studies can" (176). Schilb looks forward to a time when composition studies becomes "what it deserves to become: not a plodding servant of other disciplines but a key force in the diagnosis of the contemporary world" (188). Phelps expresses equally high hopes for composition studies when she says that the "potential contributions of composition to contemporary intellectual life arise, first, from the 'discourse connection,' through which composition touches base with the root metaphor of contextualism; and second, from the commitment to open this new relation between human and world to every developing person" (41).

Robin Varnum
American International College

Works Cited

Connors, Robert J. 1983. "Composition Studies and Science." *College English* 45: 1–20.

Flynn, Elizabeth A. 1991. "Composition Studies from a Feminist Perspective." *The Politics of Writing Instruction: Postsecondary.* Ed. Richard Bullock and John Trimbur. Portsmouth NH: Boynton/Cook. 137–154.

Lauer, Janice M. 1984. "Composition Studies: Dappled Discipline." *Rhetoric Review* 3: 20–29.

Lindemann, Erika and Gary Tate, ed. 1991. "Preface." *An Introduction to Composition Studies.* New York: Oxford University Press. v–vi.

Lunsford, Andrea A. 1992. "Rhetoric and Composition." *Introduction to Scholarship in Modern Languages and Literatures.* Ed. Joseph Gibaldi. 2nd. ed. New York: Modern Language Association. 77–100.

Miller, Susan. 1991. *Textual Carnivals: The Politics of Composition.* Carbondale, IL: Southern Illinois University Press.

Murphy, James J., James Berlin, Robert Connors, Sharon Crowley, Richard Enos, Susan Jarratt, Nan Johnson, Jan Swearingen, and Victor Vitanza. 1988. "Octalog: The Politics of Historiography." *Rhetoric Review* 7: 5–49.

North, Stephen M. 1987. *The Making of Knowledge in Composition: Portrait of an Emerging Field.* Upper Montclair, NJ: Boynton/Cook.

Park, Douglas B. 1979. "Theories and Expectations: On Conceiving Composition and Rhetoric as a Discipline." *College English* 41: 47–56.

Phelps, Louise Wetherbee. 1986. "The Domain of Composition." *Rhetoric Review* 4: 182–195.

————. 1988. *Composition as a Human Science: Contributions to the Self-Understanding of a Discipline.* New York: Oxford University Press.

Phillips, Donna Burns, Ruth Greenberg, and Sharon Gibson. 1993. "*College Composition and Communication*: Chronicling a Discipline's Genesis." *College Composition and Communication* 44: 443–465.

Schilb, John. 1991. "Cultural Studies, Postmodernism, and Composition." *Contending with Words: Composition and Rhetoric in a Postmodern Age.* Ed. Patricia Harkin and John Schilb. New York: MLA. 173–188.

critical thinking

Critical thinking is supposed to be good for you. Students are exhorted to learn and to practice it (Elbow 37–39). Teachers are admonished to teach it (Berthoff 113–115; Aronowitz 770–771), teachers know they should teach it (Tompkins 656), and it is advocated as an act, behavior, and/or attitude that teachers ought to practice themselves in order to judge and evaluate what and how they *do* teach (Selfe 5–16). In 1996, what critical thinking *is* and what critical thinking is *for*, however, are as varied and contested as the diverse factions of scholars that have kept at least one foot in composition studies during the past twenty years.

The meaning of the term *critical thinking* has gathered complexity through time, evolving from a set of thinking/reasoning skills that may be objectified, codified, and taught, to discipline-specific strategies and attitudes that resonate with political overtones. A historical accounting of the term helps to reveal its beginnings and points to the disparate directions in which its multiple and often conflicting usages find themselves moving today.

Toni-Lee Capossela credits John Dewey with coining the term *critical thinking* in the thirties. Dewey defines critical thinking as "active, persistent, and careful consideration of any belief or supposed form of knowledge in the light of the grounds that support it and the further conclusions to which it tends" (qtd. in Capossela 2). "In short," Capossela concludes, "Dewey describe[s] critical thinking as a complex, transactional, context-based web of activity involving the whole person, an activity which writing both demonstrates and promotes." In the forties, "an absorption in quantification and assessment" encouraged educators to transform Dewey's holistic concept into measurable "subskills" (2). In the eighties, a growing interest in interdisciplinarity encouraged a return to Dewey's holistic approach: "when critical thinking, like writing, becomes everybody's business, then it begins to look like a meta-subject rather than a set of subskills" (3).

"[C]ritical thinking is both a propensity and a skill; both affective and cognitive" (McPeck, qtd. in Capossela 3). It is not "a series of steps"; but rather it is "the way" of "seeing the facts in their most persuasive and vulnerable lights" (McPeck qtd. in Capossela 3). Critical thinking is "the ability to formulate generalizations, entertain new possibilities, and suspend judgment" (Meyers, qtd. in Capossela 3). Critical thinking and its "synonym 'reflective thinking,' " presuppose "a speculative or questioning stance towards knowledge and experiences" (Petrosky, qtd. in Capossela 3–4). Critical thinking is seen as interdisciplinary, an approach reinforced in writing across the curriculum programs that have made critical thinking a practice and program goal (Berthoff 113–116; Fulwiler 3).

For others, critical thinking occurs through acts of revision (Murray 145) leading to "the making of meaning" (Berthoff 115). To that end, Peter Elbow would teach students "two kinds of thinking": "first order" "intuitive" thinking and "second order thinking" that "strives for logic and control." For Elbow, student-driven "[s]econd order thinking" is "critical thinking" (37). In Ann Berthoff's usage, however, critical thinking begins through teacher-directed activity: "teaching writing is a matter chiefly of teaching critical thinking" (113), as teachers model "critical thinking" which "is the capacity to see relationships methodically" (114).

A current freshman composition reader, *Rereading America*, borrows from and yet problematizes the claims made by Elbow and Berthoff by placing the teaching of composition into cultural and social contexts: "Culture shapes the way we think; it tells us what makes 'sense.' But as culture binds us together it also selectively blinds us. Becoming a critical thinker means learning how to look beyond these cultural myths and the assumptions embedded in them" (Colombo, Cullen, and Lisle 3). Min-zhan Lu advocates a "multicultural approach to student writing style" based "on the kind of 'critical thinking' advocated by . . . *Rereading America*" (449). Kenneth Bruffee also claims that cultural assumptions may get in the way of critical thinking. "Critical thinking . . . is playing off alternatives against one another, rather than playing them off against criteria of rationality, much less against eternal verities" (Rorty qtd. in Bruffee 788).

Indeed, as early as 1977, Stanley Aronowitz puts forward a politicized social science strain of critical thinking. Aronowitz advocates a critique of mass culture by means of critical thinking: "critical thinking is the fundamental precondition for an autonomous and self-motivated public or citizenry[;] its decline would threaten the future of democratic social, cultural, and political forms" (770). Donald Lazere, Lynn Troyka, and John Trimbur express similar concerns. Lazere argues that "critical thinking" is required to circumvent "mass-mediated political thought control and the reason-numbing effects of mass culture" (8). Troyka claims that "the essence of critical thinking is thinking beyond the obvious—beyond the flash of images on the television screen, . . . the half-truths of some propaganda, the manipulations of slanted language and faulty reasoning" (112). Trimbur (1994) posits that students' "*resistance*" to the critique of mass culture may "refer to something radical teachers need to overcome in order to promote critical thinking," yet maintains that a "positive sense" of "*resistance*" may also "signify a central goal of radical pedagogy, namely eliciting counter-readings of the codes and practices of the dominant culture" (202).

Ira Shor ties critical thinking to responsible democratic citizenship. In a dialogic conversation with Paolo Freire, Schor claims that "[t]he teacher needs to model an active skeptical learner . . . who invites students to be curious and critical . . . and creative." Both men agree that it is imperative to understand and act upon the distinction between "*producing* knowledge" and "*knowing* the existing knowledge" as "schools are set up as delivery systems to market official ideas and not to develop critical thinking" (8).

Some composition theorists have taken "liberal" theorists and practitioners to task over ideological differences hinged implicitly on differing conceptions of the term "critical thinking" (Donahue and Quandahl 9). Maxine Hairston, for example, decries the "politically focused course" (181) "that puts dogma before diversity, politics before craft, [and] ideology before critical thinking" (180). She envisions classroom as "a forum for the free exchange of ideas, a place where students can examine different points of view in an atmosphere of honest and open discussion, and, in the process, learn to think critically" (188). Responding to Hairston's criticism, Trimbur (1993) argues that rhetoric, with its goals of "fostering critical thinking and open debate," is implicitly what Hairston would resist (248–249). Paradoxically, like Elbow, Berthoff, and Hairston, the "liberal" and the "radical" ask students to think critically by re-envisioning their writing. The difference is that the *radical* theorists/practitioners ask students to "re-see" writing as a function of cultural codings and psychoanalytically and socially inscribed subjectivities (Lu 449).

"Critical thinking requires us to reflect further, trying to support our position *and also* trying to see the other side" (Barnett and Bedau 4). Given that requirement, the future of composition studies will be tied to redefinitions and reenactments of critical thinking.

Lisa L. Hill
Southeastern Oklahoma State University

Works Cited

Aronowitz, Stanley. 1977. "Mass Culture and the Eclipse of Reason: The Implications for Pedagogy." *College English* 38: 768–774.

Barnett, Sylvan, and Hugo Bedau. 1993. *Current Issues and Enduring Questions: A Guide to Thinking and Argument, with Readings.* Third Edition. Boston: Bedford Books of St. Martin's Press.

Berthoff, Ann. 1981. *The Making of Meaning: Metaphors, Models, and Maxims for Writing Teachers.* Upper Montclair, New Jersey: Boynton/Cook.

Bruffee, Kenneth. 1986. "Social Construction, Language, and Knowledge." *College Composition and Communication* 48: 773–790.

Capossela, Toni Lee. 1992. "Writing and Critical Thinking: Points of Convergence, Points of Divergence." ERIC ED 345 242.

Colombo, Gary, Robert Cullen, and Bonnie Lisle. 1992. *Rereading America: Cultural Contexts for Critical Thinking and Writing.* Boston: St. Martin's.

Donahue, Patricia, and Ellen Quandahl. 1989. *Reclaiming Pedagogy: The Rhetoric of the Classroom.* Carbondale, IL: Southern Illinois University Press.

Elbow, Peter. 1983. "Teaching Thinking by Teaching Writing." *Change* 5: 37–40.

Fulwiler, Toby. 1986. "The Politics of Writing across the Curriculum." ERIC ED 276 061.

Hairston, Maxine. 1992. "Diversity, Ideology, and the Teaching of Writing." *College Composition and Communication* 43: 179–193.

Lazere, Donald. 1982. "Composition for Critical Thinking: A Course Description." ERIC ED 273 959.

Lu, Min-zhan. 1994. "Professing Multiculturalism: The Politics of Style in the Contact Zone." *College Composition and Communication* 45: 442–458.

Murray, Donald M. 1982. "Teaching the Other Self: The Writer's First Reader." *College Composition and Communication* 33: 140–147.

Selfe, Cynthia L. 1985. "Slouching toward Bethlehem: Where Are We Going?" (Working Draft). ERIC ED 267 407.

Shor, Ira, and Paolo Freire. 1987. *A Pedagogy for Liberation: Dialogues on Transforming Education.* New York: Bergin and Garvey.

Tompkins, Jane. 1990. "Pedagogy of the Distressed." *College English* 52: 653–660.

Trimbur, John. 1993. "Responses to Maxine Hairston." *College Composition and Communication* 44: 248–249.

———. 1994. "The Politics of Radical Pedagogy: A Plea for a Dose of Vulgar Marxism." *College English* 56: 194–206.

Troyka, Lynn. 1993. *Simon and Schuster Handbook for Writers.* New Jersey: Prentice Hall. 112–144.

cultural studies

"In serious critical intellectual work," Stuart Hall cautions, "there are no absolute beginnings and few unbroken continuities" (57). The work of describing intersections between composition and cultural studies is a particularly problematic case in point. James A. Berlin writes that "[c]omposition studies, since its formation in college English departments a hundred years ago, has in many of its manifestations attempted to become a variety of cultural studies[,] . . . an activity that studies the construction of subjects within social formations, focusing on . . . signifying practices . . . and the implications of those practices in power and ideology" (1993, 102).

But it was not until the 1980s that explicit institutional connections were established between composition and cultural studies. These connections emerged in the contexts of the social constructionist movement in composition, the renewed interest in rhetoric among literary theorists, the critique of disciplinarity in both institutions, and the increasing diversity of student populations. Compositionists who accepted Kenneth Bruffee's assertion "that entities that we normally call reality, knowledge, thought, facts, texts, selves and so on are constructs generated by communities of like minded peers" (774) looked to cultural studies for ways of describing those communities and explaining their like-mindedness. At the same time, in response to post-structuralist and neo-Marxist challenges, literary theorists like Terry Eagleton began to rethink English Studies, emphasizing similarities between rhetoric and cultural studies in their "concern for the kinds of effects . . . discourses produce, and how they produce them" (205); such concerns worked to blur boundaries among traditional university formations such as film studies, literary studies, and composition studies as well as to problematize definitions of the term "text." The critique of disciplinarity in knowledge formation (see, in composition studies, e.g., Bizzell, Bruffee, Fish, Harkin) shifted attention from traditional institutional formations to their cultural contexts. Additionally, as John Schilb points out, students who varied "in gender, ethnic background, financial status, and age and yet share[d] an immersion in the electronic media . . . made . . . teachers doubt the relevance of traditional texts and pedagogies" (174).

When compositionists in the United States began to envision a cultural/composition studies agenda, they looked to existing theoretical statements in cultural studies. Consequently, their visions of the project(s) for cultural/composition studies reflect their efforts to come to terms with those statements and adapt them to writing courses. Probably because its members undertake what Susan Miller calls "the kind of interpretation that would repair the split—maintained by Marxist, Foucauldian, poststructuralist, and feminist theories . . . between structuralist analyses of institutions and ['culturalist'] accounts that privilege the experience of individuals," the Birmingham Centre for Contemporary Cultural Studies has been particularly influential on compositionists. Birmingham theorists (especially Stuart Hall, Matthew Hoggart, Richard Johnson) tend to foreground the ways in which "institutions—impersonal structures of procedure, common sense, and received values—regularly turn out individuals whose thinking and writing 'freely' . . . perpetuate the structure of that institution" (Miller 23) but they are careful to attend as well to ways in which individuals might develop and exercise agency to resist those structures. Among the most profoundly influenced by the Birmingham School is Berlin (1993), who places "consciousness formation at the center of cultural studies" (102) and proposes that, since "the subject is the point of intersection of various discourses—discourses about class, race, gender, ethnicity, age, religion and the like—and it is influenced by those discourses" (103), it is necessary to "examine signifying practices in the formation of subjectivities within concrete material, social, and political conditions" (104).

John Trimbur also directly addresses the culturalist/structuralist split when he proposes that the "political-intellectual project of cultural studies" is a strategy for addressing "the dilemma of postmodernism" (127). Thus, he writes, "cultural studies portrays spectators and consumers not only as subject positions . . . but also as active interpreters of their own experience who use the cultural practices and productions they encounter differentially and for their own purposes" (127). Crucial to Trimbur's project is filling "the gap left vacant by the postmodern death of the subject with a nonessential self that allows for agency and utopian aspirations" (130).

C. Mark Hurlbert and Michael Blitz concentrate on defining, describing and fostering this agency, urging composition teachers to "work with students to examine and intervene in the 'construction' which produces people as subjects and by which people subject other people to inequitable, abusive, intolerable conditions" (25). Such a dynamic is appropriately situated in composition studies, Hurlbert and Blitz believe, because writing makes it possible for students "to make learning a personal act toward taking greater control" of their lives, and it must situate this process "in and with social order" (4).

Other compositionists are disinclined to limit the domain of cultural studies exclusively to subject formation. Henry Giroux, David Shumway, Paul

Smith and James J. Sosnoski explicitly call for cultural studies to examine the academic disciplines' construction of knowledge, and David B. Downing, Patricia Harkin, and Sosnoski think the inquiry should engage the discursive formation of subjectivities, knowledge, and values. Schilb, who, like Trimbur, explicitly connects cultural studies, postmodernism, and composition studies, calls for teachers, with students as "co-inquirers" (187), to inquire into disparate accounts of cultural studies agendas. "A composition program," he writes, "[could] examine various theories of cultural studies and post-modernism as well as how they diverge or mesh" (175); the "task," as Schilb sees it, "is not to develop a program based on premature resolution of the issues [cultural studies theorists] have generated but to make investigations of these issues the program's ongoing project" (187).

These formulations of the "object" of cultural studies' inquiry lead to varying senses of its boundaries, methods, and goals. The majority of cultural studies advocates use "rhetoric for cultural critique, disclosing the ideological processes surrounding the production and consumption of texts, as well as . . . attempts . . . to deny these processes" (Berlin 1992, 4). Joel Foreman and Shumway point to cultural studies' "intent to expand humanistic studies by including texts in new media and the products of oppressed or marginalized groups" (244; see also Schriner 95; Penticoff and Brodkey *passim*). Diana George and Diana Shoos write that "cultural studies takes as its subjects of investigation the immediate world of experience as well as mediated discourse" and so "is especially well suited to a course like composition, which calls upon students to write about what they remember, what they are currently experiencing, and what they discover through observation, research, critique" (200). Critique is the crucial element for George and Shoos, who "would argue that a course that attempts to use cultural studies without its domain as an interrogator of institutions is simply a course in pop culture" (201). Some cultural studies advocates regard it as a way to break the limits of the service orientation (Harkin and Schilb, 1; Schilb, 178) without neglecting composition's traditional commitment to the classroom (Berlin 1993, 109). But Michael Murphy argues that the cultural studies orientation that Berlin and others propose merely reinscribes the service function in an unexamined commitment to "progressivism."

Among those who have reservations about cultural studies are Maxine Hairston, who believes that required writing courses should not focus on controversial topics, and the National Association of Scholars, some of whose members are concerned that "students will feel pressure to conform to . . . the assumption that Western civilization is inherently unfair to women, minority group members, and homosexuals" (Mangan A15). From another political perspective, Maśud Zavarzadeh and Donald Morton see the cultural studies curriculum at Syracuse University as merely reformist in that it fits "into the existing structure of the academy and its supporting knowledge industry" (66); James Thomas Zebroski, writing in sympathy with the

Syracuse agenda, nevertheless describes his concern that composition's traditional emphasis on "development" within inherited cultural forms fits uneasily with cultural studies' emphasis on critique of those forms. "It would be a terrible irony" he warns, "if cultural studies functioned to reinstate (or reproduce) the banking model of education" (92).

Patricia Harkin
Purdue University

Works Cited

Berlin, James A. 1992. "Introduction." *Cultural Studies in the English Classroom.* Ed. James Berlin and Michael Vivion. Portsmouth, NH: Boynton/Cook Heinemann. 3–4.

———. 1993. "Composition Studies and Cultural Studies: Collapsing Boundaries." *Into the Field: Sites of Composition Studies.* Ed. Anne Ruggles Gere. New York: MLA.

Berlin, James A., and Michael J. Vivion, ed. 1992. *Cultural Studies in the English Classroom.* Portsmouth, NH: Boynton/Cook.

Bizzell, Patricia. 1982. "Cognition, Convention, and Certainty: What We Need to Know about Writing." *Pre/Text* 3: 213–243.

Bruffee, Kenneth A. 1986. "Social Construction, Language, and the Authority of Knowledge: A Bibliographical Essay." *College English* 48: 773–790.

Downing, David B., Patricia Harkin, and James J. Sosnoski. 1994. "Configurations of Lore." *Changing Classroom Practices: Resources for Literary and Cultural Studies.* Ed. David B. Downing. Urbana: National Council of Teachers of English.

Eagleton, Terry. 1983. *Literary Theory: An Introduction.* Minneapolis: University of Minnesota Press.

Fish, Stanley. 1989. "Antifoundationalism, Theory-Hope, and the Teaching of Composition." *Doing What Comes Naturally: Change, Rhetoric, and the Practice of Theory in Literary and Legal Studies.* Durham: Duke University Press.

Foreman, Joel, and David R. Shumway. 1992. "Cultural Studies: Reading Visual Texts." Berlin and Vivion, 244–261.

Giroux, Henry, David Shumway, Paul Smith, and James J. Sosnoski. 1984. "The Need for Cultural Studies: Resisting Intellectuals and Oppositional Public Spheres." *Dalhousie Review* 64: 472–486.

George, Diana, and Diana Shoos. 1992. "Issues of Subjectivity and Resistance: Cultural Studies in the English Classroom." Berlin and Vivion, 200–210.

Hall, Stuart. 1980. "Cultural Studies: Two Paradigms." *Media, Culture, and Society* 2: 57–72.

Hairston, Maxine C. 1991. "Required Courses Should Not Focus on Politically Charged Social Issues." *Chronicle of Higher Education* 23 January: B1 and B2.

Harkin, Patricia. 1991. "The Postdisciplinary Politics of Lore." *Contending with Words: Composition and Rhetoric in a Postmodern Age.* Ed. Patricia Harkin and John Schilb. New York: MLA. 124–138.

Harkin, Patricia, and John Schilb. 1991. "Introduction." *Contending with Words: Composition and Rhetoric in a Postmodern Age.* Ed. Patricia Harkin and John Schilb. New York: MLA. 1–10.

Hurlbert, C. Mark, and Michael Blitz. 1991. *Composition and Resistance.* Portsmouth, NH: Boynton/Cook.

Mangan, Katherine S. 1990. "Battle Rages over Plan to Focus on Race and Gender in University of Texas Course." *Chronicle of Higher Education* 21 November: A15.

Miller, Susan. 1994. "Composition as a Cultural Artifact: Rethinking History as Theory." *Writing Theory and Critical Theory.* Ed. John Clifford and John Schilb. New York: MLA. 19–32.

Murphy, Michael. 1994. "After Progressivism: Modern Composition, Institutional Service, and Cultural Studies." *Composition Theory for the Postmodern Classroom.* Ed. Gary A. Olson and Sidney I. Dobrin. Albany: State University of New York Press.

Penticoff, Richard, and Linda Brodkey. 1992. " 'Writing about Difference': Hard Cases for Cultural Studies." Berlin and Vivion, 123–144.

Schilb, John. 1991. "Cultural Studies, Postmodernism, Composition." Harkin and Schilb, 173–188.

Schriner, Delores K. 1992. "One Person, Many Worlds: A Multi-Cultural Composition Curriculum." Berlin and Vivion, 95–111.

Trimbur, John. 1993. "Composition Studies: Postmodern or Popular." *Into the Field: Sites of Composition Studies.* Ed. Anne Ruggles Gere. New York: MLA. 117–132.

Zavarzadeh, Masud, and Donald Morton. 1992. "A Very Good Idea Indeed: The (Post)Modern Labor Force and Curricular Reform." Berlin and Vivion, 66–86.

Zebroski, James Thomas. "The Syracuse University Writing Program and Cultural Studies: A Personal View of the Politics of Development." Berlin and Vivion, 87–94.

deconstruction

The term *deconstruction* was coined by a French theorist, Jacques Derrida, whose rereading of the French philosophical tradition indirectly challenged many of the basic assumptions of the dominant theoretical foundation of 1960s literary studies, the New Criticism. It emerged in the conversation about writing instruction in the late 1970s among repeated calls for theoretical awareness in a field seeking disciplinary status, in part through interdisciplinary scholarship.

One of several positions loosely held under the umbrella term *post-structuralism* (sometimes even *postmodernism*), *deconstruction* vigorously resists definition. According to Derrida, "there is not one deconstruction, and deconstruction is not a single theory or a single method" (qtd. in Olson 12). Because it is used variously to refer to a philosophical position, a theory of reading, a political strategy and more, as Jasper Neel (1995) suggests, "its 'meaning' [is] complicated far beyond any sort of summary" (158). Attempts to define deconstruction inevitably presuppose the very notions that decon-struction has been used to throw into question—certain, referential meaning and the disinterested, "objective" search for knowledge. As G. Douglas Atkins and Michael Johnson would have it, "[i]f deconstruction could be neatly defined and if the boundaries of its activities could be clearly demarcated, it would hardly be different from the tradition it challenges" (10).

According to Derrida, the primary goal of Western philosophy as a discipline, the naming of Truth, depends on the assumption that words are capable of referring accurately to a transcendent reality existing outside of language. The belief in an accurate correspondence between a rational human mind and a rational universe allowed the ancient Greeks to conceive of language, Sharon Crowley (1989) suggests, "as both a representation of truth and an instrument for finding it" (2). According to this tradition, language is at once inferior to an absolute reality to which it can only refer, yet capable of being a transparent medium to that reality when free from distortion or illogic.

Derrida and other deconstructionists have argued a philosophical position which holds that there is no "transcendental signified," no reality external to language. Instead, words have meaning only in their relation to other words. As a result, meaning, logic, and reality itself are inseparably integrated with the play of language; words are intersections of meaning rather than locations, and the project of writing "the truth" is always a program in accord with a particular value or belief system.

Such a position equips deconstructionists with a powerful reading strategy which can be turned against claims of truth, whether they are made explicitly in texts or implicitly within institutional practices. The title of Sharon Crowley's third chapter in *A Teacher's Introduction to Deconstruction* (1989), "Deconstructing Writing Pedagogy," marks the predominant context in which meanings of deconstruction have been advanced in the field. In what may well be the first mention of Derrida in composition scholarship, without specifically using the term *deconstruction*, Crowley (1979) suggests that Derrida's *Of Grammatology* can be used to expose the "poverty of current-traditional rhetoric" and underscore the value of rhetorical invention. Situating deconstruction within a set of "poststructural . . . reading theories," Edward White argues that it "tends to confirm our best practice and support our most significant challenges to the worst of what our colleagues are doing" (187). Atkins and Johnson maintain that such an understanding is authorized by "Derrida himself [who] has insisted repeatedly that deconstruction *is* teaching as well as an interventionist strategy" (11).

To that end, deconstruction has been understood as a "fundamentally subversive method" that can undo failed conceptions—such as "the ideology of asymmetry" (Kaufer and Waller 69, 73)—for teachers through the professional discourse and for students by way of informed pedagogy. Paul Northam, for example, excoriates "current-traditional rhetoric" while promoting "deconstructive reading" because it "gives [students] analytical skills and a positive attitude toward language that are more likely than established methods of invention to lead to inspiration" (116). "Assuming a deconstructive perspective," Crowley (1989) argues that "to center a writing pedagogy on authors . . . is to insert an attitude into the composing act that misunderstands its focus" (35). According to Crowley, a

> deconstructive pedagogy . . . would redirect the notion of intention or purpose . . . onto its suitability to the rhetorical situation for which it was designed. Perhaps it would even reject the notion of intention altogether and substitute the task of incorporating the projected needs of audiences into the writing process. (36)

Declaring "many of the approaches we have taken in freshman English naive and misguided," Jon Harned argues that "[i]n deconstruction pedagogy the teacher is on an equal footing with the students as a fellow inquirer" as opposed to a practice in which "the teacher is at the center of the classroom as the authority on the rules of a discursive formation or interpretive community" (14).

However, like the literary critic who identifies in the work of some New Historicists a "two-stage operation in which deconstructive analysis is brought in for the ground-clearing demolition work, then moved safely off site when the reconstruction work begins" (Keesey 425), Randall Knoper argues that "under" the name *deconstruction* "we receive the familiar":

> The contrast between what looks like a radical philosophy and its translation into what looks like familiar writing pedagogies must at least make us consider the possibility that "deconstruction" in our writing about teaching has come mainly to represent only a minor deviation. . . . Perhaps adopting deconstruction as a technology of reading and as a practice allied with process pedagogy locates it where it can induce the least change. (141)

Finding that attempts to link deconstruction and composition regularly "lose the admirable 'both/and' stance of deconstructive criticism and, to their peril, fall into easy either/or, good/bad contrasts," Linda H. Peterson claims that deconstruction is often not necessarily the instrument for performing critique but a way to authorize or dress up its dissemination. "[T]oo frequently," she argues, "deconstruction serves merely to reassert the 'new paradigm' in writing or undergird it with avant-garde concepts." Peterson is "made anxious by the assumption, too enthusiastically held, that deconstructive theory can lead directly and concretely to composition pedagogy" (358).

Similarly, Neel (1990) declares that he must "take issue" with the notion that "deconstruction is an entirely benign system that brings enlightenment to the darkened world of English teaching" (158). Following the variety of moves to explain *deconstruction* during the 1980s—including his own (1988)—as a method capable of exposing bad pedagogy and devising its effective counterpart, Neel has been most consistent in using the term since. Deconstruction, he claims (1995), is "a danger to composition" (158). In a review of Crowley's *Teacher's Introduction*, Neel (1990) warns that writing pedagogies based on deconstruction are fraught with potential problems for unwary students, teachers, and administrators. Deconstruction, Neel argues, is the voice of Plato spoken by Derrida and Hillis Miller (who he claims separate deconstruction and sophistry), a voice that "privileges thinking over speaking, speaking over writing, philosophy over rhetoric, and truth over sophistry" (159).

Outside the interviews of literary critics and responses to them in the *Journal of Advanced Composition*, one is hard pressed to find mention of deconstruction in composition literature of the 1990s. Crowley's assessment in 1987, that deconstruction "is widely construed in America as a critical methodology" (170), appears to have taken hold in composition, too, obviating its delineation as a pedagogical ally of the process movement. When the term appears explicitly now it most likely appears implicitly defined as a critical method, sometimes one turned against its own authority and the interests it has been made to serve. Declaring recently that "deconstruction

put me in the habit of suspicion" (322), Crowley (1994) notes that deconstruction has often been a instrument of conservativism, specifically the recent
"business of deconstructing subjectivity . . . just when women and people of
color are discovering its uses and its power" (323).

Peter Vandenberg
DePaul University, Chicago

Works Cited

Atkins, G. Douglas, and Michael L. Johnson, ed. 1985. Introduction. *Writing and Reading Differently: Deconstruction and the Teaching of Composition and Literature.* Lawrence: University of Kansas Press. 1–14.

Crowley, Sharon. 1979. "Of *Gorgias* and Grammatology." *College Composition and Communication* 30: 279–284.

———. 1987. "Derrida, Deconstruction, and Our Scene of Teaching." *PRE/TEXT* 8: 169–183.

———. 1989. *A Teacher's Introduction to Deconstruction.* Urbana, IL: NCTE.

———. 1994. "A Letter to the Editors." *Writing Theory and Critical Theory.* Ed. John Clifford and John Schilb. New York: MLA. 319–326.

Harned, Jon. 1986. "Poststructuralism and the Teaching of Composition." *Freshman English News* 15: 10–16.

Kaufer, David, and Gary Waller. 1985. "To Write Is to Read Is to Write, Right?" In Atkins and Johnson, 66–92.

Keesey, Donald, ed. 1994. *Contexts for Criticism.* 2nd Edition. Mountain View, CA: Mayfield.

Knoper, Randall. 1989. "Deconstruction, Process, Writing." *Reclaiming Pedagogy.* Ed. Patricia Donahue and Ellen Quandahl. Carbondale: Southern IL University Press. 128–143.

Neel, Jasper. 1988. *Plato, Derrida, and Writing.* Carbondale: Southern IL University Press.

———. 1990. Rev. of *A Teacher's Introduction to Deconstruction* by Sharon Crowley. *Journal of Advanced Composition* 10: 157–160.

———. 1995. "Learning about Learning about Deconstruction: An Epi(trying-tobe)gone." *Journal of Advanced Composition* 15: 155–161.

Northam, Paul. 1985. "Heuristics and Beyond: Deconstruction/Inspiration and the Teaching of Writing Invention." In Atkins and Johnson, 115–128.

Olson, Gary A. 1990. "Jacques Derrida on Rhetoric and Composition: A Conversation." *Journal of Advanced Composition* 10: 1–21.

Peterson, Linda H. 1986. Rev. of *Writing and Reading Differently*, Ed. G. Douglas Atkins and Michael L. Johnson. *College Composition and Communication* 40: 357–359.

White, Edward M. 1984. "Post-Structural Literary Criticism and the Response to Student Writing." *College Composition and Communication* 35: 186–196.

discipline

The term *discipline* emerged in composition scholarship in the mid-1970s—amid repeated and vociferous calls for research on composing—as something like an object of desire. Perhaps because of its relationship to *research* and *knowledge*, terms equally fluid in their meanings and implications, this keyword has often unsettled the debates in which it has been employed. Yet when it is invoked positively to stand for a united group engaged in some right act, it often escapes question despite its instability. As Stephen North would have it, "[c]haracterize Composition as paradigmatic or dialogical, coherent or chaotic as you like, but it is to everyone's advantage to treat it as a legitimate academic discipline" (363–364).

Most often, *discipline* is used as a synonym for *field, profession, community.* In such senses, it has little specific meaning, but shares with these other terms the rhetorical power of invoking collectivity. Erika Lindemann and Gary Tate use the term to imply shared purpose among "composition specialists" in *An Introduction to Composition Studies*: "This book introduces readers to the relatively new academic discipline called, variously, rhetoric and composition, rhetoric, composition, and composition studies" (v). In this sense, what Joseph Harris has said of *community* might apply equally well to *discipline*; such uses of the term are *performatives*, statements "in which saying does indeed make it so" (6). Andrea Lunsford, for example, uses the two words in tandem when she writes of "a particular disciplinary community" (5). And as Harris says of "the gambit of community," once *discipline* is offered "it is almost impossible to decline—since what is being invoked is a community of those in power, of those who know the accepted ways" (6).

The terms *research* and *discipline* were rather consistently linked in composition scholarship of twenty years ago. Nancy Sommers' usage in 1979 is typical: "Researchers have sought to give currency to a discipline without its own theoretical base by grasping on to whatever is culturally or intellectually in vogue" (46). Robert Connors wrote in 1983 that "the use of scientific terms cannot be accidental or meaningless at this point in the history of our discipline" (6). While Connors does not seem to consider *discipline* itself a "scientific term," he does argue against the "tacit message" of claims borrowing terms such as Thomas Kuhn's paradigm, "that composition studies should be a scientific or prescientific discipline" (5).

Whether one wrote in favor of or in opposition to "research," disciplinarity was often made to stand for a destination while *research*—typically interpreted as "empirical research"—constituted the vehicle. In 1979 Robert Gorrell wrote that "the research activity of recent years, whether or not the results are conclusive, has done a great deal to establish the validity of composition as a respectable academic discipline" (35–36). Four years earlier, Janice Lauer argued that

> freshman English will never reach the status of a respectable intellectual discipline unless both its theorizers and its practitioners break out of the ghetto.... Unless both the textmakers and the teachers of composition investigate beyond the field of English, beyond even the area of rhetorical studies for the solution to the composition problem, they will find themselves wandering in an endless maze. (qtd. in Park 49)

According to Douglas Park, Lauer's "notion" of composition theory and research as "scientific" is "explicit" (49). Yet for Park, "[w]hat composition research does not offer is a shapely coherence that makes it definable as a discipline" (47); a discipline is an entity "whole and defined," one with its "intellectual substance tied to the practical applications" (48). "Yet the whole notion," Park argues, "derived as it is from the sciences and from technology, is illusory and inappropriate for the complex, imprecise business of teaching writing" (54). "Properly speaking," Park goes on, "composition and rhetoric is not a discipline but a whole network of potentially related disciplines and activities" (55).

The debate over Lauer's use of *research* continues (see Lauer 1992 and Arrington), yet the debate seems to have more to do with meanings of *discipline*. While Park equates a discipline with a single method, Lauer (1984) is far more inclusive:

> a discipline has a special set of phenomena to study, a characteristic mode or modes of inquiry, its own history of development, its theoretical ancestors and assumptions, its evolving body of knowledge, and its own epistemic courts by which knowledge gains that status.... [The] epistemic court, which Toulmin describes as a community of experts who reach consensus in accord with their interpretations of the discipline's basic tasks ... [in] composition studies consists of scholars who are both knowledgeable about the range of existing research and contributing to one or the other types of inquiry about written discourse. (22–24)

In Lauer's sense of the term, what *kind* of research is being done has little bearing on her understanding of *discipline*. The production and control of *research*, very broadly conceived, is what constitutes disciplinary boundaries. According to Lauer, in composition studies the epistemic court is distinct from "those writing instructors and pedagogical advocates who are neither in touch with existing scholarship nor contributing to it." Those who are not publishing "research" or reading it are among those who "can impede if not altogether frustrate the progress of a discipline" (24).

While Lauer seems to equate *research* with published scholarship in the maintenance of disciplinary boundaries, Robert Connors (1984) equates published scholarship directly with knowledge and, therefore, "the" discipline:

> [o]ur discipline, composition studies, was formed by and largely exists through the professional journals in which our work appears.... The selective perpetuation of new ideas that is carried on by these wielders of institutional power has an immense effect on what constitutes the body of knowledge defining the discipline itself. (352)

Yet Connors implies, and Lauer makes explicit, that knowledge is authorized in a matrix of restrictions, and in this sense *discipline* is almost always employed pejoratively.

Elizabeth A. Flynn argues that such constraints, indeed disciplinarity itself, is male-centered. In describing composition studies prior to 1978 as "androcentric," Flynn identifies the predominance of males in traditional disciplinary roles—as authors of canonized texts, leaders of dominant professional organizations, and editors of leading journals. According to Flynn, androcentric disciplines inevitably yield androcentric knowledge: "the male perspective prevails because positions of power and authority within society have been held by males rather than females" (142). "Far from looking to the disciplines as the place where knowledge properly gets made," Kurt Spellmeyer suggests, "we might see them instead as social sites where this making has become artificially constrained" (801). In this sense, discipline connotes uniformity, consistency, and standardization in the training of graduate students, what John Schilb warily calls "getting disciplined."

Certainly, *discipline* has been a hotly contested term because it emerged in discussions about writing instruction at the very moment that disciplinarity was undergoing a vigorous critique throughout the academy (Harkin and Schilb). Thus, terms like *multidisciplinary* and *interdisciplinary* were typically invoked concurrently with *discipline* (see Phelps). Necessarily, however, such variations are defined in terms of disciplinarity itself, establishing that which is to be erased. Anne Ruggles Gere, for example, asserts that "as composition interacts with other disciplines ... the boundaries between them fade, becoming more permeable" (3). Definitions such as "interdisciplinarity—in its current form, an overriding concern with textuality and interpretive studies" (Moglen 87), leave one to conclude that one's disciplinary constraints often govern how the intermixing is to be understood.

Some authors have explicitly chosen to avoid the term altogether, yet in attempting to explain "what goes on in composition studies" (Harkin and Schilb 5) inevitably pull its trace along through the tacit establishment of composition studies as institutional space. Perhaps whenever two or more scholars are gathered together in the act of someone's composing, the term *discipline* will not be far removed. According to Rex Olson, following Aristotle's *Metaphysics*, writing itself is "the foundation of all disciplines. . . . [D]efinition is the first principle of disciplinarity, and composition its very foundation. Composition is the mother tongue of disciplinarity" (31).

Peter Vandenberg
DePaul University, Chicago

Works Cited

Arrington, Phillip. 1992. "The Agon Continues: A Reply to Janice Lauer." *Journal of Advanced Composition* 12: 422–424.

Connors, Robert J. 1983. "Composition Studies and Science." *College English* 45: 1–20.

———. 1984. "Journals in Composition Studies." *College English* 46: 348–365.

Flynn, Elizabeth A. 1991. "Composition Studies from a Feminist Perspective." *The Politics of Writing Instruction: Postsecondary.* Ed. Richard Bullock and John Trimbur. Portsmouth, NH: Boynton/Cook. 137–154.

Gere, Anne Ruggles. 1993. Introduction. *Into the Field: Sites of Composition Studies.* New York: MLA. 1–6.

Gorrell, Robert M. 1979. "Like a Crab Backward: Has the CCCC Been Worth It?" *College Composition and Communication* 30: 32–36.

Harkin, Patricia, and John Schilb. 1991. Introduction. *Contending with Words.* New York: MLA. 1–10.

Harris, Joseph. 1988. "Community: A Keyword in the Teaching of Writing." Conference on College Composition and Communication. St. Louis, MO. 17 March.

Lauer, Janice. 1984. "Composition Studies: Dappled Discipline." *Rhetoric Review* 3: 20–29.

———. 1992. "A Note to *JAC* Readers." *Journal of Advanced Composition* 12: 421–422.

Lindemann, Erika, and Gary Tate, ed. 1991. Preface. *An Introduction to Composition Studies.* New York: Oxford. v–vi.

Lunsford, Andrea A. 1991. "The Nature of Composition Studies." In Lindemann and Tate. 3–14.

Moglen, Helene. 1989. "Crossing the Boundaries: Interdisciplinary Education at the Graduate Level." *The Future of Doctoral Studies in English.* Ed. Andrea Lunsford, Helene Moglen, and James F. Slevin. New York: MLA. 84–90.

North, Stephen M. 1987. *The Making of Knowledge in Composition: Portrait of an Emerging Field.* Portsmouth, NH: Boynton/Cook.

Olson, Rex. 1988. "Derrida (f)or Us?" *PRE/TEXT* 9: 27–60.

Park, Douglas B. 1979. "Theories and Expectations: On Conceiving Composition as Rhetoric and a Discipline." *College English* 41: 47–56.

Phelps, Louise Wetherbee. 1986. "The Domain of Composition." *Rhetoric Review* 4: 182–195.

Schilb, John. 1994. "Getting Disciplined?" *Rhetoric Review* 12: 398–405.

Sommers, Nancy. 1979. "The Need for Theory in Composition Research." *College Composition and Communication* 30: 46–49.

Spellmeyer, Kurt. 1994. "Travels to the Heart of the Forest: Dilettantes, Professionals, and Knowledge." *College English* 56: 788–809.

discourse community

The term *discourse community* emerged in composition scholarship in the early 1980s, but its antecedents are various, much older, and just as vigorously contested. Both John Swales and Valerie Balester trace the use of *community* in the work of writers as methodologically diverse as Wittgenstein, Thomas Kuhn, Richard Rorty, Clifford Geertz, and Charles Willard. Yet sociolinguists and the matrix of scholars working at the intersection between philosophy and literary theory appear to have had the biggest influence on those writing in composition and rhetoric.

Though he doesn't use the term *discourse community*, in 1982 Martin Nystrand introduced the concept of "writer's speech communities" in which "the special relations that define written language functioning and promote its meaningful use . . . are wholly circumscribed by the systematic relations that obtain in the speech community of the writer" (17). Swales, also a sociolinguist, has argued that however tight the definition becomes for "speech community," it does not obviate the need for an alternative definition of *discourse community*. According to Swales, "[a] speech community typically inherits its membership by birth, accident or adoption; a discourse community recruits its members by persuasion, training or relevant qualification" (24). Swales claims to "appropriate" the work of "social perspectivists" to define characteristics "necessary and sufficient" for identifying a discourse community: "a broadly agreed set of common public goals"; participatory mechanisms of intercommunication that "provide information and feedback"; and a specifically appropriate genre or genres and a specialized vocabulary (24–27).

The influence of literary criticism, or perhaps more properly the texts that have been important to literary critics, on the evolution of *discourse community* has been profound. As early as 1964 Richard Ohmann mentions Northrup Frye in claiming that "[t]he community that a piece of genuine writing creates is one, not only of ideas and attitudes, but of fundamental modes of perception, thought, and feeling. That is, discourse works within

and reflects ... a world view" (301). In addition to Frye, compositionists
have invoked the speculative work on communities done by Roland Barthes,
Raymond Williams, Michel Foucault, Julia Kristeva, Edward Said, and others.
In particular, Stanley Fish's *interpretive community*—focusing as it does on
reading rather than writing per se—has played a large role in helping to
define *discourse community* by opposition (see Schilb).

Within composition studies, *discourse* and *community* by themselves
each constitute keywords of the first order—definitions of both are frequently
bound up with the problems they are used to discuss. Fusing the terms
together would seem to radically intensify the potential for slippage. Yet
according to M. Jimmie Killingsworth, a combination of the two terms "is
useful in the theory and analysis of writing because it embraces the rhetorical
concern with social interchange (discourse) and with situation or context
(community)" (110).

A *discourse*, according to David Bartholomae, is a "peculiar way of
knowing, selecting, evaluating, reporting, concluding, and arguing." Discourses are plural, various, and constrictive; they constitute a variety of
rule-based "voices and interpretive schemes" (135) with discreet "projects
and agendas that determine what writers can and will do" (139). Bruce
Herzberg has written that "language use in a group is a form of social
behavior, that discourse is a means of maintaining and extending [a] group's
knowledge and of initiating new members into the group, and that discourse
is epistemic or constitutive of the group's knowledge" (qtd. in Swales 21).

Notwithstanding the manifold questions that arise from uses of the term
discourse—for example, is it enabling or prohibitive? in what sense is *discourse*
co-terminous with *rhetoric, language* and/or *knowledge*?—the term *community*
has drawn far greater attention in composition scholarship for its instability.

"In *community*," Joe Harris (1988) writes, "we find a concept both
seductive and powerful, one that offers us a view of shared purpose and
effort and that also makes a rhetorical claim on us that is hard to resist. Yet
there is also something maddening and vague about the term" (6). John Schilb
finds that Elaine Maimon "uses the word so freely ... [that] she labels as
communities the whole academy, the various disciplines, subfields within the
disciplines, individual classes," and contributors to and readers of the book
in which her essay appears (44). Harris (1988) refers to such uses of
community as "gambits," "*performatives*—statements ... in which saying
does indeed make it so" (6). He argues that "the 'communities' to which our
theories refer all exist at one remove from actual experience. ... They are
all literally utopias—nowheres, meta-communities—that are tied to no particular time or place" (6–7).

Killingsworth laments the sometimes uncritical acceptance of *community*
in composition scholarship, but argues that use of the term *discourse* alone,
"without the ballast of *community*, which designates a (real or imagined) site

for production," leads to abstraction. He distinguishes, then, between local and global communities. Local communities are defined

> simply as the place where writers ordinarily work . . . , the site of the occupational practice by which he or she is identified in demographic descriptions. Global communities . . . are defined by likemindedness, political and intellectual affiliation, and other such "special interests" and are maintained by widely dispersed discourse practices made possible by modern publishing and other communication technologies. The global discourse community [is] mental. (111–112).

Any speaker or writer, Killingsworth maintains, is "involved simultaneously in both local and global discourse communities and will feel challenged to favor one over the other" (115). A local discourse community—presumably even "the individual as community"—is a specific site for conflicting discourse practices (117).

Killingsworth here articulates a definition of *discourse community* as a site of fragmentation and discord, an opposition to the earliest uses of the term in the field. In a powerfully influential 1982 article, Patricia Bizzell argued that "[g]roups of society members can become accustomed to modifying each other's reasoning and language use in certain ways. Eventually, these familiar ways achieve the status of conventions that bind the group in a discourse community" (214). Just two years later Kenneth Bruffee suggested that a "community of knowledgeable peers is a group of people who accept, and whose work is guided by, the same paradigms and the same code of values and assumptions" (642). Harris (1989) finds in similar constructs "the sense of like-mindedness and warmth that make community at once such an appealing *and* limiting concept" (21). "*Community*," Harris suggests, can function as a "stabilizing term, used to give a sense of shared purpose and effort to our dealings with the various discourses that make up the university" (14).

> A similar stress on a shared or collaborative project runs through most other attempts to define 'discourse community'. . . . Abstracted as they are from almost all other kinds of social and material relations, only an affinity of beliefs and purposes, consensus, is left to hold such communities together. (Harris 1988, 8–9)

Harris argues that "change and struggle within a community" constitute "normal activity," that "[o]ne does not need consensus to have community" (13).

When used to authorize a writing pedagogy, Vandenberg and Morrow argue that consensus-based conceptions "concretize the concept of community, making it a static target at which students can be aimed" (21). Such a pedagogy "tacitly supports the preservation of institutional authority by privileging discursive authority, a gesture that renders a community an oligarchy, an exclusive rather than inclusive construct" (22). Bizzell (1991) has come to argue for an interdependency between rhetorically-constructed institutions and discourse features that create and preserve each other.

Discourse community can come "to seem like an oppressive affirmation of one—and only one—set of discursive practices." According to Bizzell,

> community seems to be an utterance that helps middle-class teachers fend off criticism from those both above and below them in the social order. To those below, it seems to promise that we're not excluding anyone. To those above, it seems to ensure that we're not admitting anyone truly disruptive of the status quo, either. (59)

Killingsworth argues that competing constructions of *discourse community* must be kept alive "as a defense against an uncritical adoption of the community concept" (110). One need look no further than her stack of contemporary composition textbooks and journals to find that, uncritical or otherwise, the perceived explanatory power of *discourse community* shows no signs of abating.

Peter Vandenberg
DePaul University, Chicago

Works Cited

Balester, Valerie. 1986. "What's all this Fuss about Communities?" Annual Meeting of the National Conference of Teachers of English. San Antonio, TX. 21 Nov.

Bartholomae, David. 1985. "Inventing the University." *When a Writer Can't Write.* Ed. Mike Rose. New York: Guilford. 134–165.

Bizzell, Patricia. 1982. "Cognition, Convention, and Certainty: What We Need to Know about Writing." *Pre/Text* 3: 213–243.

———. 1991. "Marxist Ideas in Composition Studies." *Contending with Words.* Ed. Patricia Harkin and John Schilb. New York: MLA. 52–68.

Bruffee, Kenneth A. 1984. "Collaborative Learning and the 'Conversation of Mankind.'" *College English* 46: 635–652.

Harris, Joseph. 1988. "Community: A Keyword in the Teaching of Writing." Conference on College Composition and Communication. St. Louis, MO. 17 March 1988.

———. 1989. "The Idea of Community in the Study of Writing." *College Composition and Communication* 40: 11–22.

Killingsworth, M. Jimmie. 1992. "Discourse Communities—Local and Global." *Rhetoric Review* 11: 110–122.

Nystrand, Martin. 1982. Introduction. *What Writers Know: The Language, Process, and Structure of Written Discourse.* New York: Academic. 1–28.

Ohmann, Richard. 1964. "In Lieu of a New Rhetoric." Reprinted in *Professing the New Rhetorics.* 1993. Ed. Theresa Enos and Stuart Brown. Englewood Cliffs, NJ: Blair.

Schilb, John. 1992. "'Traveling Theory' and the Defining of New Rhetorics." *Rhetoric Review* 11: 34–48.

Swales, John. 1990. *Genre Analysis.* New York: Cambridge.

Vandenberg, Peter, and Colette Morrow. 1994. *Inter*textuality or *Intra*textuality? Rethinking Discourse Community Pedagogy." *The Writing Instructor* 14: 17–24.

empowerment

In 1991, Kathryn T. Flannery claims that "[t]here is much talk of empowerment in English studies. . . . Writing and reading are said to open up greater possibilities for learners to act in the world . . . , or to understand [themselves] in some fuller, richer way" (701). Madeleine Picciotto adds: "[t]he term empowerment has become central to the discourse of composition studies. Facility with certain forms of language . . . is a prerequisite for the achievement of social, economic, and intellectual power" (59). Still, Flannery cautions that the implicit meanings—and thus the perceived value—of the word "empowerment" in the literature of composition studies vary radically from one scene of writing to another (702–710).

Flannery underscores the complexities of definitions of empowerment by claiming that any model of pedagogy with a goal of "[e]mpowerment . . . has built into it a presumption of human beings as agents," a problematic category for "postmodern theory" which defines humans as culturally "produced" and thus to some extent "disempowered" (701–706). Picciotto pairs "power" with "powerlessness", a move that allows her to use "empowerment" to gauge the measures of authority oscillating between teacher, student, and institutional and social contexts (59–60).

Working within such contexts, Ira Shor claims that "[e]mpowering education . . . is a critical-democratic pedagogy for self and social change" (15); thus empowerment becomes a function of education in which the individual and the social intercreate each other. John Trimbur also advocates the power of the collective for the individual by arguing that the writing classroom is a site in which "the empowering sense of collectivity and the isolating personalization of an individual's fate" occur all at once (615). Within the social scene of the Writing Center, Gail Okawa argues for multi-ethnic peer tutors and maintains "that the very presence of such a . . . group [provides] visible evidence that students of different cultural, linguistic, and economic backgrounds can work together towards a common goal of empowerment" (10).

"Transformative visions of empowerment are central to feminist pedagogy as well" (Picciotto 60); often, these "transformative visions" correlate empowerment with "coming to voice." Susan Jarratt, for example, advocates "Productive Conflict" (118), and draws on bell hooks, who "encourage[s] students to work at coming to voice in an atmosphere where they may be afraid or see themselves at risk" (qtd. in Jarratt 120). Empowerment, in this usage, indicates an overcoming of fear in the face of critique (cf. Clark and Connnelly 3; Picciotto 59–60). Beth Daniell interviews women in Al-Anon who have "come to voice" through writing. Arguing that spiritual and religious motives have traditionally impelled human beings to literacy, for Daniell, "empowerment" is "making meaning" at "the intersection of literacy and spirituality" (245). In another reflection on the relation of women to language and literacy, Elizabeth Flynn offers a commentary on Cinthia Gannett's work connecting women, journal writing, and voice: "Gannett's writing to heal is a form of intellectual empowerment which allows for the development of a self that is sufficiently integrated to be capable of knowing" (206). Here empowerment becomes a healing and an integration prerequisite to knowing and to voice.

Randall K. Albers connects power to "voice acceptance," claiming that "issues of voice acceptance and empowerment in the classroom are related to wider issues of power in society" (6) and "that language is connected to a speaker whose empowerment involves an interaction between personal and social forces" (7). Advocating "Students' Right to Their Own Language," Albers argues that "[d]enial of voice is a denial of the very right to empowerment" (14; cf. Frisk 10–11).

For teachers of writing, "literacy somehow means empowerment" (Moshenberg 4). And Nancy Sommers claims that "[g]iven the opportunity to speak their own authority . . . , students can . . . be empowered not to serve the academy . . . , but rather to write essays that will change the academy" (30). Harriet Malinowitz, however, problematizes any definition of empowerment as the direct result of literacy instruction or as the "opportunity to speak." Malinowitz's definition addresses the power dynamics of literacy: "there can be a contradiction in the idea that writing is a tool of empowerment" for those in society who are "relatively powerless" such as "workers, people of color, and women" (152). Malinowitz sees empowerment as a collaborative effort in which "teachers must be willing to give up some of their own power," where "[t]o give up power means to question the assumptions that have delimited one's worldview" (155; cf. Brodkey 140). Malinowitz's definition suggests that empowerment begins with change in the teacher rather than with change in the student.

Sherrie Gradin underscores the need for teacher change by imagining empowerment as a function of our metaphors for teaching writing. Gradin claims that the "empowering of our students" may depend on the metaphors of our teaching models (3). Gradin advocates a model based on the metaphor of "the web" that "grants students power from the outset" (Belenky *et al.* qtd. in Gradin 17). Tamara Fish, in a critique of "masculine terms" (5), "suggest[s] that we are further diminished when the language in which we rhetoricians choose to write is a source of disempowerment or exclusion" (2) and argues for "metaphors of engagement and relationality" "in place of metaphors of combat and force" (7). In this usage, student and teacher "disempowerment" results from unexamined masculinist metaphors.

Other usages of empowerment also foreground the problematics of power relations and language within institutional scenes. Victor Vitanza sees empowerment as a deception practiced by the hegemonic discourse of the authorities in the university: " 'empowering students' . . . is the biggest hoax ever perpetrated on 'the student body' " (157). David Bartholomae problematizes empowerment by asking, "Whose desire is this, this desire for freedom, empowerment, an open field?" (64). For Bartholomae, empowerment is a "utopian" unethical "lie" that "reproduce[s] the ideology of sentimental realism" (66–69). Bartholomae chooses not to tell this "lie," even if it could be an "empowering one for . . . writers . . . at a certain stage of their education" (70).

Another site of instruction examining issues of empowerment is the CAI classroom. According to Sabine Groote, "InterChange is an empowering experience, for the students as well as for the teacher. The pressure of having to perform is taken off our shoulders" (7). In this usage, empowerment is the result of a lessening of performance anxiety for teachers and students, as audience contact is mediated by the computer. Similarly, Shirley Logan, emphasizing "technology's instrumental power in a proper *human* context" (10), claims that the CAI classroom has the potential to be an "empowering environment," a site in which "the interaction among students, teachers, subject matter, and milieu . . . promotes, authorizes, or enables all persons involved" (4).

Finally, the "actual relations empowerment comes from" are examined by Eve Sedgwick: "[s]ometimes what makes somebody able to speak in the short term might do the opposite in the long term; sometimes what absolutely shuts somebody up . . . , a year later can move into a relation of identification that is empowering to them" (qtd. in Chinn, DiGangi, and Horrigan, 92). Empowerment, in Sedgwick's usage, is an unpredictable and idiosyncratic dynamic that may—and may not—be transformative for a given subject, that may—or may not—provide the condition for the possibility that enables a subject to speak.

What the term empowerment *is* becomes a function of the literal and figurative, local and global scenes of writing and composition pedagogy in which it finds itself. Philip Smith claims that "empowerment" is an "ideological term" informed by principles that we must continue "to critique and revise [even] as we carry them out" (62–63). In the multiplicitous contexts in which power figures, such conscious critique and revision in the use of the word "empowerment" may result in both the limitation and the proliferation of the term.

Lisa L. Hill
Southeastern Oklahoma State University

Works Cited

Albers, Randall K. 1989. "No More Lip Service: Voice as Empowerment in a Story Workshop Composition Class." ERIC ED 311 440.

Bartholomae, David. 1995. "Writing with Teachers." *College Composition and Communication.* 46: 62–71.

Brodkey, Linda. 1989. "On the Subjects of Class and Gender in 'The Literacy Letters.' " *College English* 51: 125–141.

Clark, Carol Lea, and Colette Connelly. 1993. "Collaboration: Mutual Empowerment/ Silencing? Or Both?" ERIC ED 360 639.

Chinn, Sarah, Mario DiGangi, and Patrick Horrigan. 1992. "A Talk with Eve Kosofsky Sedgwick." *Pre/Text* 13: 79–95.

Daniell, Beth. 1994. "Composing (as) Power." *College Composition and Communication* 45: 238–246.

Fish, Tamara. 1989. "Is There a Sex in This Text? Gender and Value in the Rhetoric of Ethics." ERIC ED 305 682.

Flannery, Kathryn T. 1991. "Review: Composing and the Question of Agency." *College English* 53: 701–713.

Flynn, Elizabeth. 1995. "Review: Feminist Theories/Feminist Composition." *College English* 57: 201–212.

Frisk, Philip. 1989. "Black English and the Henry Higgins Project: Avoiding Disempowering Interventions into 'Black English.' " ERIC ED 348 673.

Gradin, Sherrie, L. 1989. "English Studies and the Metaphors We Live By." ERIC ED 306 574.

Groote, Sabine. 1993. "Can InterChange Write/Right Itself?" ERIC ED 359 529.

Jarratt, Susan. 1991. "Feminism and Composition." *Contending with Words.* Ed. Patricia Harkin and John Schilb. New York: MLA. 105–123.

Logan, Shirley W. 1990. "Facilitating Student and Teacher Empowerment in a Writing Computer Lab." ERIC ED 318 020.

Malinowitz, Harriet. 1990. "The Rhetoric of Empowerment in Writing Programs." *The Right to Literacy.* Ed. Andrea Lunsford, Helene Moglen, and James Slevin. New York: MLA. 152–162.

Moshenberg, Daniel. 1992. "The Problem with Note-Taking." *Composition Studies/ Freshman News* 20: 3–28.

Okawa, Gail Y. 1988. "Dimensions of Diversity: Peer Tutoring in a Multi-Cultural Setting." ERIC ED 295 190.

Picciotto, Madeleine. 1992. "Educational Literacy and Empowerment: An Experiment in Critical Pedagogy." *The Writing Instructor* 11: 59–69.

Shor, Ira. 1992. *Empowering Education: Critical Teaching for Social Change.* Chicago: University of Chicago Press.

Smith, Philip E. II. 1992. "Composing a Cultural Studies Curriculum at Pitt." *Cultural Studies in the English Classroom.* Ed. James A. Berlin and Michael J. Vivion. Portsmith, NH: Boynton/Cook. 46–65.

Sommers, Nancy. 1992. "Between the Drafts." *College Composition and Communication* 43: 23–31.

Trimbur, John. 1989. "Consensus and Difference in Collaborative Learning." *College English* 51: 602–616.

Vitanza, Victor. 1991. "Three Countertheses: Or, A Critical In(ter)vention into Composition Theories and Pedagogies." In *Contending with Words: Composition and Rhetoric in a Postmodern Age.* Ed. Patricia Harkin and John Schilb. New York: MLA. 139–172.

epistemology

In 1975, Ann E. Berthoff wrote, "What we [compositionists] need, it seems to me, is an epistemology—as pragmatic as we can make it!" (13). She was responding specifically to an article by Richard M. Coe, which claimed that "Even the 'lowly' freshman composition course, in addition to transmitting certain writing skills," has traditionally taught "the necessary . . . epistemological problem-solving skills" (1). Unlike Coe, who saw writing as supplemental to thinking, Berthoff believes that writing *embodies* the "epistemological dimension of language": "the role of language in all acts of knowing" (14). Some two decades later, most compositionists accept as commonplace Berthoff's assertion that "Composing is knowing" (13), and discussions of epistemology—pragmatic and otherwise—are central to our scholarship. But in Stephen M. North's view, composition's rapid growth as a discipline has encompassed "such different modes of inquiry, with such divergent epistemological and ontological assumptions" that it must now self-critically sort things out (337).

In its broadest sense, epistemology has to do with what Sharon Crowley calls a "worldview": "some currently accepted theory of knowledge" (2, 4). In composition, *epistemology* refers more specifically to the roles that language, writing, and pedagogy play in constructing and communicating knowledge. James A. Berlin (1987) argues that "every rhetorical system is based on epistemological assumptions about the nature of reality, the nature of the knower, and the rules governing the discovery and communication of the known" (4). Because "knowledge itself is a rhetorical construct," he reasons—that is, "because knowledge is always knowledge for someone standing in relation to others in a linguistically circumscribed situation"—rhetoric is "epistemic," and writing "is at the center of epistemic rhetoric" (165, 166; see also 1988, 488–493). Furthermore, says Richard Fulkerson, "teaching writing implicitly involves teaching epistemology" because "our perceptions of how texts are created and of what classroom methods are effective depend on assumptions about what counts for knowledge" (411).

Definitions of *epistemology* range from the philosophical and "meta-rhetorical" (Kameen 73) to the pedagogical and ideological; consequently, its usages, connotations, and distinctions from other terms vary widely. Berlin, for example, says that unlike *ideology*, *epistemology* "allows for a closer focus on the rhetorical properties—as distinct from the economic, social, or political properties—of the [meaning] systems considered" (1987, 4). North, on the other hand uses *epistemology*, *ideology*, and *methodology* seemingly interchangeably (see, e.g., 356–57; 365)—perhaps suggesting that all knowledge is contingent, for it is always limited by our politics. Fulkerson, however, is critical of such ambiguities, arguing that compositionists' "[f]ailure to recognize the essential independence of [such terms] . . . is one cause of problems and inconsistencies that crop up whenever scholars attempt to categorize approaches to teaching composition" (420–421).

One reason a consistent definition of *epistemology* is elusive within composition scholarship is that so many "kinds" of epistemology are discussed. Crowley alone identifies several, including "modern epistemology," which "is permeated with patriarchal assumptions about the way the world works" (174 n4); "classical epistemology," in which "knowledge was contained in the collected wisdom of the community" (2); and "empirical epistemology," which emphasized "powers of perception . . . [to learn] as much as possible about the world by means of observation and study" (78). Her "current-traditional epistemology" is similar to John Clifford and John Schilb's "traditional epistemologies," which assume that "an objectively distinct reality exists and that it can best be rendered by a prose that aims to be utterly transparent" (60). Berlin names "Plato's epistemology," in which truth "is beyond the resources of language" (1982, 771). Both Berlin and Bruce Herzberg describe something they call "the new epistemology," in which "knowledge comes from perception and reflection" (Herzberg 100), and is "discovered through the experimental method" (Berlin 1982, 769). The list goes on and on.

But epistemologies don't just change from one historical context to the next; they also exist simultaneously. Indeed, since the mid-1980s, many compositionists have dismissed as naive nostalgia the desire for "the one, true system" (Berlin 1987, 3), and write instead of "competing epistemologies" (Hobson 65), "clashing epistemologies" (Bridwell-Bowles 109), or, more innocuously, "several epistemological systems" (Crowley 173 n1). Despite this embrace of multiplicity, some epistemologies emerge as better than others. For Herzberg, the news is mostly bad: "the epistemological preference in the [university writing] curriculum has changed" from one "that reflected the ideology of the state-church power" to one that serves "the new power team: state and business" (97, 98).

Mike Rose believes that while this may be true of "objective" learning activities that are grounded in "a limited theory of knowledge," writing

> assumes a richer epistemology and demands fuller participation. It requires
> a complete, active, struggling engagement with the facts and principles of

> a discipline, an encounter with the discipline's texts and the incorporation
> of them into one's own work, the framing of one's knowledge within the
> myriad conventions that help define a discipline, the persuading of other
> investigators that one's knowledge is legitimate. (359)

For Rose, epistemologies create conditions that constrain or enrich interaction
among individual knowers, texts, and discursive conventions; more vigorous
interactions produce more sophisticated forms of knowledge. Peter Elbow
holds a similar view, but laments that many students seem to believe that
communicating one's thoughts results only in "distortion and loss," and thus
"[is] not worth the effort"—an "epistemological individualism" or "epistemological arrogance" that he characterizes as "wrongheaded" and "parochial"
(81). However, Elbow also sees the potential of something better: an "epistemological megalomania" that encompasses many forms of knowing and
promotes "the process of trying out interpretations or lenses" (296, 299). He
likens this kind of epistemology to "our family silver" (296), and describes
its task as nothing less than helping us to figure out the nature of "figuring
out" (296).

Lynn Worsham represents an exception to this trend toward embracing
multiple epistemologies. In composition studies, she says, "the epistemological
attitude" (e.g., 83) is reductive and homogeneous. It treats discourse as "an
object of knowledge and a repository of truth" (84); "maintains the propriety
of thesis and position, origin and closure" (90); and "position[s] the speaker
or writer in a phallic position of mastery over discourse" (93). Its practitioners, epistemologists, "live" in universities and practice the gate-keeping
function of "epistemological justification"—that is, they sanction certain
discourses as meaningful (92, 101). By contrast, the French feminist discourse
practice of *écriture feminine* "raises the specter of epistemological . . . anarchy"
and rejects "the epistemological stance[,] . . . the economy of proper meaning,
proper nouns, and common nouns," by "refusing to become an object of
knowledge . . . and a spectacle for the gaze of the epistemologist" (86, 90,
92). Worsham depicts *epistemology* as an oppressive, monolithic term that,
in its singular desire for meaning, denies the possibility that "our deepest
relation to language and to the world is not epistemic but emotional and
material" (92). More ambivalently, Robert J. Connors attributes this under-
cutting of "meaning systems" to "epistemological radicals" or "epistemological anarchist[s]" within composition (67).

Clearly, composition is not free from what North describes as the
"scramble for the power and prestige that go with being able to say what
constitutes knowledge" (3). Nowhere are these ongoing disciplinary power
struggles more apparent than in conflicts between theory and practice, what
Schilb calls "the issue of 'theory's' epistemological authority"—its ability to
provide "firm, objective, universal, bedrock principles for our practice" (92).
North and others claim the same authority for practitioners of composition,
placing them "at the center of the field's knowledge-making explosion,
exerting a sort of epistemological gravitational pull" (371). Eric H. Hobson

dismisses both positions as misguided disciplinary insecurity, reflecting our need for a disciplinary rationale and identity, knowledge of "from where [we] came intellectually and to where [we] are headed" (73). But since our search for "a pristine epistemological home" is futile, Hobson believes, we should instead negotiate the "epistemological tightropes" and "epistemological mix[es]" that are conditions of postmodernism (73, 74). And as Steven Lynn sees it, this means articulating a "divided epistemology" that allows us "to move beyond . . . either/or choices, into a realm of both/and" (909).

Elizabeth Ervin
University of North Carolina at Wilmington

Works Cited

Berlin, James A. 1982. "Contemporary Composition: The Major Pedagogical Theories." *College English* 44: 765–777.

———. 1987. *Rhetoric and Reality: Writing Instruction in American Colleges, 1900–1985.* Carbondale: Southern Illinois University Press.

———. 1988. "Rhetoric and Ideology in the Writing Class." *College English* 50: 477–494.

Berthoff, Ann E. 1975. "Reclaiming the Imagination." *Freshman English News* 3: 13–14.

Bridwell-Bowles, Lillian. 1991. "Research in Composition: Issues and Methods." *An Introduction to Composition Studies.* Ed. Erika Lindemann and Gary Tate. New York: Oxford University Press. 94–117.

Clifford, John, and John Schilb. 1985. "Composition Theory and Literary Theory." *Perspectives on Research and Scholarship in Composition.* Ed. Ben W. McClelland and Timothy R. Donovan. New York: Modern Language Association. 45–67.

Coe, Richard M. 1974. "Rhetoric 2001." *Freshman English News* 3: 1–3, 9–13.

Connors, Robert J. 1991. "Writing the History of Our Discipline." *An Introduction to Composition Studies.* Ed. Erika Lindemann and Gary Tate. New York: Oxford University Press. 49–71.

Crowley, Sharon. 1990. *The Methodical Memory: Invention in Current-Traditional Rhetoric.* Carbondale: Southern Illinois University Press.

Elbow, Peter. 1986. *Embracing Contraries: Explorations in Teaching and Learning.* New York: Oxford University Press.

Fulkerson, Richard. 1990. "Composition Theory in the Eighties: Axiological Consensus and Paradigmatic Diversity." *College Composition and Communication* 41: 409–429.

Herzberg, Bruce. 1991. "Composition and the Politics of the Curriculum." *The Politics of Writing Instruction: Postsecondary.* Ed. Richard Bullock and John Trimbur. Portsmouth, NH: Boynton/Cook. 97–117.

Hobson, Eric H. 1992. "Maintaining Our Balance: Walking the Tightrope of Competing Epistemologies." *The Writing Center Journal* 13: 65–75.

Kameen, Paul J. 1980. "Rewording the Rhetoric of Composition." *Pre/Text* 1: 73–93.

Lynn, Steven. 1987. "Reading the Writing Process: Toward a Theory of Current Pedagogies." *College English* 49: 902–910.

North, Stephen M. 1987. *The Making of Knowledge in Composition: Portrait of an Emerging Field.* Portsmouth, NH: Boynton/Cook.

Rose, Mike. 1985. "The Language of Exclusion: Writing Instruction at the University." *College English* 47: 341–359.

Schilb, John. 1991. "What's at Stake in the Conflict between 'Theory' and 'Practice' in Composition?" *Rhetoric Review* 10: 91–97.

Worsham, Lynn. 1991. "Writing against Writing: The Predicament of *Écriture Féminine* in Composition Studies." *Contending with Words: Composition and Rhetoric in a Postmodern Age.* Ed. Patricia Harkin and John Schilb. New York: MLA. 82–104.

error

The written history of *error* leaves one with the sense that the phenomenon is, first, negative, and second, distinguished by its divergence from standard dialect more so than by its relation to other issues of acceptable school writing such as tone, consideration of audience, *ethos*, and the like. Albert R. Kitzhaber describes the teaching of writing in the late nineteenth and early twentieth centuries as "dominated by an ideal of superficial correctness, of conformity to rules chiefly for the sake of conformity" (188). He points out that the Harvard entrance examination in English helped spark avid attention to such surface-level aberrations as indications of poor writing (200). In fact, L. B. R. Briggs, in 1882, fully equates "bad English" with "ungrammatical" English when commenting on results of the entrance examination (qtd. in Kitzhaber 203). Robert J. Connors and Andrea A. Lunsford (1993) also describe much of the teaching of writing in the twentieth century as involved with correcting and editing student papers, noting that the definition and counting of errors is associated with objectivity (202–203).

While the mid-century brought about a shift from looking almost exclusively at such sentence-level turbulence to examining student writing as a rhetorical device with the teacher as a responsive audience, the idea of *error* continues to elicit images of unconventional grammar, spelling, punctuation, and diction. In 1963, for example, James W. Ney construes error as exclusively a "sentence-level" problem. Writing in 1990, Gary Sloan likewise finds it necessary to base his definition of *error* on the guidance of grammar handbooks (300), although he gives a nod to the tentativeness of such a definition by sometimes enclosing *error* in quotation marks. Paramount to Sloan's study of the *frequency* of errors, though, is the *quantifiability* of errors; sentence-level errors are more readily countable than structural ones (see also Peckham 18, 21). Similarly, Connors and Lunsford (1993) distinguish between the "content of the paper[,] . . . specifically rhetorical aspects of its organization," and "formal and mechanical errors," which nearly always tend to be indicated "using either handbook numbers or the standard set of mysterious phatic grunts: 'awk,' 'ww,' 'comma,' etc." (205).

Mina Shaughnessy's *Errors and Expectations* seems to be at the fulcrum of contested contemporary perceptions of *error.* Shaughnessy notes that the perception of *error* as an occurrence in written discourse that calls attention to itself due to its lying outside the bounds of acceptability has no doubt been common among compositionists (12). But "the guiding metaphor of error was transformed" by her work as scholars began to deal more fully with the political issues of student diversity and open admissions (Laurence 21). Before her book, *error* was used primarily, if not exclusively, in a pejorative sense. Errors were to be avoided, and the teaching of writing was shaped by the intent to eradicate such errors. Shaughnessy, however, advocated exploring student errors, making them the subject of inquiry "in order to determine at what point or points along the developmental path error should or can become the subject of instruction" (13). While she defines errors as anomalies (12), Shaughnessy delves into a course of action centered around the reasons for those errors. This perception of error, referred to as error-analysis, reflects Piaget's view that learning spawns a system of errors or "signals of the learner's way of coping with new challenges" (Foster 39).

Barry M. Kroll and John C. Schafer extend the perception of *error* as a point of inquiry, and their definition is fused with their attitude towards errors. In an effort to dispel the myth of the "composition teacher as revenge-thirsty monster wielding pen and red ink," they delineate a shift from product-oriented to process-oriented remedies. The latter approach, which is informed by cognitivist theory and views errors as "windows into the mind" of the writer, calls for treating each type of error as a useful starting point in discovering which linguistic strategies led to the error. But the former approach, grounded in behaviorist learning theory, involves identifying those types of errors, labeling them "bad," and promoting habits of accepted discourse (242–243).

Some scholars have attempted to delineate among kinds or degrees of error. Sidney Greenbaum and John Taylor, for example, offer a scheme in which errors fall into three categories: "clearly unacceptable," "divided usage," and "clearly acceptable" (169–170). In like manner, Muriel Harris and Tony Silva distinguish between global errors—surface features that interfere with the intended audience's reading of a text—and local errors—surface features that do not interfere even though they defy convention (526).

Other compositionists emphasize that error is better understood as a manifestation of a rhetorical intention. David Bartholomae argues, for instance, that "[a]n error (and I would include errors beyond those in decoding and encoding sentences) can only be understood as evidence of intention" and, thus, an indication of control (255). Gary Sloan likewise acknowledges error as a matter of intention and rhetorical choice: the "gap between prescription and practice make the word 'error' something of a misnomer. A number of the 'errors' . . . are perhaps better viewed as manifestations of rhetorical choice" (306).

Joseph M. Williams correlates the dissonance created by errors of grammar and usage with that of social errors. He suggests "[turning] our attention from error as a discrete entity, frozen at the moment of its commission, to error as part of a flawed transaction" (153). Williams notes the great diversity in definitions of error and a similar diversity in the feelings associated with particular categories of error: "The categories of error all seem like [sic] they should be yes-no, but the feelings associated with the categories seem much more complex" (155). Thus, he defines error as occurring in the interaction of the writer, the reader, and the formulators of handbooks (159). Connors and Lunsford (1988) likewise locate error in the interaction between writer and reader (396), an interaction that changes according to its historical context. In emphasizing "features of writing styles which are commonly displaced to the realm of 'error' and thus viewed as peripheral to college English teaching" (448), Min-zhan Lu likewise accentuates the social epistemic quality of error. She concludes that writing conventions are not essentially prescribed and constant through the ages; students must be taught how to operate within these conventions in order to succeed in their particular writing situations (457–458; see also Lazere 12; Owens 227–231).

Since conventions do not remain rigid over time or across different writing situations, error is an inherently relative and localized phenomenon. It is, nonetheless, one that is consistently construed as an artifact on the page or a product of the interaction among reader, writer, and rulebook.

Bill Bolin
East Texas State University

Works Cited

Bartholomae, David. 1980. "The Study of Error." *College Composition and Communication* 31: 253–277.

Connors, Robert J., and Andrea A. Lunsford. 1988. "Frequency of Formal Errors in Current College Writing, or Ma and Pa Kettle Do Research." *College Composition and Communication* 39: 395–409.

———. 1993. "Teachers' Rhetorical Comments on Student Papers." *College Composition and Communication* 44: 200–223.

Foster, David. 1992. *A Primer for Writing Teachers: Theories, Theorists, Issues, Problems.* Portsmouth, NH: Boynton/Cook Heinemann.

Greenbaum, Sidney, and John Taylor. 1981. "The Recognition of Usage Errors by Instructors of Freshman Composition." *College Composition and Communication* 32: 169–174.

Harris, Muriel, and Tony Silva. 1993. "Tutoring ESL Students: Issues and Options." *College Composition and Communication* 44: 525–537.

Kitzhaber, Albert R. 1990. *Rhetoric in American Colleges, 1850–1900.* Dallas: Southern Methodist University Press.

Kroll, Barry M., and John C. Schafer. 1978. "Error-Analysis and the Teaching of Composition." *College Composition and Communication* 29: 242–248.

Laurence, Patricia. 1993. "The Vanishing Site of Mina Shaughnessy's *Errors and Expectations.*" *Journal of Basic Writing* 12: 18–28.

Lazere, Donald. 1992. "Back to Basics: A Force for Oppression or Liberation?" *College English* 54: 7–21.

Lu, Min-zhan. 1994. "Professing Multiculturalism: The Politics of Style in the Contact Zone." *College Composition and Communication* 45: 442–458.

Ney, James W. 1963. "On Not Practicing Errors." *College Composition and Communication* 14: 102–106.

Owens, Derek. 1994. *Resisting Writings (and the Boundaries of Composition).* Dallas: Southern Methodist University Press.

Peckham, Irvin. 1993. "Beyond Grades." *Composition Studies* 21.2: 16–31.

Shaughnessy, Mina P. 1979. *Errors and Expectations: A Guide for the Teacher of Basic Writing.* New York: Oxford.

Sloan, Gary. 1990. "Frequency of Errors in Essays by College Freshmen and by Professional Writers." *College Composition and Communication* 41: 299–308.

Williams, Joseph M. 1981. "The Phenomenology of Error." *College Composition and Communication* 32: 152–168.

essay

For writing teachers (and students), the word rolls off the tongue as easily as any, and why not: essays, it seems to go without saying, are those works of nonfiction prose students try to write, often by reading other published essays. But this accommodating word, used interchangeably by teachers with terms like "paper," "composition," "project," and "exercise," is as ambiguous as it is adaptable. Consequently, researchers have tried to "explain" the rhetoric of the essay from a variety of angles. One researcher classifies essays as texts with abstract, philosophical, and multisyllabic vocabularies, distinguishing them from "literary discourse" (Stotsky). Another defines the essay as a single "macroparagraph," the test of its worth found somehow in the way its paragraphs hang together (D'Angelo). Elsewhere, one contends that the essay is not at all the hierarchical presentation of information according to conventional outlines but rather a horizontal progression of meaning in stages (Larson). And both vertical and horizontal renderings of "compositional unfolding," argues another, are equally at home in this discursive space best understood as something comparable to a musical composition (Hesse).

Interestingly, Montaigne, the "creator" of the medium, is frequently invoked to promote conflicting definitions of the essay. In one case Montaigne's writings are used as support for the idea of the essay as a laboratory for testing but not proving ideas (Zeiger). Some see in Montaigne a kindred spirit whose private ruminations take on potentially universal implications, the true mark of an essay (Atkins). These privilegings of the private-made-public, sometimes unapologetically "romantic" (Elbow 1995, 82), "egocentric" and "self-indulgent" (Atkins 637), are definitions fashioned partly in opposition to the "academic essay," a mode of discourse many consider tainted by dishonest objectification. These definitions are in turn challenged by those who applaud Montaigne's dispassionate attempts to unveil the truth through clear and independent thinking but adamantly reject proponents of the "personal" or "familiar" essay as succumbing to "misplaced passion, sentimentality, and even dishonesty" (Marius 40). And there are those who, less concerned with positioning themselves specifically on one side or the other of the academic-personal debate, cite Montaigne's critique of scholastic discourse (its fragmented disciplines limiting the exchange of ideas with their artificial boundaries) to advance the notion of the essay as a site of authorial experience ever situated within and thus contributing to a distinct community (Spellmeyer).

Some views of the essay are primarily aesthetic: one sees the essay as an art form ideal for meditating on the self (Simonson); another entertains an apparently eros-driven reading of the essay which "tries to open, to stimulate, to inject multiple overtones so that insight is expanded and pleasure is aroused" (Brashers 155). Lynn Z. Bloom argues that ideally essays should be regarded as literary nonfiction, and not just articles, which are devices intended for passing along information. In contrast, the essayist is given permission to wander, comment on the process of the text's evolving composition, and in the words of Peter Elbow, "render experience rather than explain it" (1991, 136).

But critics of the familiar essay and autobiographical academic writing, like Gordon Harvey, charge that such definitions lend themselves to narcissism and bad thinking. Even the authorial "presence" Harvey claims all good essays must possess is more subtle than overt, and ought not to detract from the essay's primary goal of "academic analysis." Like Harvey, Gesa E. Kirsch and Joy S. Ritchie criticize the popularity of the personal essay among feminist scholarship, claiming that such attempts tend not to be innovative or alternative but simply offer essentialist renderings of a confessional voice leading to more master narratives. Joel Haefner argues that the essay is not the class-less, neutral vehicle promoting democracy through individualistic expression many claim, but always a "cultural product."

Others would maintain that personal writing is not always solipsistic, but can in fact be a tool for intellectual growth and social change. Margaret Byrd Boegeman argues that the function of the personal essay is to instill "self-reliance" and "self-possession," antidotes to rampant conformism in the predominating culture. Allan Brick sees the essay as simultaneously personal and political, arguing for a "revolution" in which "personal writing" plays a fundamental role towards "an overall institutional commitment to the individual's democratic right to an education [where] personal identity, self-exploration, active creativity, and 'praxis' [are] essential to learning in all fields" (515).

One thing many of the above have in common is their assumption that the essay—whether interpreted as an aesthetic of the personal, a search for ontological truths, or a medium for social construction—remains separate from poetry, fiction, drama, and so on. Others are more critical of such distinctions. According to Shirely Brice Heath, the essay was originally epigrammatic in nature and consciously poetic, but has since evolved into a perversion where its unacknowledged function is to serve as a gatekeeper keeping certain classes and cultures outside of the academy. Although Winston

Weathers has introduced the idea of "grammar A" (classical modes of persuasion, objective voice, linear progression, etc.) as distinct from "grammar B" (experimental tropes derived largely from modernist literature), he insists that our understanding of the essay is incomplete until it includes both traditional and experimental styles. Lillian Bridwell-Bowles argues that essays should be thought of as "diverse discourse," critically experimental writing receptive to textual manipulation and language play more representative of our pluralistic society. And, arguing along with modernist and postmodern poets that grammar is content and vice versa, Derek Owens has read the essay as an open zone crying out for textual, performative, and technological innovation of the most extreme kind. Definitions such as these tend to blur the line between "poet" and "writer," and assume both "academic" and "personal" manifestations of discourse as too often elitist, patriarchal, ethnocentric, and psychologically debilitating. All of these writers and definitions have one thing in common, and that is a faith in the written word (constructed in some container labeled "essay") as a viable medium for information exchange and construction of the world. This faith contrasts sharply with what Ron B. Scollon and Suzanne B. K. Scollon have learned in their study of Athabaskan Indians and other ethnic communities where people are prone to reject much of written discourse, and instead privilege face-to-face dialogue over transmission of meaning through writing. Here, writers of essays and those schooled in what the authors refer to as "essayist literacy" (the necessary fictionalization of both author and reader in order to write for a large, hypothetical audience) are always suspect. Studies like this suggest that our own rituals of writing are always localized, culturally specific acts of self-promotion.

As we scan different readings (and thus, always, engenderings) of this word and its origins, it would appear that the essay can not signify any bona fide genre. Rather, the term might best be considered an "open rubric" the intention of which can only be defined locally by the "rule makers" of specific discourse communities: i.e., the teacher, the test maker, the editor, the publishing company. As paradigm shifts in our technology and culture continue to force us to revamp our definitions of literacy and writing, the debates over the appropriate meanings for the "essay" will most likely become even more heated and, perhaps to those outside academic communities, increasingly irrelevant.

Derek Owens
St. John's University

Works Cited

Atkins, G. Douglas. 1994. "Envisioning the Stranger's Heart." *College English* 56: 629–641.

Bloom, Lynn Z. 1991. "What We Talk about When We Talk about Literary Nonfiction." *College English* 53: 944–948.

Boegeman, Margaret Byrd. 1980. "Lives and Literacy: Autobiography in Freshman Composition." *College English* 41: 662–669.

Brashers, Howard C. 1971. "Aesthetic Form in Familiar Essays." *College Composition and Communication* 22: 147–155.

Brick, Allan. 1981. "First Person Singular, First Person Plural, and Exposition." *College English* 43: 508–515.

Bridwell-Bowles, Lillian. 1992. "Discourse and Diversity: Experimental Writing within the Academy." *College Composition and Communication* 43: 349–68.

D'Angelo, Frank J. 1974. "A Generative Rhetoric of the Essay." *College Composition and Communication* 25: 388–396.

Elbow, Peter. 1991. "Reflections on Academic Discourse: How It Relates to Freshmen and Colleagues." *College English* 53: 133–153.

———. 1995. "Being a Writer vs. Being an Academic: A Conflict in Goals." *College Composition and Communication* 46: 72–83.

Haefner, Joel. 1992. "Democracy, Pedagogy, and the Personal Essay." *College English* 54: 127–137.

Harvey, Gordon. 1994. "Presence in the Essay." *College English* 56: 642–654.

Heath, Shirley Brice. 1993. "Rethinking the Sense of the Past: The Essay as Legacy of the Epigram." In Odell, Lee, ed. *Theory and Practice in the Teaching of Writing: Rethinking the Discipline.* Carbondale: Southern Illinois University Press: 105–131.

Hesse, Douglas. 1989. "Essay Form and *Auskomponierung*." In Butrym, Alexander J., ed. *Essays on the Essay: Redefining the Genre.* Athens: University of Georgia Press.

Kirsch, Gesa E., and Joy S. Ritchie. 1995. "Beyond the Personal: Theorizing a Politics of Location in Composition Research." *College Composition and Communication* 46: 7–29.

Larson, Richard L. 1971. "Toward a Linear Rhetoric of the Essay." *College Composition and Communication* 22: 140–146.

Marius, Richard. 1995. *A Writer's Companion.* 3rd ed. NY: McGraw-Hill, Inc.

Montaigne, Michel Eyquemde. 1957. *The Complete Works of Montaigne.* Trans. Donald M. Frame. Stanford, CA: Stanford University Press.

Owens, Derek. 1994. *Resisting Writings (and the Boundaries of Composition).* Dallas: Southern Methodist University Press.

Scollon, Ron, and Suzanne B. K. Scollon. 1981. *Narrative, Literacy, and Face in Interethnic Communication.* Norwood, NJ: ABLEX.

Simonson, Harold P. 1964. "The Essay as Art." *College Composition and Communication* 15: 34–37.

Spellmeyer, Kurt. 1989. "A Common Ground: The Essay in the Academy." *College English* 51: 262–276.

Stotsky, Sandra. 1981. "The Vocabulary of Essay Writing: Can It Be Taught?" *College Composition and Communication* 32: 317–326.

Weathers, Winston. 1980. *An Alternate Style: Options in Composition.* Rochelle Park, NJ: Hayden.

Zeiger, William. 1985. "The Exploratory Essay: Enfranchising the Spirit of Inquiry in College Composition." *College English* 47: 454–466.

evaluation

In composition studies, *evaluation* typically represents the act of a teacher or peer placing value on the work of a student. Yet, James C. Raymond contends that composition scholars "have not even agreed on what it is we are trying to evaluate—whether it is the mastery of editorial skills, or indices of cognitive development, or success in communicating a semantic intention" (399). Thus, although composition studies has watched an ever-expanding list of evaluation methods and techniques develop and has seen the emphasis shift from evaluation as "judging" to evaluation as "coaching" (Faigley 395), the meaning of *evaluation* continues to vary (see also Siegel 303).

According to Robert J. Connors and Andrea Lunsford, teachers saw themselves primarily as editors in the first part of the century, correcting student papers and assigning grades, "rating" instead of "responding" to student writing (445–446). The subsequent proliferation of rating scales (for an extreme example of mathematical assessment, see Leahy) that occurred was met with some criticism, most notably by Fred Newton Scott, who stated that "whenever a piece of scientific machinery is allowed to take the place of teaching . . . the result will be to artificialize the course of instruction" (qtd. in Connors and Lunsford 447). Scott's disdain for the reduction of evaluation to mathematical scales finds resonance in composition studies' continued struggle today with evaluation's conflicted goals of assessment and instruction. Elaine O. Lees contends that evaluation is a paradox forcing teachers to assess "students as writers," using their papers as the "evidence" of their abilities. This practice relies on the assumption that "students have already succeeded in creating personas which suitably represent them" (373). According to Lees, in order to fulfill their goal of teaching students to write, instructors have to evaluate (respond to) students in such a way that students learn to "ignore the evidence that their ability has so far produced and believe in the possibility of producing something else" (374). Susan Miller further highlights the conflicted meanings inherent in *evaluation*, claiming that when methods of evaluation "separate the writer from the writing" to insure a "fair" assessment, they move further away from the intentions of composition studies: *"learning to* write, *getting better* at writing, and *being good* at it" (176).

Mary K. Healy distinguishes between evaluation and response, defining evaluation as the "final 'assessment' of a work" and response as "a reaction to an initial or working draft" (qtd. in Lape and Glenn 439). However, Nancy Sommers contends that, even when assessing student rough drafts, many teachers formulate their comments as if they are assessing a final product instead of responding to a work in progress (154). Their comments reflect their sometimes conflicted desires to defend the grade given on one hand and to lead the student toward further discovery as a writer on the other, to both judge and respond at the same time. According to Lester Faigley, the writing-as-process movement has resulted in a change in meaning of evaluation from "summative" to "formative" (395), shifting the concept of evaluation to that of a pedagogical tool. Denise Lynch asserts that evaluation as a process to facilitate the educational goals of composition instructors can make students better writers, while evaluation as justification can "alienate or discourage" these very students (310). A teacher's evaluation, for Sommers, should ultimately act as a model "to help our students to become that questioning reader themselves[,] . . . to help them evaluate what they have written and develop control over their writing" (148).

According to Anne Greenhalgh, a "responsible teacher" is a "responsive reader," whose comments "respect the differences between a teacher's and a student's responsibility to an emerging text" (401). Writing of the different voices of response offered by teachers, Greenhalgh breaks response into two categories: "interruptive" (based on reader response) and "interpretive" (based on external realities) (404). She claims that teachers tend to use more interpretive comments than interruptive, grounding their authority in "external realities" such as handbooks, instead of "responding to a particular text" (405). Lil Brannon and C. H. Knoblauch assert that evaluation should involve an exploration of the student's purpose, giving the student increased control over their work (163). They contend that evaluation is a vehicle for helping writers achieve their own purposes instead of a medium for teachers to "dictate choices that properly belong to the writers" (159).

Evaluation is often seen as the power to decide what is deemed good writing. According to Francine Hardaway, transferring partial power and responsibility from the teacher to the students through peer evaluation allows students to influence and apply evaluation criteria, demystifying the evaluation process and revealing to students its inherent subjectivity (577–578). Removing the power of evaluation from the teacher completely, Miller advocates the practice of self-evaluation, a process by which students assess their writing using their own individual criteria, as a way "to internalize new images of ourselves" (182). She asserts that "[w]ithout such judgments, new events are not occasions for growth; those who cook only to eat do not become chefs" (182). Self-evaluation privileges the individual growth of the student as writer in contrast to many traditional evaluation methods that assess students in relation to each other. Barrett John Mandel argues for the removal of qualitative evaluation altogether, contending that "judgment in the form of grades and measurement (against 'standards') does more to prevent education than to encourage it" (623). Instead he advocates a quantitative concept of evaluation, claiming that this non-punitive system encourages students and produces writing that is "enormously superior" to that received under traditional qualitative evaluation (630).

Regardless of the assessment technique, evaluation typically results in a paper being returned to a student with marks and comments. According to Sommers, there exists within composition studies an "accepted, albeit un-written cannon for commenting on student texts." Sommers contends that at the moments when instructors charge their students with vagueness, their own comments often ironically comprise vague, general suggestions such as "choose precise language" or "think more about your audience," causing students to view evaluation as a presentation of "rules for composing" and leading them to view writing as "a matter of following the rules" (153).

Michael Platt and John V. Knapp argue that evaluation should be construed as a public, immediate, interactive, highly personal form of com-munication among students and teachers. Evaluation often baffles students who begin each class frantically attempting to determine what evaluation means to this particular instructor. Platt suggests transforming evaluation into a method of public review in small groups where both students and teacher give the writer immediate feedback on a paper (22–23). In a similar vein, Knapp proposes conference grading that brings the student and teacher together for the purpose of evaluation and allows the teacher to question the student about any items the instructor would generally ask herself if grading the paper alone (650–651). For Knapp and Platt, evaluation becomes an act of communication or miscommunication between a teacher and a student, between reader and writer.

Because each act of evaluation typically involves at least two human beings, this practice quickly becomes part of a complicated human relation-ship. As the context changes with each teacher, each student, each paper, evaluation becomes a dynamic act, and at times, the center of consternation.

Jennifer A. Clough
DePaul University, Chicago

Works Cited

Brannon, Lil, and C. H. Knoblauch. 1982. "On Students' Right to Their Own Texts: A Model of Teacher Response." *College Composition and Communication* 33: 157–167.

Connors, Robert J., and Andrea Lunsford. 1992. "Teachers' Rhetorical Comments on Student Papers: Ma and Pa Visit the Tropics of Commentary." *The St. Martin's*

Guide to Teaching Writing. Ed. Robert Connors and Cheryl Glenn. New York: St. Martin's Press. 445–469.

Faigley, Lester. 1989. "Judging Writing, Judging Selves." *College Composition and Communication* 40: 395–412.

Greenhalgh, Anne M. 1992. "Voices in Response: A Postmodern Reading of Teacher Response." *College Composition and Communication* 43: 401–410.

Hardaway, Francine. 1975. "What Students Can Do to Take the Burden Off You." *College English* 36: 577–580.

Knapp, John V. 1976. "Contract/Conference Evaluations of Freshman Composition." *College English* 37: 647–653.

Lape, Sue V., and Cheryl Glenn. 1992. "Responding to Student Writing." *The St. Martin's Guide to Teaching Writing.* Ed. Robert Connors and Cheryl Glenn. New York: St. Martin's Press. 437–444.

Leahy, Jack Thomas. 1963. "Objective Correlation and the Grading of English Composition." *College English* 25: 35–38.

Lees, Elaine O. 1979. "Evaluating Student Writing." *College Composition and Communication* 30: 370–374.

Lynch, Denise. 1982. "Easing the Process: A Strategy for Evaluating Compositions." *College Composition and Communication* 33: 310–314.

Mandel, Barrett John. 1973. "Teaching without Judging." *College English* 34: 623–633.

Miller, Susan. 1982. "How Writers Evaluate Their Own Writing." *College Composition and Communication* 33: 176–183.

Platt, Michael. 1975. "Correcting Papers in Public and in Private." *College English* 37: 22–27.

Raymond, James C. 1982. "What We Don't Know about the Evaluation of Writing." *College Composition and Communication* 33: 399–403.

Siegel, Muffy E. A. 1982. "Responses to Student Writing from New Composition Faculty." *College Composition and Communication* 33: 302–309.

Sommers, Nancy. 1982. "Responding to Student Writing." *College Composition and Communication* 33: 148–156.

expressive writing

Richard Young articulates the problematic nature of "expressive discourse" when he notes that the term has been "variously defined, meaning anything from uncritical effusion about the self for those who are critical of romantic theory and pedagogy, to, for the more sympathetic, an aim of discourse prerequisite to all other aims of discourse" (30). Lester Faigley attaches the qualities "sincerity," "spontaneity," and "originality" to expressive writing, which, he notes, have also been used to define " 'expressive' poetry" (528–531). Implicit here is the connection of "expressive" forms of writing to literary forms, a connection also made by James Kinneavy (393). In expressive writing, Kinneavy says, "it is the speaking self that dominates the discourse, and it is by discourse that he expresses and partially achieves his own individuality" (398). Kinneavy's definition incorporates three attributes of expressive writing that are common to most accounts: its connection to speech, its correlation to the "self" of the writer, and its function as a means of identity formation for the writing "self."

In associating expressive writing with speech, Kinneavy provides a common link to the theory of James Britton, who, along with his co-authors in *The Development of Writing Abilities, 11–18*, devise "a dynamic three-term scale" of language functions moving from "communicative" to "expressive" to "poetic," with the expressive function being of particular interest because of its connections to speech (10–11). According to Britton, language that "invites the listener to enter into [the writer's] world and respond to him as a person is revealing of self inasmuch as, being informal, and leaving much implicit, it is closer to the way the individual thinks when he thinks by himself than more developed or more mediated utterance. It is this function of language," Britton says, "which we have called *expressive*" (141). The expressive function, then, reflects the individuality of the writing "self" and is characterized by its informality and inexplicitness.

Britton also believes that the expressive function is at the core of all discourse production, citing it as "a kind of matrix from which differentiated forms of mature writing are developed": as more complex writing tasks develop, "expressive writing changes to meet the demands" of those tasks (83). Janet Emig (citing Britton's model) agrees, stating that "the notions that all student writings emanate from an expressive impulse and that they then bifurcate into two major modes is useful and accurate" (37). Kinneavy, too, places "the expressive component" at the heart of all discourse, because it "is, in effect, the personal stake of the speaker in the discourse." (393) Samples of the sort of discourse that Kinneavy would deem "expressive"—in which the expressive component often dominates—take such diverse forms as diaries, journals, cursing, and suicide notes (393).

Jeanette Harris's 1991 study *Expressive Discourse*, however, is devoted to the notion that "the writing presently categorized as expressive is . . . more accurately and more usefully viewed as four different phenomena" which she labels "the interior text, the generative text, aesthetic discourse, and experience-based discourse" (x), the former two being "form[s] that a text assumes rather than type[s] of completed discourse," and the latter two being "types" of discourse that are "static and completed entities" (xi). While aware of the confusion and ambiguity that has surrounded the term "expressive writing," Harris believes that "one can accept an expressive approach to teaching writing without believing that the approach produces writing that constitutes a category of discourse" (170). Harris refers to the "rhetorical expressionists," those who employ an expressive approach, as seeing "writing not as a rhetorical act or a practical means of communication but as a way of helping students become psychologically healthier and happier, more fulfilled and self-actualized" (28). Peter Elbow (1991), as one of the "rhetorical expressionists" cited by Harris, has taken exception with this depiction (84). Harris' representation of "rhetorical expressionism" draws upon the taxonomies of theorists like James Berlin who, in *Rhetoric and Reality*, divides theories of composing into the categories of "expressionistic," "cognitive," and "social-epistemic." An expressionistic rhetoric, Berlin says, is distinguished by "its emphasis on the cultivation of the self" (73), and he adds that such a rhetoric "falls short of being epistemic . . . because it denies the place of intersubjective, social processes in shaping reality" (146). (For similar taxonomies that include "expressive" or "expressionistic" components, see Berlin 1982, 1988, 1990.)

Christopher C. Burnham, on the other hand, argues that an expressive rhetoric does indeed promote an epistemic view of language. He adds that "[i]ts aim is to better understand how writing comes to be in order to help individuals use language to create an identity and to act effectively in the world" (154). Citing Britton's work as his foundation, Burnham states: "As a functional category, expressive writing represents a mode rather than a form; it is a purpose that must be realized in the process of creating a text rather than a description of a text itself. . . . In short, the expressive function creates texts—notes, drafts, correspondence with collaborators, additional drafts—that map out the process through which formal discourse evolves" (157). Despite the confusion of terminology, what Burnham here calls "a mode rather than a form" is similar to what Harris calls the "forms" of "interior text" and "generative text," expressive writing seen as a step in the process of developing other forms of completed texts.

Stephen Fishman, like Burnham, suggests that "there is more to expressivism than personal writing and self-discovery," that attention to the social realm is inherent in an expressive rhetoric (660). Using Elbow's work as a model, Fishman sees expressivism, with its "emphasis upon believing," or "the sympathetic hearing of diverse languages," as being "rooted in a romanticism that seeks not isolation but new ways to identify with one another and, thereby, new grounds for social communion" (654). Like Fishman, Maureen Neal (45–47) and Elbow (1990, 13–15) suggest the theoretical intersections between "expressionist" and social-constructionist theories of composing. *[the attempt to connect w/ the larger world]*

Among the theoretical developments that have contributed to the complication of the term "expressive writing" during the last decade have been the destabilization of the notion of the autonomous "self" and the related debate over the distinction between the terms "objective" and "subjective." David Bartholomae voices both of these concerns when he refers to "expressive discourse" as "a mode whose fundamental purpose, as many see it, is to perpetuate a figure of the writer as a free-agent, as independent, self-authorizing, a-historical, a-cultural; where writing is the expression of the thoughts and feelings of a particularly privileged sensibility" (123). He goes on to say that the "dangers of the expressive mode" are that it "makes everything an idealized human story, a story of 'common' humanity" and that it "resists and erases its own position within a discursive practice" (126); by so doing it attempts to be "objective" when objectivity itself is not possible. *[how?]* Elbow (1990) wishes to suggest, however, that critics of expressive writing often "give in to hierarchical thinking and assume that one side of any dichotomy must always win or dominate the other" (15). Just because personal expressive writing "invites feeling does not mean that it leaves out thinking; and because it invites attention to the self does not mean that it leaves out other people and the social connection" (10).

Donald E. Bushman
University of North Carolina at Wilmington

Works Cited

Bartholomae, David. 1990. "A Reply to Stephen North." *PRE/TEXT* 11: 121–30.

Berlin, James A. 1982. "Contemporary Composition: The Major Pedagogical Theories." *College English* 44: 765–777.

———. 1987. *Rhetoric and Reality*. Carbondale: Southern Illinois University Press.

———. 1988. "Rhetoric and Ideology in the Writing Class." *College English* 50: 477–494.

————. 1990. "Writing Instruction in School and College English: 1890–1985." *A Short History of Writing Instruction*. Ed. James J. Murphy. Davis, CA: Hermagoras Press.

Britton, James, *et al.* 1977. *The Development of Writing Abilities (11–18)*. New York: Macmillan.

Burnham, Christopher C. 1993. "Expressive Rhetoric: A Source Study." In *Defining the New Rhetorics*. Ed. Theresa Enos and Stuart C. Brown. Newbury Park, CA: Sage.

Elbow, Peter. 1990. "Forward: About Personal Expressive Academic Writing." *PRE/TEXT* 11: 7–20.

————. 1991. "Some Thoughts on *Expressive Discourse*: A Review Essay." *Journal of Advanced Composition* 11: 83–93.

Emig, Janet. 1971. *The Composing Processes of Twelfth Graders*. Urbana, IL: NCTE.

Faigley, Lester. 1986. "Competing Theories of Process: A Critique and a Proposal." *College English* 48: 527–542.

Fishman, Stephen M., and Lucille Parkinson McCarthy. 1992. "Is Expressivism Dead? Reconsidering Its Romantic Roots and Its Relation to Social Constructionism." *College English* 54: 647–661.

Fulkerson, Richard. 1979. "Four Philosophies of Composition." *College Composition and Communication* 30: 344–348.

Harris, Jeanette. 1990. *Expressive Discourse*. Dallas: Southern Methodist University Press.

Knoblauch, C. H. 1988. "Rhetorical Constructions: Dialogue and Commitment." *College English* 50: 125–140.

Kinneavy, James L. 1971. *A Theory of Discourse*. Englewood Cliffs, NJ: Prentice-Hall.

Neal, Maureen. 1993. "Social Constructionism and Expressionism: Contradictions and Connections." *Composition Studies* 21: 42–48.

Young, Richard. 1987. "Recent Developments in Rhetorical Invention." In *Teaching Composition: Twelve Bibliographic Essays*. Ed. Gary Tate. Fort Worth: Texas Christian University Press.

feminism

In composition studies, feminism has been constructed as a classroom pedagogy, a research methodology, a rhetoric, and a social critique linked to other movements for social change and transformation. Theorists generally agree that feminism is a political movement designed to alleviate the patriarchal oppression of women; however, multiple debates have been waged over the relative meaning of the term *feminism* as well as over the multiple meanings of terms associated with feminism: *experience, femininity, gender*, and *identity politics*, as well as the categories *woman* or *women*. Given the contested nature of these terms, it is perhaps better to speak of feminisms—rather than feminism—in order to signify the contested, multiple sites of feminist teaching and theorizing.

From 1970 to 1985, pedagogical strategies identified as "feminist" began to make their way into writing courses taught by women's studies advocates. True to the feminist consciousness-raising movement that prevailed in the late 1960s and early 1970s, Florence Howe portrays the feminist writing classroom as a collaborative, open-ended space designed to break women students out of "passive-dependent patterns and assumptions of inferiority," thus liberating them "to analyze sexual stereotyping and to grow conscious of themselves as women" (865). Likewise, Adrienne Rich encourages women teachers and students to empower themselves by learning to believe "in the value of women's experience, traditions, perceptions" (240). Similarly, Pamela J. Annas heralds feminism as a liberatory pedagogy that encourages women students to "discover or rediscover a new women's language, a kind of writing which is confident in asserting the particulars of women's experience—both in content and form" (370). Metaphors of discovery—as well as liberation—are deployed by feminists to represent the exploratory, transformative potential of feminism.

Not surprisingly, feminist pedagogical methods—an emphasis on personal voice, shared pedagogical authority, and collaboration—have much in common with expressivist approaches to writing instruction. Cynthia L.

Caywood and Gillian R. Overing represent feminism and expressivism as compatible socio-political movements since both revise current-traditional authority relations and both re-value the power of students' experiences and voices (xii). But while expressivist pedagogies emphasize the search for individual voice, feminism radicalizes the "personal" into a subversive, political act. Elisabeth Daumer and Sandra Runzo, for instance, argue that feminism is a way of "battling" gender inequities. Feminism, they contend, enables "students to find a voice to combat the pervasive forces in our culture that silence women and others, who because of race, class, or other circum-stances have been permitted less visibility and whose concerns have been suppressed" (53). In this representation of feminism (which has historical and theoretical roots in liberal and cultural feminisms), women students' authentic feminine voices are depicted as fettered by or lost in patriarchal discourse and must be freed or recovered by the feminist teacher. Feminism becomes a way of empowering women to "come to voice" by deconstructing the binary between public/private and personal/political writing (see Annas 37, Frey).

The general dearth of feminist research in composition studies provoked Elizabeth Flynn (1988) to remark that "[f]or the most part . . . the fields of feminist studies and composition studies have not engaged each other in a serious or systematic way." Critical of the androcentrism present in traditional research on the composing process, Flynn deploys the gender differences research paradigm from the social sciences (Belenky *et al*; Chodorow; Gilligan) to study male and female ways of composing and knowing. Thus, she constructs feminism as a research methodology that highlights "what it means to compose as a woman" (425), that encourages women students "to become self-consciously aware of what their experience in the world has been and how this experience is related to the politics of gender" (434).

Flynn (1991) further portrays feminism in composition studies as a methodology that identifies "androcentrism in all its varieties, including the androcentrism of cognate fields." Feminism, Flynn continues, recuperates "those modes of thinking within the field that are compatible with a feminine epistemology" (143). In fact, she co-mingles the terms *feminine* and *feminism* to invent a new term—*femininism*—a feminine approach to language study "characterized by modalities of relatedness and mutuality, indistinct boundaries, flexibility, and non-oppositional styles" (147). The co-mingling of these terms however, has caused controversy among feminists who see feminism as a critique of traditional feminine virtues, not a reinscription of femininity (see Bizzell, Looser).

Likewise equating "feminine" epistemologies with "feminist" episte-mologies, Clara Juncker calls for teachers of composition to adopt French feminist theories of *ecriture féminine* or feminine writing (Cixous). Juncker represents *ecriture féminine* as a seductive and subversive "force" that can "dislocate" the phallic order by enabling student writers "to (re)invent them-selves and to inscribe difference in(side) academia" (434). Juncker's appropriation of French feminism, however, has been a point of contention between feminists in composition studies. Lynn Worsham warns that attempts to import French feminism into composition studies "unwittingly contain and neutralize it within an ideological space that it resists and refuses" (94). She asserts that composition studies, an agent of modernist thought driven by the "will to pedagogy," tames and domesticates the wild, unruly, radical potential of *ecriture féminine*, "swallow[ing] up its specific force in the epistemological desires of a discipline that would rather not be questioned" (97).

Despite the widespread tendency to appeal to "personal" or autobiographical writing as a feminist genre, rhetorical theorist Catherine E. Lamb questions the favoring of autobiography over argument in feminist composition studies (13). Lamb wishes to deflect the adversarial approach to argument with a feminist approach grounded in the principles of mediation, negotiation, and "maternal thinking," the ability to exercise "attentive love" or "the ability to think or feel as the other" (16, see Ruddick). Through argumentative styles that rely upon "maternal thinking," Lamb constructs feminism as a rhetoric that eschews adversarial argument and dissolves the binary between autobiography and argument.

Feminist pedagogical theorists influenced by poststructural and postmodern critiques of essentialism, however, contend that "maternal thinking" may reinscribe stereotypical notions of femininity, thus disabling the counter-hegemonic power and authority of the feminist writing teacher. "Because most high school teachers are women and may be seen as maternal figures," Susan Jarratt contends, "the role of the supportive, nurturing composition teacher repeats that childish pattern and puts the teacher at a disadvantage in any attempt to assert a counterhegemonic authority as a woman" (111). bell hooks also rejects the maternal model in favor of a confrontational feminist pedagogic stance: "Unlike the stereotypical feminist model that suggests women best come to voice in an atmosphere of safety, one in which we are all going to be kind and nurturing, I encourage students to work at coming to voice in an atmosphere where they may be afraid or see themselves at risk" (53). Both hooks and Jarratt represent feminism as an oppositional pedagogy designed to boldly and unapologetically confront—rather than avoid—issues of gender, race, class, and sexuality.

Indeed, feminists influenced by poststructural and postmodern critiques of identity politics (see Fuss, Ritchie, Spivak) have become suspicious of the tendency to essentialize gender differences in feminist research and pedagogy. Arguing that "[m]any of the feminist paradigms on which our composition theories are based have been rendered suspect by recent feminist (particularly poststructuralist) theories" (54), Devoney Looser urges feminist researchers and teachers to question the historical and cultural assumptions commonly made about the categories *woman, women*, and *women's experience* because they risk positing a universal female essence. Indeed, concern over representations of "women's experience," "women's identity," and the "personal" prompted Gesa E. Kirsch and Joy S. Ritchie to remark that feminists need to "examine just what a politics of location means for research, what are its implications, and its limitations" (9).

Feminist theorists have also attempted to understand the connection between the devalued status of composition teaching and the female gender of many of its workers, the majority of whom are part-time and non-tenure track faculty. Sue Ellen Holbrook argues that feminism serves as an interpretive lens through which we can understand the "feminization" of composition—a process whereby "the field has become associated with feminine attributes and populated by the female gender" (201). Susan Miller also examines the implications of feminization—the "feminized actual, historical, and symbolic status of composition professionals and their students"—in order to "reveal existing counterhegemonic structures in the field's existing practices and intellectual positions" (51). Feminism thus becomes a strategy for not only understanding the relationship between gender and the status of writing teachers, but also for transforming the feminized status of composition into counterhegemonic political practices that dismantle gender imbalances and inequities.

Feminism's complexity as a social, political, and historical movement cannot be contained within fixed categories and classification schemes in composition studies; rather, we must pay attention to the local contexts and contingencies that currently influence feminist theory and practice.

Eileen E. Schell
Syracuse University

Works Cited

Annas, Pamela J. 1985. "Style as Politics: A Feminist Approach to the Teaching of Writing." *College English* 47: 360–371.

Belenky, Mary Field, Blythe McVicker Clinchy, Nancy Rule Goldberger, and Jill Mattuck Tarule. 1986. *Women's Ways of Knowing: The Development of Self, Voice, and Mind.* New York: Basic Books.

Bizzell, Patricia. 1994. "Review of Anxious Power: Reading, Writing, and Ambivalence in Narratives by Women." *Rhetoric Review* 13: 192–196.

Caywood, Cynthia L., and Gillian R. Overing, ed. 1987. *Teaching Writing: Pedagogy, Gender, and Equity.* Albany: SUNY Press.

Chodorow, Nancy. 1978. *The Reproduction of Mothering: Psychoanalysis and the Sociology of Gender.* Berkeley: University of California Press.

Cixous, Hélène. 1981. "The Laugh of the Medusa." *New French Feminisms: An Anthology.* Ed. Elaine Marks and Isabelle de Courtivron. New York: Schocken. 245–264.

Daumer, Elisabeth, and Sandra Runzo. 1987. "Transforming the Composition Classroom." *Teaching Writing: Pedagogy, Gender, and Equity.* Ed. Cynthia L. Caywood and Gillian R. Overing. Albany: SUNY Press. 45–62.

Flynn, Elizabeth. 1988. "Composing as a Woman." *College Composition and Communication* 39: 423–435.

———. 1991. "Composition Studies from a Feminist Perspective." *The Politics of Writing Instruction: Postsecondary.* Ed. Richard Bullock and John Trimbur. Portsmouth, NH: Boynton/Cook. 137–154.

Frey, Olivia. 1990. "Beyond Literary Darwinism: Women's Voices and Critical Discourse." *College English* 52: 507–526.

Fuss, Diana. 1989. *Essentially Speaking: Feminism, Nature, and Difference.* New York: Routledge.

Gilligan, Carol. 1982. *In a Different Voice: Psychological Theory and Women's Development.* Cambridge, Mass.: Harvard University Press.

Howe, Florence. 1971. "Identity and Expression: A Writing Course for Women." *College English* 3: 863–871.

Holbrook, Sue Ellen. 1991. "Women's Work: The Feminizing of Composition." *Rhetoric Review* 9: 201–229.

hooks, bell. 1989. "Toward a Revolutionary Feminist Pedagogy." *Talking Back: Thinking Feminist, Thinking Black.* Boston: South End Press. 49–54.

Jarratt, Susan. 1991. "Feminism and Composition: The Case for Conflict." *Contending with Words: Composition and Rhetoric in a Postmodern Age.* Ed. Patricia Harkin and John Schilb. New York: Modern Language Association. 103–123.

Juncker, Clara. 1988. "Writing with Cixous." *College English* 50: 424–436.

Kirsch, Gesa E., and Joy S. Ritchie. 1995. "Beyond the Personal: Theorizing a Politics of Location in Composition Research." *College Composition and Communication* 46: 7–29.

Lamb, Catherine E. 1991. "Beyond Argument in Feminist Composition." *College Composition and Communication* 42: 11–24.

Looser, Devoney. 1993. "Composing as an 'Essentialist'? New Directions for Feminist Composition Theories." *Rhetoric Review* 12: 54–69.

Miller, Susan. 1991. "The Feminization of Composition." *The Politics of Writing Instruction: Postsecondary.* Ed. Richard Bullock and John Trimbur. Portsmouth, NH: Boynton/Cook. 39–54.

Rich, Adrienne. 1979. "Taking Women Students Seriously." *On Lies, Secrets, and Silence: Selected Prose, 1966–1978.* New York: W.W. Norton. 33–49.

Ritchie, Joy S. 1990. "Confronting the 'Essential' Problem: Reconnecting Feminist Theory and Pedagogy." *Journal of Advanced Composition* 10: 249–273.

Ruddick, Sara. 1980. "Maternal Thinking." *Feminist Studies* 6: 70–96.

Spivak, Gayatri. 1987. *In Other Worlds: Essays in Cultural Politics.* New York: Methuen.

Worsham, Lynn. 1991. "Writing against Writing: The Predicament of Ecriture Féminine in Composition Studies." *Contending with Words: Composition and Rhetoric in a Postmodern Age.* Ed. Patricia Harkin and John Schilb. New York: Modern Language Association. 84–103.

form/structure

"Few issues in the teaching of writing . . . are less well understood than the nature of form," Joseph M. Williams has written (474). The "mere slipperiness of the word 'form,' " (Winterowd 1971, 39) is compounded by its being conflated with what Frank J. D'Angelo calls its "obvious analogs"—*shape, design, pattern, plan, archetype*, and the like (9). Indeed, D'Angelo (1974) himself uses *arrangement, dispositio, organization, structure*, and *form* interchangeably on a single page of an earlier text (396). Many have likewise noted that *coherence* and *form* "are virtually synonymous" (Winterowd 1970, 828); form, in this sense, means the "set of relationships between the parts which creates the whole" (Stalter 341). A further complication is that form is something normally invisible, something "we ordinarily become conscious of . . . only when we are troubled by it" (Colomb and Williams 89). Or as Paul Rodgers puts it, form is something we recognize "as if by instinct or intuition. . . . We may not know precisely *what* structure is, but we know *where* it is" (178).

Form in writing has been represented: as what results when an "invariable deep structure" of discourse is transformed into a "variety of surface realizations" (Winterowd 1971, 41); as the "result of two cooperating-competing sets of principles," the "principles of design" (which "have the effect of complicating the product") and the "principles of pattern" (which cause us "to see not the parts, but the whole") (Brashers 147); as "hierarchical, [as] units embedded within or added to larger units embedded within or added to still larger units" (Pitkin 141); as vertical, as units of "higher and lower levels of abstraction" connected by means coordination and subordination, and as horizontal, " 'linear,' or directional . . . [as] a succession of steps, taken in a temporal sequence" (Larson 141); and as a three-dimensional matrix of interconnected discourse units (Nold and Davis 142). Furthermore, some, like Willis L. Pitkin, Jr., have noted that form is "not a static entity." Instead, he writes, the structure of discourse is one of "stages and substages, junctures and subjunctures" (139). Phenomenological accounts likewise posit "text structure as a *layered* experience" of multiple strata (Colomb and Williams 90).

While "the subject of arrangement, organization, or form, whichever term one likes best," has been studied since antiquity as the second of the five canons of classical rhetoric (Stewart 92), one result of the process movement was that "everything that smacked of . . . the F-word, 'Form' . . . became suspect" (Coe 1993, 264). Form became "associated with conformity, with rigid rules and 'boiler plate' prose" (Chapman 73), became known as "the most dismal stuff that students and teachers must deal with" (Winterowd 1975, 163).

According to Richard M. Coe (1987), the traditional conception posits that "form is a *container* to be filled (hence the term *content*)," with form and content being independent entities (15–16), a definition that Winston Weathers, for one, finds problematic: "I may be free to put 'what I have to say' in the plain box or in the ornate box, in the large box or in the small box, in the fragile box or in the sturdy box. But always *the box*—squarish and rectangular" (1–2). This view contributes to the schism between mechanical and organic representations of form, which respectively imagine "parts of discourse joined together like machine parts" and "the structure of a discourse . . . [as] evolv[ing] like a plant from a seed" (Stewart 94).

William Zeiger distinguishes between organic form—the "inner correspondences . . . unique to the work"—and abstract form—which "is transferable, . . . [and] represents a pattern not of art but of life" (210). Like Kenneth Burke, who believed that phenomena like "the cycle of a storm . . . [and] the ripening of crops" provide humans with "the formal equipment" by which they produce art (141), Zeiger maintains that "prose patterns generally derive from 'natural' schemata dwelling within the mind and projected outward, . . . from physical sensations which underlie and precede conscious thought" (210–211), from "basic conceptual orders and the truths that they embody" (218). His suggestion that "bodily transactions might underlie our allegiance to logical or any other form" (213) seems to correspond with the French feminist notion of "writing the body": "Like the feminine sexuality from which it originates, *l'ecriture féminine* (over)flows in endless expulsions of blood, milk, child, and orgasms" (Duren, qtd. in Juncker 426).

Coe (1987)—contending that "[t]here is no meaning without form," that information is data put "*in formation*, by forming"—argues that we should "define form in terms of its function in a process of forming. . . . [W]hatever is used to inform—to impose pattern on noise, cosmos on chaos—is form" (16–17). Ann E. Berthoff likewise portrays linguistic, syntactical, and rhetorical structures

> as speculative instruments. Forms are not cookie cutters superimposed on some given, rolled-out reality dough; forms are not alien structures that are somehow made appropriate to "what you want to say." Forms are our means of abstracting; or, rather, forming *is* abstracting. (77)

In this vein, D'Angelo (1975) notes, "form in discourse is both the informing principle as well as the shape or structure" (79). Form thus has heuristic force. As Coe (1987) puts it, "Form, in its emptiness, is heuristic, for it guides a structured search. Faced with the emptiness of form, a *human* being seeks matter to fill it" (18). D'Angelo (1976) states simply that "any theory of invention is a theory of form" (359).

Of late, scholars have been emphasizing that discursive forms are "social structures" (Coe 1987, 18). According to Coe (1987), forms are "the social memory" of a community's "standard responses," attitudes, and expectations (19). Form is thus also ideological. A form can constrain "against the discovery of information . . . [and] against the communication of a message contrary to the interests of some power elite" (20). Thus, "[o]ppressed social groups often find it necessary to invent new forms because the socially dominant forms will not readily carry their ideas" (25). In like manner, Keith Fort argues that the form of the traditional, critical essay "both reflects and perpetuates attitudes that generate structures in our society" (629). According to Fort, the form of the essay conditions "students to think in terms of authority and hierarchy" and manifests the same " 'proper' attitude towards authority that would be found in almost any of the institutions in our society." Moreover, he notes, since "the form has internal competition as its motive force"—the writer "competing against his subject to claim his mastery over it"—the form "will thus also generate external competition" (635). Furthermore, he contends, "form establishes a relation between self, object, and audience that satisfies needs" (633), the "form of the standard essay rest[ing] on a self-deceptive need for an authority whom we don't consciously believe can exist" (636). He contends that the "form of the critical essay has . . . evolved in large part as a strategy that will seem to solve [the] contradiction" between our "unconscious need to believe in the reality of a transcendent authority . . . [and our] conscious belief that such authority cannot exist." The form of the critical essay does so by allowing "subjective interpretation to presented in such a way that it does not appear to be dependent on the mind of fallible human being" (633–634).

Form in composition studies has long stood for a generic kind or type of discourse which can be classified "based on aims, audiences, subject matter, rhetorical situations, or formal characteristics of some kind," has long served as a synonym for genre (D'Angelo 1987, 131). It has, moreover, been construed as "a product of inspiration" (Chapman 73), as being "of utmost importance in all good writing" (D'Angelo 1974, 396), as "inseparable" from and "synonymous" with style (D'Angelo 1975, 104, 109), and as something which students equate with "[c]ontrol over texts and readers" (Podis and Podis 439). Most recently, form has been represented as a disciplinary lack. Lillian Bridwell-Bowles has written that the multiple perspectives and the "cloudy" concept of truth in our postmodern world means that "we need a wide variety of forms of writing," that we "need to investigate new forms" (55–56).

Paul Heilker
Virginia Tech

Works Cited

Berthoff, Ann E. 1981. *The Making of Meaning: Metaphors, Models, and Maxims for Writing Teachers.* Portsmouth, NH: Boynton.

Brashers, Howard C. 1971. "Aesthetic Form in Familiar Essays." *College Composition and Communication* 22: 147–155.

Bridwell-Bowles, Lillian. 1995. "Freedom, Form, Function: Varieties of Academic Discourse." *College Composition and Communication* 46: 46–61.

Burke, Kenneth. 1953. *Counter-Statement.* 2nd ed. Los Altos CA: Hermes.

Chapman, David W. 1991. "Forming and Meaning: Writing the Counterpoint Essay." *Journal of Advanced Composition* 11: 73–81.

Coe, Richard M. 1987. "An Apology for Form; or, Who Took the Form Out of the Process?" *College English* 49: 13–28.

———. 1993. Review of *Beyond Outlining: New Approaches to Rhetorical Form*, by Betty Cain. Lantham, MD: University Press of America, 1992. In *College Composition and Communication* 44: 264–266.

Colomb, Gregory G., and Joseph M. Williams. 1985. "Perceiving Structure in Professional Prose: A Multiply Determined Experience." *Writing in Nonacademic Settings.* Ed. Lee Odell and Dixie Goswami. New York: Guilford. 87–128.

D'Angelo, Frank J. 1974. "A Generative Rhetoric of the Essay." *College Composition and Communication* 25: 388–396.

———. 1975. *A Conceptual Theory of Rhetoric.* Cambridge, MA: Winthrop.

———. 1976. "Notes toward a Semantic Theory of Rhetoric within a Case Grammar Framework." *College Composition and Communication* 27: 359–362.

———. 1987. "Aims, Modes, and Forms of Discourse." *Teaching Composition: Twelve Bibliographical Essays.* Ed. Gary Tate. Fort Worth: Texas Christian University Press. 131–154.

Fort, Keith. 1971. "Form, Authority, and the Critical Essay." *College English* 32: 629–639.

Juncker, Clara. 1988. "Writing (with) Cixous." *College English* 50: 242–436.

Larson, Richard L. 1971. "Toward a Linear Rhetoric of the Essay." *College Composition and Communication* 22: 140–146.

Nold, Ellen W., and Brent E. Davis. 1980. "The Discourse Matrix." *College Composition and Communication* 31: 141–152.

Pitkin, Willis L., Jr. 1969. "Discourse Blocs." *College Composition and Communication* 20: 138–148.

Podis, JoAnne M., and Leonard A. Podis. 1990. "Identifying and Teaching Rhetorical Plans for Arrangement." *College Composition and Communication* 41: 430–442.

Rodgers, Paul. 1967. "The Stadium of Discourse." *College Composition and Communication* 18: 178–185.

Stalter, William. 1978. "A Sense of Structure." *College Composition and Communication* 29: 341–345.

Stewart, Donald. 1987. "Some Thoughts on Arrangement." *Journal of Advanced Composition* 7: 92–100.

Weathers, Winston. 1980. *An Alternate Style: Options in Composition.* Rochelle Park, NJ: Hayden.

Williams, Joseph M. 1988. Review of *Toward a Grammar of Passages*, by Richard M. Coe. Carbondale: Southern Illinois University Press, 1988. In *College Composition and Communication* 39: 474–478.

Winterowd, W. Ross. 1970. "The Grammar of Coherence." *College English* 31: 828–835.

———. 1971. "*Dispositio*: The Concept of Form in Discourse." *College Composition and Communication* 22: 39–45.

———. 1975. *Contemporary Rhetoric.* New York: Harcourt.

Zeiger, William. 1990. "The Circular Journey and the Natural Authority of Form." *Rhetoric Review* 8: 208–219.

freshman English

The many meanings of this keyword—used synonymously with *freshman rhetoric, freshman composition,* and *first-year writing*—reflect what Sharon Crowley (1991) calls "the deep institutional and cultural embeddedness of Freshman English" (158). Most commonly, freshman English is portrayed as a " 'service' course, a course that should 'cover' grammar, spelling, punctuation, . . . term paper writing, . . . library introduction," critical reading, and other aspects of academic literacy for faculty in other departments (Tighe 33). Dudley Bailey has noted that this likens freshman English to "the janitors [who] perform a 'valuable service' for our various colleges . . . [but] are not really a part of any of them" (qtd. in Crowley 1986, 14). Gary Tate, for one, rejects this definition: "Does the vast apparatus of our discipline—all the journals, books, conferences, graduate programs—exist in the cause of nothing more than better sociology and biology papers?" (319).

Freshman English is sometimes represented positively: as "the University's most important single course" (Hoblitzelle 600); as "the Best Course in the University to Teach" (Fulweiler 104); as "one of the most rewarding and stimulating courses" a student can take (Moyer 169); as perhaps "the most important part of the [English] curriculum, calling for the highest degree of experience, skill, and dedication" (Nash 130); as "one of the most difficult jobs in the university" (Shaw 159); as "the student's first introduction to the world of the mind and the serious discussion of ideas" (Moyer 169); or as "a training of the whole person" (Purdy 795) which is "essential in any system of liberal education" (Kitzhaber 3). Hence, Crowley (1991) notes, "Freshman English is a sentimental favorite in America, like big bands and Norman Schwartzkopf" (156).

But freshman English is far more often constructed as a "failure" (Macrorie 629), "an educational and intellectual scandal" (Roellinger 326), a "monumental error, . . . [an] insurmountable problem" (Greenbaum 186), "a continuing dilemma" (Nash 125), and a "peril" to English departments that is "clearly in need of radical and sweeping reforms" (Kitzhaber 26). Indeed, published calls for the complete abolition of freshman English began as early as 1931 (see Greenbaum 177). Thus, negative representations of freshman English abound. The general conception, as Toby Fulweiler notes, is that

> teaching freshman English is the worst chore in the university. So bad, in fact, that only part-timers and graduate students should have to do it. Or so bad that everyone on the faculty should share The English Teacher's Burden. (104)

"For years," George Stade says, "the course justified its existence by disenchanting more students, harrying more administrators, breaking in (or down) more apprentice teachers, and enriching more publishers, than any other" (143). Freshman English, he maintains, is also notable for its "schizophrenia," its "hebephrenia beyond therapy" (144). It is, he contends, something as "embarrassing and superfluous as it is difficult to part with, . . . like a bridegroom's . . . pornography collection" (143). Crowley (1986) writes that "Freshman English has been a black hole ever since its inception, swallowing up students, teachers, and money without giving much in return" (11). Moreover, Crowley (1991) says,

> Freshman English is a lot like "hell night" in fraternity initiations: people do it because it was done to them, everybody sentimentalizes it by forgetting it more painful aspects, and nobody notices its potentially deleterious effects until somebody complains or gets hurt. (156)

Ken Macrorie has characterized freshman English as an "essentially punitive and negative course" in which "dumb, bored, and boring teachers" create "laborious piddling routines for students" (630). It has also been described as an "academic boondoggle" (Bullard 373); "a Frankenstein's monster with four heads and three right arms, . . . a garbage dump of non-study with no underlying philosophy" (Tighe 33–34); a "disease" (Greenbaum 187); a "bad joke," and as "shit" (Pichaske 118).

Freshman English has furthermore been figured as an unfortunate psychological space, one of "disgust[,] . . . defeat, and resignation" (Tighe 32–33), "shame[,] . . . self-debasement[,] . . . self-denigration" (Shaw 158), "cynicism and despair" (Stade 144), "desperation[,] . . . unfounded hope[,] . . . guilt feelings" (Macrorie 630), and "paralyzing indifference" (Roellinger 326). Leonard Greenbaum maintains that "the trauma of the course can live with people the rest of their unnatural days" (186). In short, as Francis X. Roellinger puts it, "anxiety over freshman English, like anxiety over radioactive fallout, cigarette smoking, and cholesterol, rises and falls and never quite goes away" (325).

Freshman English is also frequently invoked as an empty space notable for its various lacks, as an absence. According to Crowley (1986), "When teachers of English write about the course in their professional journals it is to complain about it: its teachers' lack of training and motivation; its students ill-preparedness and lack of motivation; its low status; its lack of intellectual integrity" (11). Crowley, herself, remarks on the "the intellectual poverty" of "the ordinarily unproductive vineyards of freshman English" (14–15). For Stade, freshman English is "singularly devoid of either the profitable or the playful,... has no content at all... [and] is not a subject" (144–145). Moreover, Greenbaum argues, freshman English is a course designed "to develop in the student an overwhelming sense of his own inadequacies." It is, he writes, the place "where a person learns that he can't write," and it thus serves as "the crown on thirteen hapless years of composition education that has taken expressive children and molded them into wordless adults" (186). This portrayal of freshman English as primarily an absence or lack is perhaps inevitable since, according to Crowley (1986), freshman English was conceived at Harvard, beginning in 1874, "in the midst of an awareness of lack[,] ... [conceived of] as a response to perceived deficiencies in students' literate skills, rather than as an area in which to study a body of received knowledge." This origin in lack, she says, has always "plagued" freshman English, fueling the repeated attempts "to make the course teachable and respectable by grounding it in some discipline" (11).

Moreover, American culture's class-based fear of illiteracy, Crowley (1991) argues, constructs freshman English "as cultural capital—as the mutual property of all persons who conceive of education as a site for transmission (or criticism) of a received dominant culture" (159), including faculty in other disciplines and the general public as well. Since the grapholect taught in freshman English "signifies that its possessors are suitable for admission to the class of educated persons," Crowley says (161), the course functions "as a repressive instrument of student... legitimation" (170), as a "period of atonement" (160), an "initiation rite" (166), and "as a border checkpoint, the institutional site wherein students either provide proper identification or retreat to wherever they came from" (160). In this way, freshman English is also constructed "as something that is done to the students for their own good" (173). Or, as Albert R. Kitzhaber, puts it, "Freshman English is one of those things like spinach and tetanus shots that young people put up with because their elders say they must" (1).

University administrators, it has been argued, see "freshman writing courses as havens for the halt and the lame" of the faculty (Purdy 795), "as a place to economize" (Hoblitzelle 600), and as a cause of "dwindling enroll-ment figures" (Shaw 155). Crowley (1991) contends that for faculty in other disciplines, freshman English "serves as a convenient scapegoat for their guilt about refusing to teach discipline-specific literacy" (157) and as "a cheap way ... to salve their guilt about their own teaching" since it "is the one place in the academy where students presumably get some individual attention" (165). It has also been construed as an exercise in "empire building"—since it "is chiefly this course that makes the English department one of the largest in most colleges" (Bullard 373)—and as the "daily bread" of the "newly-enfranchised persons" of a "new academic discipline," despite its "lowly intellectual position at the bottom of the academic pecking order" (Crowley 1991, 165–166).

Most recently, as Crowley (1991) notes, freshman English has come to be seen "as a venue for radical instructional politics" (164), as a place to "sensitize students to the fact that they live in an oppressive culture ridden with sexism, racism, and classism" (173). Finally, Crowley notes, the very size of freshman English as a universal requirement "subjects its administrators, teachers, and students to unprofessional and unethical working practices on a scale that is replicated nowhere else in the academy" (157).

Paul Heilker
Virginia Tech

Works Cited

Bullard, Catherine. 1964. "Academic Boondoggle." *College English* 25: 373–375.

Crowley, Sharon. 1986. "The Perilous Life and Times of Freshman English." *Freshman English News* 14: 11–16.

———. 1991. "A Personal Essay on Freshman English." *Pre/Text* 12: 155–176.

Fulweiler, Toby. 1986. "Freshman Writing: It's the Best Course in the University to Teach." *The Chronicle of Higher Education.* 5 Feb. 1986: 104.

Greenbaum, Leonard. 1969. "The Tradition of Complaint." *College English* 31: 174–187.

Hoblitzelle, Harrison. 1967. "A Study of Freshman English: An Informal Summary." *College English* 28: 596–600.

Kitzhaber, Albert R. 1963. *Themes, Theories, and Therapy: The Teaching of Writing in College.* New York: McGraw-Hill.

Macrorie, Ken. 1966. "A Letter to One More Newly-Elected Committee Set Up to Plan and Administer a Course in Freshman Composition." *College English* 27: 629–630.

Moyer, Charles R. 1969. "Why I Gave Up Teaching Freshman English." *College English* 31: 169–173.

Nash, George. 1976. "Who's Minding Freshman English at U. T. Austin?" *College English* 38: 125–131.

Pichaske, David R. 1976. "Freshman Comp: What Is This Shit?" *College English* 38: 117–124.

Purdy, Dwight. 1986. "A Polemical History of Freshman Composition in Our Time." *College English* 48: 791–796.

Roellinger, Francis X. 1964. "The Present State of Freshman English: An Interim Report." *College English* 25: 325–330.

Shaw, Patrick W. 1974. "Freshman English: To Compose or Decompose, That Is the Question." *College Composition and Communication* 25: 155–159.

Stade, George. 1969. "Hydrants into Elephants: The Theory and Practice of College Composition." *College English* 31: 143–154.

Tate, Gary. 1993. "A Place for Literature in Freshman Composition." *College English* 55: 317–321.

Tighe, Donald J. 1963. "The Shame of Freshman English." *College Composition and Communication* 14: 32–35.

grammar

Twenty-five years ago, Charlton Laird lamented that "nobody knows what grammar is," that scholars "cannot agree how it works, how it is related to men and mental processes, or even how one should go about studying it, once it can be identified and defined" (181). In the time since, scholarship in composition studies has come to understand *grammar* as a keyword whose definitions are legion.

In 1985, for instance, Patrick Hartwell delineated five distinct kinds of grammar. Grammar 1, he said, is "the grammar in our heads," the internalized system of unconscious rules which speakers of a language share (111). Grammar 2 is "scientific grammar" (110), that is, the "attempt to approximate the rules or schemata of Grammar 1 by writing fully explicit descriptions that model the competence of a native speaker" (115). Next comes Grammar 3, the popular (mis)understanding of grammar as (mis)usage, as "linguistic etiquette." Hartwell defined Grammar 4 as " 'school grammar' . . . meaning, quite literally, 'the grammars used in the schools.' " Finally, he distinguished Grammar 5, " 'stylistic grammar,' defined as 'grammatical terms used in the interest of teaching prose style' " (110).

The discussion of grammar in composition studies over the last thirty years seems to amount to a long series of responses to a single quotation. In 1963, Richard Braddock, Richard Lloyd-Jones, and Lowell Schoer wrote:

> In view of the widespread agreement of research studies based on many types of students and teachers, the conclusion can be stated in strong and unqualified terms: the teaching of formal grammar has a negligible or, because it displaces some instruction and practice in actual composition, even a harmful effect on the improvement of writing. (37–38)

But since this conclusion contradicts the commonsense belief that one's writing must be improved by a knowledge of grammar, this construction of grammar has been repeatedly attacked or ignored. Many teachers and scholars have maintained, despite the evidence to the contrary, that grammar would indeed help students write better, if only they studied the right kind of grammar.

Fueled by the belief that "because the newest form of grammar is so superior to the bad old grammars it will succeed where the others have failed" (Lester 227), scholars embarked on a quest for the "right kind" of grammar by means of a tremendous proliferation of redefinitions. Hence, in the last three decades, the literature in composition studies has manifested a great many new constructions of *grammar* through the addition of prefatory adjectivals such as *technical, functional, formal, systemic, prescriptive, true, applied, semantic, case, junction, text, instrumental, rhetorical, immediate constituent, comparative, streamlined writer's, Latinate, X-bar, Old, New, Montague, neo-Bloomfieldian, neo-Firthian, Interactive, function-word Structural, phonological Structural, Transformational-Generative, Tagmemic, Stratificational,* and, of course, *Traditional* (including *old-line Traditional, much-revised scholarly-traditional,* and *pragmatic traditional surface structure*).

More problematic than this sheer number of contesting (re)constructions of grammar, however, have been the occasions when scholars and teachers (re)defined and attempted to construe a Grammar 2 (scientific grammar) as the field's collective Grammar 4 (school grammar). In the case of generative grammar, for instance, when one scholar ultimately found that it had "not been an effective means for teaching skillful use of the language," he redefined it back into being solely a Grammar 2, concluding that since "transformational grammar is not a theory of rhetoric or usage or even competence in writing," we should study it instead for the insights it offers into our minds and our linguistic facility (Luthy 352–355).

In like manner, many have urged compositionists to understand grammar as "a subject in its own right . . . a discipline worthy of the name, a challenge worthy of the intellect" (Stockwell 59), as a theory which we should study for its own sake rather than as a practice which we study to avoid errors in writing. Grammar has also come to mean "a theory of generation," as in Richard M. Coe's "grammar of passages." Here, grammar refers to the system of constituent structure rules underlying whatever phenomenon is being examined which explains which patterns are preferred and which are proscribed. A similar meaning is apparent in constructions like Kenneth Burke's, where grammar refers to "the purely internal relationships" among the units of a system, their range of possible transformations, permutations, and combinations (xvi). For Winston Weathers, grammar refers to nothing less than "the set of conventions governing the construction of a whole composition," its subject matter, organization, development, structure, style, and communication goals (2).

Such expansive definitions obviously clash with more fundamental representations. For instance, grammar is frequently imagined as a useful tool, as in Jim W. Corder's description of "grammar as a sprightly instrument in composition" (480). As Laird points out, grammar has also come "to refer to elements and to matters elementary" (181), that is, foundational. In this vein, grammar has long been represented as being the center of the English curriculum (recalling its status as one part of the classical trivium), as the key to control over and mastery of written language, as the chief indicator of competence in written English, and thus as a central element of every "back to basics movement." In contrast, other constructions of grammar as foundational include grammar as drill-and-practice exercises—the stuff of workbooks, as a crisis staved off by means of "grammar hotlines," as an illness in need of remediation in writing "labs" and "clinics," and as a stigma and a source of "Toxic shame—overwhelming embarrassment, usually triggered by becoming aware of a mistake" (Farrell 270).

Through the use of such contested meanings, grammar has come to be understood as being situated at the crux of the shifting power relation between teachers and students. As Hartwell has said, "At no point in the English curriculum is the question of power more blatantly posed than in the issue of formal grammar instruction" (127).

Paul Heilker
Virginia Tech

Works Cited

Braddock, Richard, Richard Lloyd-Jones, and Lowell Schoer. 1963. *Research in Written Composition.* Champaign, IL: National Council of Teachers of English.

Burke, Kenneth. 1969. *A Grammar of Motives.* Berkeley: University of California Press.

Coe, Richard M. 1988. *Toward a Grammar of Passages.* Carbondale: Southern Illinois University Press.

Corder, Jim W. 1977. "Outhouses, Weather Changes, and the Return to Basics in English Education." *College English* 38: 474–482.

Farrell, Thomas J. 1992. Review of *Rhetorical Grammar: Grammatical Choices, Rhetorical Effects*, by Martha Kolln. *College Composition and Communication* 43: 269–270.

Hartwell, Patrick. 1985. "Grammar, Grammars, and the Teaching of Grammar." *College English* 47: 105–127.

Laird, Charlton. 1969. "A Simpleminded Look at Grammar and Language." *College Composition and Communication* 20: 181–186.

Lester, Mark. 1967. "The Value of Transformational Grammar in Teaching Composition." *College Composition and Communication* 18: 227–231.

Luthy, Melvin J. 1977. "Why Transformational Grammar Fails in the Classroom." *College Composition and Communication* 28: 352–356.

Stockwell, Robert P. 1964. "Grammar? Today?" *College Composition and Communication* 15: 56–59.

Weathers, Winston. 1976. "Grammars of Style: New Options for Composition." *Freshman English News* 4: 1–18.

history

Any account of past events may be described either as *a* history or as *the* history of those events. Thus the very structure of our language encourages us to imagine that some histories are definitive. However, as Kenneth Burke has observed, any account in language, including accounts of history, operates as a "terministic screen," both reflecting and deflecting reality (45). It is possible to conceptualize history as a record of the past, or as a story about the past, or as a story with a message that may serve political ends. John Schilb has observed that history can either be conceptualized as "something that lies outside of the human imagination, waiting to be discovered" or as "something constructed by historians, and hence open to the kind of study we can accord to human meaning-making activities" (13).

Kathleen Welch complains that historical narratives of all kinds "continue to be produced with apparently omniscient writers presenting objective realities" (71). Nan Johnson, however, has described historiography as both a rhetorical *and* an archaeological enterprise. Johnson has characterized her own historiographic position as falling "somewhere in the middle of the continuum of beliefs ranging from an orthodox confidence in the expository nature of history" to "a poststructuralist self-consciousness of history as a form of literary narrative" (Murphy *et al.* 9). Sharon Crowley has observed that even when a historian acknowledges the constructed nature of her account, readers may assume it corresponds unproblematically to the reality it attempts to represent. Crowley says she and other historians "often find that the intellectual categories we introduce in our histories, or the figures we study, are reified by our readers in such a way as to award them quasi-metaphysical status" (Murphy *et al.* 7).

Hayden White has argued that "all historical narratives contain an irreducible and inexpungeable element of interpretation" (51). History, according to White, is a story with a moral, and historiography is a poetic enterprise. White advocates "subjecting any historical discourse to a *rhetorical* analysis, so as to disclose the poetical understructure of what is meant to pass for a modest prose representation of reality" (105). According to White, historians interpret their materials in at least two ways: "by the choice of a plot structure, which gives to their narratives a recognizable form, and by the choice of a paradigm of explanation, which gives to their arguments a specific shape, thrust, and mode of articulation" (67). Available plot structures include: the "comedy, tragedy, romance, epic, or satire" (59). Alternative models for historical explanation include: "the ideographic, the contextualist, the organicist, and the mechanist" (66). White suggests that both the choice of plot structure and the choice of explanatory paradigm "are products of a third, more basic, interpretive decision: a moral or ideological decision" (67).

There are historians, however, who while acknowledging the interpretive nature of all historiography, contend that history can and should remain free of ideological bias. Cases in point are provided by Robert J. Connors and Stephen M. North. Connors (1984) observes that "all historical interpretation is partly value judgment" (166). Even so, in a review of James Berlin's *Writing Instruction in Nineteenth-Century American Colleges,* Connors (1986) accuses Berlin of having "an axe to grind" and of filtering events "through powerful terministic screens." Connors adds that "to his credit," Berlin "admits his biases early in the book" (247). North, for his part, both concedes that "historians are no more objective than anyone else" (77) and objects to what he describes as a "propagandistic agenda" (88) in Connors' "The Rise and Fall of the Modes of Discourse." North appears to draw a sharp line between interpretation and ideology when he observes that "to favor some interpretive bias in Historical inquiry is one thing" but "to move outside the bounds of that inquiry in the name of reform, however subtly, is quite another" (90). Be that as it may, he makes no attempt to pinpoint just where interpretation ends and ideology begins.

History, in James Berlin's view, is inescapably ideological. Berlin argues that any historical account is "inscribed with a particular ideology—a version of what exists, what is good, and what is possible" and that any historian makes rhetorical choices "in a play of power with consequences for the present and the future, doing so, moreover, whether she chooses to or not" (56). In a review of Berlin's *Rhetoric and Reality,* however, Sharon Crowley observes that despite Berlin's sensitivity to ideology, "he never questions the repressive institutional situations which have shaped composition instruction since its beginnings." Crowley faults Berlin for failing to explain either "what ideological strictures mandate that most teachers of composition are (and always have been) part-time, untenured and untenurable instructors or graduate students" or "what ideological strictures have worked, historically, to confine research in composition to inferior status" (247). Crowley's critique is based on two premises. The first is that history should serve to promote productive change. The second is that historical data should be examined within their political and social contexts.

Schilb shares these assumptions and draws, moreover, a sharp contrast between intellectual and sociopolitical history. While he classifies most recent histories of rhetoric as intellectual histories (20), he argues that "a great variety of sociopolitical factors could and should be taken into account in charting developments in rhetorical theory" (21). He concludes that a sociopolitical history of composition is necessary "if we are to understand teachers' modern 'socializing imperatives' and challenge them for the betterment of writing instruction" (31).

Susan Miller observes that most histories of composition "elevate composition" above its surroundings "in problematic attempts to turn the low, excluded carnival of writing into a legitimate theater of the text" (35). It is the separation of composition from its social and educational contexts that, in Miller's view, is problematic. She does not question the validity of using history as an avenue to power and improved status. In fact, she suggests that the alternative to marginalization "is to look for one's own story" (36). She argues, however, that if composition is "to answer some important political questions and to gain support from the peers it wishes to persuade of its value," its historians must "use data from analyses of actual social situations, privileging mechanisms, discursive practices, and verifiable outcomes from writing" (120).

Margaret Strain, like Miller and Schilb, stresses the importance of context, and she insists moreover that the historian herself is an integral part of the contextual field of whatever she studies. Strain advocates a hermeneutic model for historiography in composition and says that a historian working with such a model "situates a focal text within larger social and cultural networks with a self-conscious awareness of her own prejudgments with regard to the historical context she constructs." The historian's interpretive presence, Strain argues, should be "seen as a positive value, inviting multiple readings" (220). "The multivocality of a hermeneutic history," she argues, "prods us to ask questions, to engage the ambiguities, and to listen to the marginalized and silenced texts" (234).

Victor Vitanza would probably classify Strain's model as "Revisionary Historiography." According to Vitanza, there are three categories of historiography: Traditional, Revisionary, and "Sub/Versive" (84). As Vitanza defines it, traditional historiography ranges "from a naive, unselfconscious practice to a more popular, highly-conscious, positivistic practice of History Writing" (85). Revisionary historiography, by contrast, springs either from the impulse to correct established interpretations of history or from the hermeneutical principle that "all facts are always already 'interpretations' " (95). Sub/Versive historiography, however, is rooted in the understanding "that the overthrow of a political position (or, as far as that goes, any position or ideology) is only a capitulation to eventual recapitulation" (107). Vitanza himself writes Sub/Versive historiography. The political goal of such historiography, according to Vitanza, is "to find a non-fascistic way to attenuate fascism" (108). It also seeks to counter "the hollow voice of Authority, which speaks of the 'bedrock grounding' of knowledge" (109).

Vitanza identifies six purposes of Sub/Versive historiography, dividing them into two sub-sets, one originated by Michel Foucault and the other by Vitanza himself. The first of the purposes in Foucault's sub-set is, in Foucault's own terms, "parodic, directed against reality," and opposed to "the theme of history as reminiscence or recognition." The second is "dissociative, directed against identity," and opposed to "history given as continuity or representative of a tradition." The third is "sacrificial, directed against truth," and opposed to "history as knowledge" (160). The first of the purposes in Vitanza's sub-set "is to dispel" or "expel the influence of philosophy." The second is to replace the "conceptual framework of 'Philosophical Rhetoric' " with a "competing, contrary framework." The third is to replace "representative anecdotes" with "mis/representative antidotes" (Vitanza 112–113). Histories constructed on the Sub/Versive model, Vitanza says, will be "curative fictions" informed by "the therapeutic power of laughter" (113).

Robin Varnum
American International College

Works Cited

Berlin, James A. 1987. "Revisionary History: The Dialectical Method." *Pre/Text* 8: 47–61.

Burke, Kenneth. 1966. *Language as Symbolic Action: Essays on Life, Literature, and Method.* Berkeley: University California Press.

Connors, Robert J. 1984. "Historical Inquiry in Composition Studies." *The Writing Instructor* 3: 157–167.

———. 1986. Review of *Writing Instruction in Nineteenth-Century American Colleges* by James A. Berlin. *College Composition and Communication* 37: 247–249.

Crowley, Sharon. 1988. Review of *Rhetoric and Reality: Writing Instruction in American Colleges, 1900–1985* by James Berlin. *College Composition and Communication* 39: 245–247.

Foucault, Michel. 1977. *Language, Counter-Memory, Practice: Selected Essays and Interviews.* Trans. Donald F. Bouchard and Sherry Simon. Ithaca, NY: Cornell University Press.

Miller, Susan. 1991. *Textual Carnivals: The Politics of Composition.* Carbondale, IL: Southern Illinois University Press.

Murphy, James J., James Berlin, Robert Connors, Sharon Crowley, Richard Enos, Susan Jarratt, Nan Johnson, Jan Swearingen, and Victor Vitanza. 1988. "Octalog: The Politics of Historiography." *Rhetoric Review* 7: 5–49.

North, Stephen M. 1987. *The Making of Knowledge in Composition: Portrait of an Emerging Field.* Upper Montclair, NJ: Boynton/Cook.

Schilb, John. 1986. "The History of Rhetoric and the Rhetoric of History." *Pre/Text* 7: 11–34.

Strain, Margaret M. 1993. "Toward a Hermeneutic Model of Composition History: Robert Carlsen's 'The State of the Profession 1961–1962.' " *Journal of Advanced Composition* 13: 217–240.

Vitanza, Victor J. 1987. " 'Notes' towards Historiographies of Rhetorics; or, Rhetorics of the Histories of Rhetorics: Traditional, Revisionary, and Sub/Versive." *Pre/Text* 8: 63–125.

Welch, Kathleen E. 1990. *The Contemporary Reception of Classical Rhetoric: Appropriations of Ancient Discourse.* Hillsdale, NJ: Lawrence Erlbaum.

White, Hayden. 1978. *Tropics of Discourse: Essays in Cultural Criticism.* Baltimore: Johns Hopkins University Press.

ideology

The term *ideology* enters composition studies from Marxist discussions, where it may generally be said to point to ways in which ideas function as "a set of discursive strategies for legitimating a dominant power" (Eagleton 1994, 8). In compositionists' conversations, three very broad and interrelated areas of emphasis may be delineated; within each lie contrasting and contesting definitions of this keyword.

I. Ideology and "False" Consciousness

Some compositionists, especially those influenced by Marxist thought, define ideology as "false consciousness"—that is, in Ira Shor's definition, "manipulated action and reflection which lead people to support their own repression" (1980, 55)—and point unabashedly to "real" economic relations that are masked by its illusions. Richard Ohmann (1976) works from what he calls "a general principle of ideology"—that "a privileged social group will generalize its own interests so that they *appear* to be universal social goals" (86; emphasis added). Susan Miller (1991), focussing on subjectivity in *Textual Carnivals*, writes that "[i]ndividuals are placed, or given the status of subjects by ideological constructions that tie them to *fantasized* functions and activities, not to their actual situations . . . [and that] *mask very real* needs to organize societies in particular ways" (123, emphasis added). Miller here invokes Althusser's conception of interpellation, a process by which (in James Berlin's words) "ideology . . . addresses and shapes [subjects] through discourses that point out what exists, what is good, and what is possible" (1993, 103). In Miller's analysis, a culture would mask its need for cheap instruction in usage and orthography by interpellating its (poorly paid and predominantly female) composition teachers as nurturing mother figures who prepare students to take their place in literate society. Linda Brodkey draws an analogy between the ideological narratives through which a culture knows itself and Kenneth Burke's representative anecdotes, explaining that a representative anecdote (about, for example, the artist as solitary genius) "generates ideology" in its selectivity, reduction, and scope and (thereby) constitutes a model to which students are taught (interpellated) to aspire (1987, 401).

But not every compositionist—or even every Marxist—who uses the word ideology places this emphasis on "false" consciousness. Some include Marx in their postmodern distrust of master narratives and use ideology to refer to any system of beliefs about the actual, the good, and the possible. Patricia Bizzell (1991) foregrounds this distinction in her assertion that compositionists tend to "use the term *ideology* to demonstrate that no person has access to unfiltered reality. . . . We do not really use *ideology* in Marx's sense, as an explanation that distorts reality. . . . Rather, we tend to adhere more to Louis Althusser's notion of ideology as an interpretation that constitutes reality" (55). In *Rhetoric and Reality*, Berlin stipulates that he will use the term

> simply to refer to the pluralistic conceptions of social and political arrangements that are present in a society in any given time. These conceptions are based on discursive (verbal) and nondiscursive (nonverbal) formations designating the shape of social and political structures, the nature and role of the individual within these structures, and the distribution of power in society. (4–5)

In non-Marxist usage, ideology can refer to any narrow or constricting system of belief, as in E. D. Hirsch's claim that national cultures and national languages transcend ideologies (1987, passim) and Maxine Hairston's (1992) distress at what she sees as "the cultural left['s] belief . . . [that] any teacher should be free to use his or her classroom to promote any ideology" (188).

II. Ideology, Hegemony, and Critical Consciousness

Discussions of "false" or restrictive consciousness occasion questions about the degree to which an individual is aware (or could choose to become aware) of ideology and, from the perspective of that awareness, resist. To the extent that ideology names the boundaries of what is known or knowable at a given moment in history, it might be understood as a "misrecognition" from which one cannot entirely escape. Several left-oriented compositionists emphasize the "invisibility" of ideology and its "naturalizing" function. David Kaufer and Gary Waller, for example, point out that ideological formations not only prescribe actual behaviors but also "define or 'naturalize' possible ones," such that ideology becomes "a kind of sociocultural epoxy-resin" that holds a culture together (75). Ohmann (1987) approvingly alludes to Terry Eagleton's definition of ideology as that complex of beliefs and values and habits which makes the existing power relations of the society seem "natural" or "invisible" (Eagleton 1976, 4–5; Ohmann, 121). J. Elspeth Stuckey emphasizes Eagleton's observation that ideology reflects "those misperceptions of the 'real' which contribute to the reproduction of the dominant social relations" (Eagleton, 1984, 54; Stuckey, 22) to support her assertion that "the ways in which literacy is thought about in this country are reductive and dangerous" (21). Stuckey (22) and Kathleen McCormick (1994, 34) point to ways in which ideology covers up (and/or appears to resolve) a culture's contradictions, those "fragmented . . . and incomplete sets of ideas that people use to get on in the world" (Faigley 1992a, 100). For example, (as McCormick points out) many first year students (and their teachers) believe both that the research paper should present an original point of view and that it should assemble as many sources as possible, without reflecting on the potential contradictions implicit in those beliefs. Indeed, David Shumway writes that "ideology is precisely what the culture makes us accept without reflection" (153).

That acceptance might usefully be considered in the context of what Antonio Gramsci calls hegemony. According to Victor Villanueva, "hegemeny equals ideological domination . . . by consent" (20) in which the world view of the dominant class is understood to be "truth" and consented to by the dominated who are then (in Nancy Mack's words) "controlled by it internally. Ideology becomes our mental police" (Mack and Zebroski 91). The leftist project then becomes an effort to promote reflection on, and resistance to, ideological assumptions, although Bizzell (1991) asserts that "[w]e may indeed free ourselves from a particular ideology, but the lever that pries us loose can only be another ideology, which manages at that moment to be more persuasive for reasons . . . that are culturally conditioned" (55).

Ideology may also be regarded as a consciously held set of ideas that one knows about but chooses not to abandon. Faigley (1989), for example, writes that a student who follows the formulae for writing a letter of application given in a standard business writing textbook "has voluntarily [accepted] the dominant ideology . . . by presenting himself as a commodity" (251).

III. IDEOLOGY AND/AS PRACTICE

A third strain of discussion addresses the question whether ideology is more usefully understood (exclusively) as a set of ideas or as a practical political force to be met with specific strategies of resistance. In composition studies, the tendency is overwhelmingly toward the latter construction. For Berlin, (1993) "ideology . . . includes a version of power formations governing the agent" (103). Faigley points approvingly to Althusser's "redefinition" of "ideology as sets of cultural practices rather than as systems of ideas" (1992b, 40) and notes that Michael Halliday's "social-semiotic view . . . [of ideology] gives language a very active role in coding experience and mediating social meanings" (1992a, 100). Throughout their extensive work, Shor and Giroux inscribe ideology as a force that constructs students and offer strategies for resistance. Similarly, Ohmann (1976, 1987) shows how ideology constructs the general public's notions about the importance and usefulness of writing courses; Berlin (1988, 1996), Sharon Crowley, Miller (1989, 1991), McCormick (1990, 1994) explain how ideology constructs teachers' and administrators' notions about writing curricula. John Clifford (1991), Crowley (1991),

McCormick (1990), Ohmann (1976), Berlin (1988, 1996), Faigley (1992a), and Kathleen E. Welch (1987) describe some ways in which text- books and curricula interpellate the teachers and students to whom they are marketed. Michael Blitz and C. Mark Hurlbert look at such university communications as course catalogues and memos.

Patricia Harkin
Purdue University

Works Cited

Berlin, James A. 1987. *Rhetoric and Reality: Writing Instruction in American Colleges, 1900–1985.* Carbondale: Southern Illinois University Press.

———. 1988. "Rhetoric and Ideology in the Writing Class." *College English* 50: 477–494.

———. 1993. "Composition Studies and Cultural Studies: Collapsing Boundaries." *Into the Field: Sites of Composition Studies.* Ed. Anne Ruggles Gere. New York: MLA. 99–116.

———. 1996. *Rhetorics, Poetics and Cultures: Refiguring College English Studies.* Urbana: NCTE.

Bizzell, Patricia. 1991. "Marxist Ideas in Composition Studies." *Contending with Words: Composition and Rhetoric in a Postmodern Age.* Ed. Patricia Harkin and John Schilb. New York: MLA. 52–68.

Brodkey, Linda. 1987. "Modernism and the Scene(s) of Writing." *College English* 49: 396–418.

Clifford, John. 1991. "The Subject in Discourse." Harkin and Schilb, 38–51.

Clifford, John, and John Schilb, ed. 1994. *Writing Theory and Critical Theory.* New York: MLA.

Crowley, Sharon. 1990. *The Methodical Memory: Invention in Current Traditional Rhetoric.* Carbondale: Southern Illinois University Press.

Eagleton, Terry. 1976. *Marxism and Literary Criticism.* Berkeley: University of California Press.

———. 1984. *Criticism and Ideology: A Study in Marxist Literary Theory.* London: Verso.

———. 1994. "Introduction." *Ideology.* Ed. Terry Eagleton. London: Longman. 1–20.

Faigley, Lester. 1989. "The Study of Writing and the Study of Language." *Rhetoric Review* 7: 240–256.

———. 1992a. *Fragments of Rationality: Postmodernity and the Subject of Composition.* Pittsburgh: University of Pittsburgh Press.

———. 1992b. "The Left in New Times." *Pre/Text* 13: 37–56.

Giroux, Henry. 1985. *Theory and Resistance in Education.* South Hadley, MA: Bergin and Garvey.

———. 1992. *Border Crossings: Cultural Workers and the Politics of Education.* New York: Routledge.

Hairston, Maxine. 1992. "Diversity, Ideology, and Teaching Writing." *College Composition and Communication* 43: 179–193.

Halliday, M. A. K. 1978. *Language as a Social Semiotic.* London: Edward Arnold.

Hirsch, E. D., Jr. 1987. *Cultural Literacy: What Every American Needs to Know.* Boston: Houghton Mifflin.

Hurlbert, C. Mark, and Michael Blitz. 1992. "The Institution('s) Lives!" *Pre/Text* 13: 59–78.

Kaufer, David, and Gary Waller, 1985. "To Write is to Read is to Write, Right?" *Writing and Reading Differently: Deconstruction and the Teaching of Composition and Literature.* Ed. G. Douglas Atkins and Michael L. Johnson. Lawrence; University Press of Kansas.

Mack, Nancy, and James Thomas Zebroski. 1992. "Remedial Critical Consciousness?" *Pre/Text* 13: 81–101.

McCormick, Kathleen. 1990. "The Cultural Imperatives Underlying Cognitive Acts." Ed. Linda Flower *et al. Reading to Write: Exploring a Cognitive and Social Process.* New York: Oxford University Press.

———. 1994. "On a Topic of Your Own Choosing . . . " *Writing Theory and Critical Theory.* Ed. John Clifford and John Schilb. New York: MLA.

Miller, Susan. 1989. *Rescuing the Subject: A Critical Introduction to Rhetoric and the Writer.* Carbondale: Southern Illinois University Press.

———. 1991. *Textual Carnivals: The Politics of Composition.* Carbondale: Southern Illinois University Press.

Ohmann, Richard. 1976. *English in America: A Radical View of the Profession.* New York: Oxford University Press.

———. 1987. *Politics of Letters.* Middletown, CT: Wesleyan University Press.

Shor, Ira. 1980. *Critical Teaching and Everyday Life.* Chicago: University of Chicago Press.

———. 1986. *Culture Wars: School and Society in the Conservative Restoration, 1969–84.* Boston: Routledge.

———. 1992. *Education and Empowerment: Critical Teaching for Social Change.* Chicago: University of Chicago Press.

Shumway, David. 1994. "Science, Theory and the Politics of Empirical Studies in the English Department." In Clifford and Schilb, 148–158.

Stuckey, J. Elspeth. 1991. *The Violence of Literacy.* Portsmouth, NH: Boynton/Cook.

Villanueva, Victor. 1992. "Hegemony: From an Organically Grown Intellectual." *Pre/Text* 13: 17–34.

Welch, Kathleen E. 1987. "Ideology and Freshman Textbook Production: The Place of Theory in Writing Pedagogy." *College Composition and Communication* 38: 269–281.

institution

Compositionists have long been sensitive to the ways in which educational institutions are both material and discursive formations—in Kurt Spellmeyer's words, "buildings and books, chairs and slates, traditions of inquiry and a language to frame them" (70). Sometimes these formations are presented in "either/or" terms: Jasper Neel, for example, characterizes institutions as places that "house" college writing courses (90), while the student writers who occupy these courses, according to Spellmeyer, understand *institution* as "the anonymity of [textual] forms and conventions" (72).

More typically, though, *institution* embodies the complex relationships between discursive *and* material constructs—what Mike Rose calls "a political-semantic web that restricts the way we think about the place of writing in the academy" (342). Rose's analysis of "institutional language about writing instruction in American higher education" reveals "a reductive, fundamentally behaviorist model of the development and use of written language" that "in various ways, keeps writing instruction at the periphery of the curriculum" (341, 345). Carl G. Herndl, however, finds that it is the curriculum itself—the "institution's demands for standards, uniformity and objectivity in the classroom" (329)—that is oppressive. Both perspectives represent the widespread view that, as Patricia Harkin puts it, "what institutions do best is regulate and, by regulating, constrain"; she calls this "the institution's will to homogenize," suggesting that hegemony and conformity are part of an institution's "nature" (109). Who, then, are the agents of this institutional gatekeeping? Patricia Bizzell (1982) says it is university administrators who frequently define the "institutional goal" of composition—its "responsibility" in service to the university—as initiating students into the norms of the "academic discourse community" (191). David Bartholomae blames both university and composition administrators, pointing out, for example, their shared unwillingness to "pay attention" to certain kinds of student writing (14–15).

Many compositionists, however, have identified writing teachers and their pedagogies as the primary "representatives of institutional power and cultural ideals" (Phelps 47), in part to foreground the ways that academic institutions and their discourses "mediate dominant values" (Clifford 521) and thus function as political sites. Bizzell (1988) has argued that most popular notions of "cultural ideals" are "totalitarian, racist, sexist, and laden with social class prejudice" (146). And as Steve North shows, "institutional power" implies a similar hegemony:

> The teacher . . . empowered by training, experience, and (usually) advanced degrees, determines what constitutes reality and how all class members are to gain access to it; represents—as a reader/evaluator—what the discipline considers an appropriate audience; and determines, too, how discourse is to be used: not only what the right things to say are, but what the right way to say them is. (4)

These "realities" are shaped by varying political interests. For example, in feminist scholarship, *institution* is roughly synonymous with *patriarchy*, or the traditionally male intellectual "establishment"; indeed, Janis Tedesco's discussion of "a male- and institutional-bias" in educational theories (248) suggests that institution-as-patriarchy and institution-as-academic-discourse-conventions are virtually indistinguishable. In its Marxist manifestation, academic institutions can be understood as part of a ruling apparatus that reproduces what James Berlin describes as "the dehumanizing effects of industrial capitalism" (486–487), or, more broadly, what Harkin calls "symbolic capital" (108). Berlin holds writing classrooms and certain composition pedagogies responsible for "the alienating and fragmenting experience of the authoritarian institutional setting" (485). Richard Ohmann asserts, furthermore, that without intervention on the part of teachers, the "main institutional form [of capitalism] . . . the giant corporation," will "continue to saturate most classrooms, textbooks, student essays, and texts of all sorts" (678, 687).

Greg Myers acknowledges that academe in general might "help provide a justification for the hierarchies of society" (156). But he dismisses the idea that institutions are vast, static monoliths, believing instead that they are unstable constructs that can be negotiated and altered, and that hold potential for reform as well as corruption (166). Lynn Worsham demonstrates this in her discussion of the "antagonism" between composition's "institutional discussion of writing," which takes place in academic settings and is driven by the need to make meaning (83), and the "flagrantly subversive" *ecriture féminine*—practiced most infamously by French writer Hélène Cixous—which resists meaning by inscribing heterogeneity rather than content (89). Worsham describes a stylistic strategy known as mimicry, which *ecriture féminine* utilizes "to hollow out the structures of a discourse from within those structures and therefore is a form of infidelity . . . that operates within an institution to ruin it" (87). She does not deny the power of disciplinary conventions and the academic "site" itself, but suggests that such institutions are not inherently patriarchal, and can be subversively invested with feminist values. Such self-conscious reimagining of institutions from the perspectives of women indicates that there are alternatives to understanding institutions as oppressive hegemonies: by defining institutions rather than being defined by them, they can be understood and inhabited differently.

This premise also informs composition scholarship influenced by the work of Michel Foucault, who characterizes *institution* as discourse that exists "within the established order of things," but that contains the means for its own destabilization and remaking (216). Les Perelman applies this definition to the "institution-based discourse" of the composition classroom, in which "both speaker and hearer exist largely as projections of institutional roles rather than as idiosyncratic individuals" (474). Perelman rejects the notion of "a true, unified, central 'self' that is the ultimate source of all discourse" in favor of one that assumes many roles within a variety of constraints, and believes that the most important skill writing teachers can offer their students is an awareness of how discourse is "determined and informed by institutional contexts. In so doing, rather than imprisoning students in specific institutional roles, we are helping them attain the tools by which those roles can be both effectively performed and transcended" (478). For Perelman, "institutionality in discourse" varies from context to context, but is determined by external rules and goals and thus largely fixed within those contexts (474). Spellmeyer, on the other hand, thinks that it is precisely this view of institutions as "knowledge received"—information that "exist[s] prior to any learner's participation" (58), or what Perelman calls "preexisting institutional conventions of discourse" (476)—that allows students to develop passive attitudes toward learning. If they were instead encouraged to see institutions as "knowledge made," and themselves as knowledge makers, these students might experience texts as generative discourse "events," multiple and mutable. Thus for Spellmeyer, institutions are "systems of exclusion and regulation which simultaneously authorize and constrain the speaking subject" (73–74), and writing teachers need to show students how these systems work.

In the increasingly sophisticated usage of *institution*, two strong themes emerge. The first is simply that "institutions are": that our experience of the world is "always already" framed by institutions; that the material and discursive conditions of, in particular, educational institutions both "authorize" us to write, think, and teach, and constrain the way we do so. But as the second theme makes clear, the definitions and manifestations of *institution*, far from inevitable, are filled with weaknesses, tensions, contradictions, and possibilities. Spellmeyer suggests that an institution

> never "belongs" to everyone equally, or to anyone once and for all.... Although one group may assert proprietary rights to an entire institution, and although custom may lend substantial weight to their claim, institutions by virtue of their public character are focal points for conflicts engendered by a host of divergent private imperatives. But these conflicts, these scrambles for ownership, no single group can ever win decisively. (70)

In other words, the "ownership" of both material and discursive institutions remains very much up for grabs. And Harkin believes that these ongoing disagreements—about what students should write and "why, historically, the institution [i.e., 'the American academy'] has held writing to be so important" in the first place—should be part of the college composition curriculum (114).

Elizabeth Ervin
University of North Carolina at Wilmington

Works Cited

Bartholomae, David. 1993. "The Tidy House: Basic Writing in the American Curriculum." *Journal of Basic Writing* 12: 4–21.

Berlin, James. 1988. "Rhetoric and Ideology in the Writing Class." *College English* 50: 477–494.

Bizzell, Patricia. 1982. "College Composition: Initiation into the Academic Discourse Community" (review essay). *Curriculum Inquiry* 12: 191–207.

————. 1988. "Arguing about Literacy." *College English* 50: 141–153.

Clifford, John. 1989. "Discerning Theory and Politics" (review essay). *College English* 51: 517–532.

Foucault, Michel. 1972. "The Discourse on Language." *The Archaeology of Knowledge*. Trans. A. M. Sheridan Smith. New York: Pantheon. 215–237.

Harkin, Patricia. 1991. "Hyperscholarship and the Curriculum." *Rhetoric Review* 10: 108–117.

Herndl, Carl G. 1991. "Writing Ethnography: Representation, Rhetoric, and Institutional Practices." *College English* 53: 320–332.

Myers, Greg. 1986. "Reality, Consensus, and Reform in the Rhetoric of Composition Teaching." *College English* 48: 154–174.

Neel, Jasper. 1988. *Plato, Derrida, and Writing*. Carbondale: Southern Illinois University Press.

North, Steve. 1985. "Journal Writing across the Curriculum: A Reconsideration." *Freshman English News* 14: 2–4, 8–9.

Ohmann, Richard. 1985. "Literacy, Technology, and Monopoly Capital." *College English* 47: 675–689.

Perelman, Les. 1986. "The Context of Classroom Writing." *College English* 48: 471–479.

Phelps, Louise Wetherbee. "A Constrained Vision of the Writing Classroom." *Profession* 93: 46–54.

Rose, Mike. 1985. "The Language of Exclusion: Writing Instruction at the University." *College English* 47: 341–359.

Spellmeyer, Kurt. 1993. *Common Ground: Dialogue, Understanding, and the Teaching of Composition*. Englewood Cliffs, NJ: Prentice Hall.

Tedesco, Janis. 1991. "Women's Ways of Knowing/Women's Ways of Composing." *Rhetoric Review* 9: 246–256.

Worsham, Lynn. 1991. "Writing against Writing: The Predicament of *Ecriture Féminine* in Composition Studies." *Contending with Words: Composition and Rhetoric in a Postmodern Age*. Ed. Patricia Harkin and John Schilb. New York: MLA. 82–104.

intertextuality

The term *intertextuality* was coined in the late 1960s by French theorist Julia Kristeva, who used it to refer to the concept that "any text is constructed as a mosaic of quotations; any text is the absorption and transformation of another" (66). Michael Worton and Judith Still suggest that because every writer is first a reader, any given text "is inevitably shot through with references, quotations, and influences of every kind." And any reader's particular interpretation of that text depends on her particular framework of textual experience. Both of these "dual axes of intertextuality," then, are "politically charged" (1–2), and their contending processes of inclusion and selection prevent any text from determining its range of signification, its "influence," its meaning. Kristeva's sense of intertextuality holds that every text is an assimilation of other texts and a reply to them; no text, in turn, can avoid this "absorption and reply."

Kristeva's theory implies that intertextuality is embedded in the very nature of textuality. Jay Clayton and Eric Rothstein point out, then, that Kristeva's "development of the term . . . was itself a complex intertextual event" (18). Kristeva "absorbs" the text of Mikhail Bakhtin by slipping "text" parenthetically into a paraphrase of his *dialogic* theory: "each word (text) is an intersection of words (texts) where at least one other word (text) can be read" (66). Yet this same move "transforms" Bakhtin; while he stressed a relationship between meaning and situational or historical context, Kristeva argues that intertextuality provokes an "endlessly expanding context"—no text can ever be contained by a single interpretation, in a single era, or for a single purpose.

Intertextuality, then, is a single word, a marker, that we can take to "stand for," to "mean," the undecidability inherent in any given term or text. Yet if this is so, *intertextuality* itself cannot escape the very operation it has been used to signify. Use of the term seems to demand acceptance of Leonard Orr's assertion that "[i]n any intertextual chain . . . a textual distortion takes place" (817). It should come as no surprise to see the term used for competing, even antithetical, "politically charged" purposes in composition studies.

Supporting a conception of the Montaignian or exploratory essay, Nancy Kline's pedagogy encourages students to think of "writing as exploration," to "write to find out what [they're] thinking" (19). To facilitate such an approach, Kline asks her students to read, in her words, "professional essays" that are intertextual—that respond to or somehow incorporate other texts— and that "approach their own page as an experimental, playful space." Martin Luther King's "Letter from Birmingham Jail," for example, "establishes its own voice" and "is a kind of dialogue" (16).

"What I want to teach my students," Kline writes, is that "there's a person speaking to us in the pages we have read . . . a human presence at play in the page" (37). By reading the professional essays, students will become aware of and perhaps go on to mimic a relationship between their own texts and others they have read in what Kline calls "intertextual play." Students, she suggests, "possess worlds of their own that may fruitfully be brought to bear on what they are reading and writing, worlds that most certainly influence the timbre of their own voices" (30). In closing, she firmly underscores Joan Didion's dictum that "Writing is the act of saying I" (36).

Intertextuality, then, can be read to function as a kind of support for what is sometimes labeled an expressivist pedagogy. Yet in "Intertextuality and the Discourse Community," James Porter—who never cites Kline's article—offers the term as something of a safeguard against the very position Kline articulates, recasting her central authority as a mythic figure:

> Intertextuality counters . . . one prevailing composition pedagogy, one favoring a romantic image of the writer, offering as role models the creative essayists, the Sunday Supplement freelancers, the Joan Didions, E. B. Whites. . . . Our anthologies glorify the individual essayist . . . an autonomous writer exercising a free, creative will through the writing act. . . . [W]e romanticize composition by overemphasizing the autonomy of the writer. (41)

Understanding what he calls "the intertext" as something of a synonym for *discourse community*, Porter stresses that "authorial intention is less significant than social context. . . . [T]he intertext *constrains* writing" (35). Rejecting out of hand the very possibility of an "individual voice," Porter argues that Intertextuality suggests that our goal should be to help students learn to write for the "discourse communities" they choose to join: "Intertextual theory suggests that the key criteria for evaluating writing should be 'acceptability' within some discourse community" (43).

Using intertextuality to refer to the functions of texts *within* given communities rather than across them is evident not only in pedagogy, but in rhetorical analysis as well. Amy J. Devitt, for example, "describes the many different text-types in the tax accounting community and interprets these texts in terms of their social and epistemological functions" (336). As Devitt makes clear, her use of the term is meant to "encapsulate the interaction of texts within a single discourse community" (337).

Considerably less arbitrary in the creation of boundaries is Charles Bazerman's examination of an article that could be taken to represent "the professional discourse of evolutionary biology." His reading, however, demonstrates how this text

> strays far beyond descriptive biology and evolutionary theory to encompass voices from the French Enlightenment, medieval Venetian art and architecture, contemporary international urban intellectual life, anthropology, forensic science, mathematical modeling, and statistical genetics. (196)

According to Bazerman, an intertext is a "strategic site of contention, . . . the site at which communal memory is sorted out and reproduced, at which current issues and communities are framed and dynamics established pushing the research front toward one future or another" (194). For Bazerman, any given field's intertext is "built upon a series of containments," resulting in "a literature set apart from other discussions, a literature following its own questions and listening to its own special evidence and arguments" (212).

Bazerman describes the intertext as an image, an implication or effect of rhetorically aware composing: an "explicit intertextual field" is itself composed in every disciplinary text through "explicit citation and discussion of other texts identified as being closely related" (194). Each text suggests a "related web of claims and counterclaims; attacks and responses, support and reliance" (116). Each text offers a "representation" of a field's intertext, a carefully sorted accumulation of references "that will be persuasive and useful for carrying forth one's own work" (212). Through such "intertextual self-fashioning," Bazerman suggests that authors attempt to reformulate their disciplines; they are successful to the extent that readers accept particular representations of their field's intertext.

Bazerman's version of intertextuality assumes a kind of interpersonal interaction, an exchange among individuals through the medium of text, which he identifies as "intersubjectivism." While Paul Hunter would find agreement with Bazerman against the concept of a single or "univocal" meaning for any text, he announces the desire to turn "away from intersubjectivism to intertextuality." For Hunter, intertextuality stresses the "interaction between and among texts," not people. Citing Paul Ricoeur, Hunter sees a text as something of a veil or barrier with "semantic autonomy"; an author's intention, he argues, is always cut off from a text's meaning or meanings. For Hunter, inscription and interpretation become aspects of textuality, and it is textuality itself that "projects" or constructs "the world of knowledge" (7–8). Intertextuality, then, is a process that escapes intersubjective attempts to control, constrain, or define it.

Like most other theoretical systems at work in composition studies, intertextuality is an "import." It was authorized or legitimized outside the purposes and concerns of American postsecondary writing instruction. Intertextuality as a critical term seems to have emerged in composition studies through the very process(es) it is often used to describe. One might say, then, that composition studies itself functions as an "intertextual matrix," as what Kristeva calls an "*intersection of textual surfaces* . . . as a dialogue among several writings" (65).

Peter Vandenberg
DePaul University, Chicago

Works Cited

Bazerman, Charles. 1994. *Constructing Experience*. Carbondale: Southern Illinois University Press.

Clayton, Jay, and Eric Rothstein, ed. 1991. *Influence and Intertextuality in Literary History*. University of Wisconsin Press.

Devitt, Amy J. 1991. "Intertextuality in Tax Accounting: Generic, Referential, and Functional." *Textual Dynamics of the Professions*. Ed. Charles Bazerman and James Paradis. Madison: University of Wisconsin Press. 336–357.

Hunter, Paul. "Intertextual Knowledge: A New Look at Rhetoric-as-Epistemic." ED 273 966.

Kline, Nancy. 1989. "Intertextual Trips: Teaching the Essay in the Composition Class." *Journal of Teaching Writing* 8: 15–37.

Kristeva, Julia. 1980. *Desire in Language: A Semiotic Approach to Literature and Art*. Ed. Leon S. Roudiez. Trans. Thomas Gora, Alice Jardine, and Leon S. Roudiez. New York: Columbia University Press.

Orr, Leonard. 1986. "Intertextuality and the Cultural Text in Recent Semiotics." *College English* 48: 811–823.

Porter, James E. 1986. "Intertextuality and the Discourse Community." *Rhetoric Review* 5: 34–47.

Worton, Michael, and Judith Still, ed. 1990. *Intertextuality: Theories and Practices*. Manchester: Manchester University Press.

invention

Invention is one of the five canons of classical rhetoric. Edward P. J. Corbett explains that "*Inventio* was concerned with a system or method for finding arguments" (22). He specifies "that there were two kinds of arguments or means of persuasion available to the speaker," the "non-artistic means" (e.g., witnesses, tortures), which "were really not part of the art of rhetoric," and the "artistic means," comprised of the three rhetorical appeals (*logos, ethos,* and *pathos*). "The method that the classical rhetoricians devised to aid the speaker in discovering matter for the three modes of appeal," Corbett adds, "was the *topics*," which "constituted a method of probing one's subject to discover possible ways of developing that subject" (22–24). In addition to the use of the topics, Thomas Sloane tells us, the *inventio* of Cicero included the "continual practice of debating one side [of an issue] and then the other" (466; see also McClish). Sharon Crowley (1994) shows how classical invention has been adapted by composition studies when she refers to inventional devices as "sets of instructions that help [speakers and writers] find and compose proofs appropriate for any rhetorical situation" (30). It has been generally accepted that these "sets of instructions" are equivalent to what are routinely called "heuristic procedures," what Richard Young, in his 1976 bibliographic essay, refers to as any "explicit plans for analyzing and searching which focus attention, guide reason, stimulate memory and encourage intuition" (1). That which is said to *qualify as* an inventional device or heuristic procedure, however, has been deliberated throughout the history of composition studies.

As an illustration of the many and disparate conceptions of invention, Young discusses four different theories—one of which is classical invention—that have found acceptance in contemporary composition studies. While each constitutes a "theory of invention," he wishes to show clear distinctions between the *function* of classical invention and the functions of the other three theories. First is Kenneth Burke's dramatistic method; unlike the classical topics, which "are aids in discovering possible arguments," this method is "an aid in discovering [i.e., identifying with] the essential features of the behavior of groups or individuals" (1978, 37). And since Burke himself conflates "persuasion" and "communication" in his *Rhetoric of Motives* (see esp. 45–46), the *function* of his method is essentially the same as that of classical invention. However, as Young's comments on D. Gordon Rohman's pre-writing method suggest, its purpose is quite different from classical invention: central to pre-writing is "the presupposition that, if writing cannot be taught, it can nevertheless be coaxed by various means," such as through journaling or meditation (1976, 17–18). Unlike the goal of classical invention, "[t]he principle goal of pre-writing is the self-actualization of the writer" (18; for an alternative view, see Autrey). As for the third of these theories, Kenneth Pike's tagmemic invention, Young describes it as combining pre-writing's focuses on "the discovery of ordering principles and on psychological changes in the writer" and classical invention's focus of "finding arguments which are likely to produce psychological changes in the audience" (23). This theory, Young (1978) says, "conceives of invention as essentially a problem-solving activity, the problems being of two sorts: those arising in one's own experience of the world and those arising out of a need to change others" (39). (See Young, Alton L. Becker, and Pike's *Rhetoric: Discovery and Change* for a textbook application of the tagmemic method.) While each of these theories constitute heuristic procedures, their differing forms and functions are the result of differing approaches to the composing process.

Absent from Young's overviews of contemporary theories of invention are references to the influence of theories from the eighteenth and nineteenth centuries, an era which, he argues, witnessed "the virtual disappearance of rhetorical invention" (1987, 37; see also Winterowd 344). The influence of eighteenth-century rhetorics, as well as developments in the fields of philosophy and psychology, had a significant impact on composition instruction through much of the twentieth century. Those who comment on this "current-traditional" theory typically see invention as being "outside of the composing process" (Berlin 64–68). Crowley (1990), though, argues "that a viable theory of invention was implicit in . . . current-traditional rhetoric and that [it] was intimately tied to modern privileging of authorial voice" (xiii). She elsewhere notes that this notion of invention has its roots in eighteenth-century ideas of "genius" or "natural ability" (1985, 51–53). Based on her studies of nineteenth-century textbooks, Crowley outlines three different methods of invention common to current-traditional rhetoric: "the utilization of prior knowledge and natural ability," both of which are unteachable; "disciplined exercise of the mental faculties" gained through such activities as reading, conversation, and meditation; and "method" or "planning," undertaken through such means as outlining or studying the works of good writers (52–56).

Crowley's description of the inventional theory implicit in current-traditional texts mirrors what Karen Burke LeFevre has called "Platonic invention," a system wherein "ideas are created in the mind of an atomistic individual and then expressed to the rest of the world" (1). But LeFevre argues that this conception of invention "sketches an incomplete view of what happens when writers invent" and that "invention is better understood as a social act" (1). Invention thus "becomes an act that may involve speaking and writing, and that at times involves more than one person; it is furthermore an act initiated by writers and completed by readers, extending over time through a series of transactions and texts" (1). LeFevre makes clear that she is drawing on theories and examples of processes of invention in a variety of fields in order to expand the definition of "rhetorical invention" (4–5). Doug Brent, too, expands "rhetorical invention" to include the "social act" of reading as a heuristic procedure, which aids in the development of a reader/writer's "belief system," and "contribute[s] to the building of further discourse" (14). For Brent, "invention must be seen as a Janus-headed process" that "looks backward [i.e., when one reads] to previous stages of the conversation," and "at the same time . . . looks forward to the audience to which the rhetor will present her knowledge" (118). Invention for Brent and LeFevre is thus a recursive, dialogic activity that one engages in during all stages of the writing process.

LeFevre and Brent are among those in composition studies that have promoted conceptions of invention that stretch the limits of classical *inventio*. Indeed, as early as 1970, the "Report of the Committee on the Nature of Rhetorical Invention," noted that the classical notion of invention "tends to rob the invention process of its dynamic character" (105). Expanded definitions of invention see it "not just as a method of retrieving what we already know, but as a process that constitutes our inquiry" (LeFevre 123). Paul Kameen uses the term "imagination" to describe these forms of "modern invention" that are strategies "for the methodical acquisition of new knowledge": classical invention is thus "a fairly mechanical 'special case' of creative thought that imagination absorbs into its broader systems," he asserts (85–86). Young (1976), however, states that "heuristic search is neither purely conscious nor mechanical" since its effective use is reliant upon "intuition, relevant experience and skill" (2).

It is this commingling of classical invention with other definitions of the process that prompted Young to state: "It is becoming increasingly apparent that as new and significant methods of invention emerge we need to develop a more adequate terminology which distinguishes various arts or methods of invention from *the* art of invention, that is, the members from the class" (1976, 17). More recently, Young and Yameng Liu characterize "the study of invention in writing" as "draw[ing] from the classical theory of *inventio* and yet go[ing] beyond many of its specific assumptions and conclusions," arguing that "invention" is most fruitfully conceived in its broader sense (xiii).

Donald E. Bushman
University of North Carolina at Wilmington

Works Cited

Autrey, Ken. 1991. "Toward a Rhetoric of Journal Writing." *Rhetoric Review* 10: 74–90.

Berlin, James A. 1984. *Writing Instruction in Nineteenth-Century American Colleges.* Carbondale: Southern Illinois University Press.

Brent, Doug. 1992. *Reading as Rhetorical Invention: Knowledge, Persuasion, and the Teaching of Research-Based Writing.* Urbana, IL: NCTE.

Corbett, Edward P. J. 1990. *Classical Rhetoric for the Modern Student.* 3rd edit. New York: Oxford University Press.

Crowley, Sharon. 1985. "Invention in Nineteenth-Century Rhetoric." *College Composition and Communication* 36: 51–60.

———. 1990. *The Methodical Memory: Invention in Current-Traditional Rhetoric.* Carbondale: Southern Illinois University Press.

———. 1994. *Ancient Rhetorics for Contemporary Students.* New York: Macmillan.

Kameen, Paul J. 1980. "Rewording the Rhetoric of Composition." *PRE/TEXT* 1: 73–93.

LeFevre, Karen Burke. 1987. *Invention as a Social Act.* Carbondale: Southern Illinois University Press.

McClish, Glen. 1991. "Controversy as a Mode of Invention: The Example of James and Freud." *College English* 53: 391–402.

Scott, Robert L., *et al.* 1975. "Report of the Committee on the Nature of Rhetorical Invention." *Contemporary Rhetoric: A Conceptual Background with Readings.* Ed. W. Ross Winterowd. New York: Harcourt Brace Jovanovich. 104–112.

Sloane, Thomas O. 1989. "Reinventing *inventio.*" *College English* 51: 461–473.

Winterowd, W. Ross. 1991. "A Philosophy of Composition." *Rhetoric Review* 9: 340–348.

Young, Richard E. 1976. "Invention: A Topographical Survey." *Teaching Composition: Ten Bibliographical Essays.* Ed. Gary Tate. Fort Worth: Texas Christian University Press. 1–43.

———. 1978. "Paradigms and Problems: Needed Research in Rhetorical Invention." *Research on Composing: Points of Departure.* Ed. Charles R. Cooper and Lee Odell. Urbana, IL: NCTE. 29–47.

———. 1987. "Recent Developments in Rhetorical Invention." *Teaching Composition: Twelve Bibliographic Essays.* Ed. Gary Tate. Fort Worth: Texas Christian University Press. 1–38.

Young, Richard E., Alton L. Becker, and Kenneth L. Pike. 1970. *Rhetoric: Discovery and Change.* New York: Harcourt, Brace & World.

Young, Richard E., and Yameng Liu, ed. 1994. Introduction. *Landmark Essays on Rhetorical Invention in Writing.* Davis, CA: Hermagoras Press. xi–xxiii.

knowledge

When Richard Braddock, Richard Lloyd Jones, and Lowell Schoer published *Research in Written Composition* in 1963, their express intent was "to review what is known and what is not known about the teaching and learning of composition" (1). By bringing scientific method to bear directly and comprehensively on a field otherwise "laced with dreams, prejudices, and makeshift operations," the authors hoped to lay a sound foundation for future research and knowledge in composition. "Much of what is known about composition teaching," they claim, "is actually known about the procedures of research," which they distinguish from "what is known about the teaching and learning of written composition" (29). By binding knowledge in the field to specific modes of research, Braddock *et al.* laid the groundwork for many future composition specialists to think of knowledge as a product of empirical investigation (see Hillocks, and Hayes *et al.*). At the same time, the report set the stage for the play of knowledge as a means of defense against the forces of irrationality threatening the field's integrity both from without (via "public pronouncements") and from within (via "irresponsible [self-serving] work").

By 1987 Stephen North characterizes knowledge in composition as a complex but "fragile" accumulation of institutional traditions, theories, and practices "lack[ing] any clear coherence or methodological integrity" (3). Like his NCTE predecessors, North worries that this institutional disarray of knowledge confounds composition's disciplinarity. "The various kinds of knowledge produced by these [disparate] modes of inquiry," writes North, "have been piled up uncritically, helter-skelter, with little regard to incompatibilities" (3). In 1992, George Dillon, constructing knowledge in composition as an underdeveloped and monolithic "body," likewise insists that knowledge will only develop fully as a result of "refining and developing its categories and distinctions, not by collapsing them" (120). Lil Brannon and C. H. Knoblauch argue that knowledge in composition should lead to "sensible and deliberate" writing instruction—a prescription that seems to assume that knowledge itself is sensible and deliberate, culminating in an orderly state of affairs (2). Informing these various constructions of knowledge—i.e., knowledge as "makeshift operation," as "pile," as underdeveloped "body," or as "sensible and deliberate"—is the tacit assumption that knowledge is stable enough to allow "knowledge making" to proceed (or develop) along linear and/or hierarchical lines.

From a post-modern or late capitalist perspective, knowledge is often conceived of as a marketplace filled with multiple and often competing products. In North's market place, for instance, practical, historical, philosophical, critical, empirical, clinical, formal, and ethnographic knowledges all compete for the scholar-teacher's time and energy. Reflecting as they do well-established forms of knowledge, such epistemological divisions, especially when organized along stated or unstated hierarchical lines, nevertheless work to figure composition studies as something other than a loose assemblage of disparate assumptions, research methodologies, and truth claims. North's titular assumption that knowledge is "made" rather than "found," a multivalent effect of research rather than its *causa finalis*, also distinguishes the postmodern view of knowledge from the modern notion reflected in the NCTE report (i.e., knowledge is something one discovers). In his tripartite taxonomy of the field, James Berlin likewise argues that "knowledge itself is a rhetorical construct . . . [just as] epistemology is rhetorical, is itself a social and historical construct" (165).

Some theorists in composition will have no truck with conventional taxonomies like North's or Berlin's. Victor Vitanza, for instance, argues for an "extreme form of pluralism," for Feyerabend's "epistemological anarchism" (82). For Vitanza, knowledge unfolds like an "unending text," an epistemological field that "would allow for outsiders, for voices of mavericks—for which there is no place in North's . . . vision of things" (82). Vitanza's post-structuralist textual metaphor offers a striking contrast to the visual metaphor that has dominated western thinking about knowledge for centuries. Instead of positing an inner eye with which we contemplate reality as it is reflected in the mirror of our mind—thus obtaining knowledge as a clear reflection of reality—post-structuralists such as Roland Barthes insist that knowledge is both strictly intertextual and inseparable from "reality" (no perspective, no mirror, no reflection, no inner eye). "We never find a state where man is separated from language," writes Barthes, "which he then creates in order to 'express' what is taking place within him: it is language which teaches the definition of man, not the reverse" (qtd. in Schilb 427).

Peter Elbow, however, regards knowledge as the product of mysterious— or at least confoundingly complex—concatenations of human experience. Knowledge is conceived as an effect, in the forms of "insight" and "growth," of intuitive, organic human machinations such as writing. In an oft-mentioned passage, Peter Elbow compares writing to cooking, to "bubbling, percolating, fermenting, chemical interaction, atomic fission" (1973, 48). Such cooking, he continues, "drives the engine that makes growing happen. . . . It's because of cooking that . . . a writer can start out after supper seeing, feeling, and knowing one set of things and end up at midnight seeing, feeling, and knowing things he hadn't thought of before" (49). The organic element in Elbow's description of knowledge as "knowing" derives from his explicit interest in challenging what he views as the false dichotomy between thought and feeling: "either we have 'knowledge' that is social, communal, socially justified, etc., etc.—or we have non- or pseudo-knowledge that is private, subjective, confessional, and so forth" (1990, 15). For Elbow, "knowledge is always both personal and social." Significantly, Elbow's embodied knowledge, like Vitanza's anarchistic knowledge, tends to resist institutional control.

David Bartholmae, in an apparently more pragmatic vein, treats knowledge as a sociohistorical phenomenon, an exterior symbolic order whose mechanical tendency is to interpellate subjects and, through them, to transmit "power, tradition and authority" in what he conceives as the real "substation"—versus the "idealized utopian space"—of the classroom (166).

For John Trimbur, knowledge is or ought to be overtly political, a "link" between critical analysis and specific movements such as civil rights and feminism (10). Gesa E. Kirsch and Joy S. Ritchie, for their part, apply the feminist link between the personal and political to knowledge in composition. One's knowledge, they contend, is political insofar as it is a "reflection" of ideology and culture, a "reinterpretation of one's experiences through the eyes of others," a recognition of one's "split selves" and "multiple and often unknowable identities" (8). Ken Bruffee's social constructionist view of knowledge—to the extent "it assumes that there is no such thing as a universal foundation, ground, framework, or structure of knowledge [and that] there is only an agreement, a consensus arrived at for the time being by communities of knowledgeable peers"—reiterates the feminist subversion of the notion that knowledge is a stable structure. For Bruffee in this context, and for Patricia Bizzell when she argues for an "anti-foundational" definition of knowledge, knowledge *is* consensus—fluid, dynamic, impermanent (Bruffee 790).

Science and/or art, process and/or product, object and/or subject, private and/or public, political and/or apolitical, organic and/or mechanical, linear and/or non-linear, empirical and/or theoretical, exclusive and/or inclusive, singular and/or multiple, cooperative and/or competitive: the apparently protean phenomenon/phenomena that constitutes knowledge in composition is, for better or worse, clearly keeping up with our postmodern times.

Thomas C. Kerr
Virginia Tech

Works Cited

Bartholomae, David. 1995. "Writing with Teachers." *College Composition and Communication* 46: 162–171.

Berlin, James A. 1987. *Rhetoric and Reality: Writing Instruction in American Colleges, 1900–1985.* Carbondale: Southern Illinois University Press.

Bizzell, Patricia. 1986. "Foundationalism and Anti-Foundationalism in Composition Studies." *PRE/TEXT* 7: 37–55.

Braddock, Richard *et al.* 1963. *Research in Written Composition.* Champaign: National Council of Teachers of English.

Bruffee, Kenneth. 1986. "Social Construction, Language, and the Authority of Knowledge: A Bibliographical Essay." *College English* 48: 773–790.

Dillon, George L. 1992. "When Reference Discourse No Longer Refers." *A Rhetoric of Doing: Essays on Written Discourse in Honor of James L. Kinneavy.* Ed. Stephen Witte *et al.* Carbondale: Southern Illinois University Press.

Elbow, Peter. 1990. "About Academic Personal Expressive Writing." *PRE/TEXT* 11: 7–19.

———. 1973. *Writing without Teachers.* New York: Oxford University Press.

Hayes, John R. *et al.* 1992. *Reading Empirical Studies: The Rhetoric of Research.* Hillsdale, NJ: Lawrence Erlbaum Associates, Publishers.

Hillocks, George Jr. 1986. *Research on Written Composition: New Directions for Teaching.* Urbana: ERIC and NCTE.

Kirsch, Gesa E., and Joy S. Ritchie. 1995. "Beyond the Personal: Theorizing a Politics of Location in Composition Research." *College Composition and Communication* 46: 7–29.

Knoblauch, C. H., and Lil Brannon. 1984. *Rhetorical Traditions and the Teaching of Writing.* Upper Montclair, NJ: Boynton/Cook Publishers, Inc.

North, Stephen M. 1987. *The Making of Knowledge in Composition: Portrait of an Emerging Field.* Portsmouth, NH: Boynton/Cook Publishers.

Schilb, John. 1989. "Composition and Poststructuralism: A Tale of Two Conferences." *College Composition and Communication* 40: 422–443.

Trimbur, John. 1988. "Cultural Studies and Teaching Writing." *Focuses* 1: 5–18.

Vitanza, Victor. 1987. " 'Notes' towards Historiographies of Rhetorics; or the Rhetorics or the Histories of Rhetorics: Traditional, Revisionary, and Sub/Versive." *PRE/TEXT* 8: 64–125.

literacy

In the collective consciousness of the United States, fueled by the media and political interests, the term literacy has come to mean competence in reading and writing. According to UNESCO, literacy is required "for effective functioning in [a] group and community" (qtd. in Winterowd 7). Over the past twenty years, theorists in both literacy and composition studies have challenged these relatively unproblematic conceptions, contesting some of the essential terms (such as *reading, writing, competency*, and *functional*).

Most scholars extend the definition of literacy to political and social domains. Citing Jenny Cook-Gumperz, Glynda Hull *et al.* point out that even within the realm of the classroom, literacy involves the "social process of demonstrating knowledgeability" (Gumperz) and that "competence in classrooms means interactional competence as well as competence with written language: knowing when and how and with whom to speak and act in order to create and display knowledge" (301).

Because literacy agonistically and antagonistically inhabits both popular and academic spheres, an uncontroversial definition is difficult to come by. The popular opinion that the United States is in the midst of a "literacy crisis," for example, stems from a particular view of what literacy is. Jimmie M. Killingsworth explains that nationally circulated editorials such as Merrill Sheils' "Why Johnny Can't Write" (first appearing in Newsweek, 1975) imply that literacy is "reified and measurable" (Killingsworth 35). Low scores on standardized tests are supposedly proof of the problem while changes in school curricula to improve test scores (by moving "back to basics") are the solution. Andrew Sledd argues that debates about literacy levels are unproductive because "there is no thing, literacy, only constellations of forms and degrees of literacy, shifting and turning as history rearranges the social formations in which they are embedded. Pieties about literacy with a capital L ought to be scrutinized: Which literacy? Whose literacy? Literacy for what?

How?" (499). Andrea A. Lunsford, Helene Moglen, and James Slevin echo Sledd's assertions, explicitly linking the implications to teaching:

> It is necessary to ask what kind of literacy we want to support. . . . Since the teaching of reading and writing can never be innocent, literacy workers must choose pedagogical methods with care, mindful of the theoretical assumptions with which those methods are informed. (2)

Further complicating the discussion are back to basics solutions in which it is increasingly unclear what "basics" are. Donald Lazere supports the teaching of "radical" basics, maintaining that "factual knowledge, mechanical and analytic skills (including remedial instruction in reading and writing standard English) . . . can help empower [students] both in gaining access to academic sources expressing oppositional ideas, and in mastering the culture of the critical discourse themselves" (19). Although Lazere's goal is toward a "liberatory literacy," enabling students to be critical of the discourse they are learning, aspects of his argument have some resonance in cultural literacy championed by E. D. Hirsch. According to Hirsch, to be truly literate, a person must be conversant with a specific body of knowledge known to educated people, or, more precisely, the cultural knowledge of the dominant society. While Hirsch's position has been attacked as being ethnocentric (see, for example, Johnson), his argument reinforces a link between language and knowledge, calling into question the traditional definition of literacy as skills acquisition. As Jeff Smith succinctly states: "If I'm going to teach words, I have to teach the world, too" (218).

But whose world? Richard Courage argues that non-school and school-based literacies compete and that learning the latter does not necessarily insure the ability to function in society: "[O]ur highly elaborated, discursive, stylistically complex literacy practices could . . . lead to our being labelled 'functionally illiterate' . . . in the workplace" (492). Courage advocates the concept of multiple literacies and suggests that teachers find ways to help students bridge the gaps between different literacies. In this vein, Patricia Bizzell contends that an "academic literacy" created through a collaboration "that successfully integrates the professor's traditional canonical knowledge and the students' non-canonical resources" (150) can circumvent both the prescriptiveness of traditional conceptions of literacy (which she calls literal literacy) and the cultural biases of Hirsch's program.

But even Bizzell's academic literacy is potentially a locus of ideological struggle. The hegemonic nature of literacy has been frequently discussed by critical pedagogues (see Freire, Roy) who, in place of traditional literacy inculcation, promote what they call critical literacy. The goal of critical literacy is to help students resist the authority and power of the dominant discourse through dialectical (and critical) approaches to language and knowledge. According to Henry Giroux:

> *Literacy* in its varied versions is . . . the practice of representation as a means of organizing, inscribing, and containing meaning. . . . Hence, literacy becomes *critical* to the degree that it makes problematic the very structure and practice of representation; that is, it focuses attention on the importance of acknowledging that meaning is not fixed and that to be literate is to undertake a dialogue with others who speak [and we may add: read, write] from different histories, locations, and experiences. (brackets in Roy; qtd. in Roy 699)

Critical literacy depends upon resistance to the status quo, and while critical pedagogy has enjoyed some popularity in composition studies (as witnessed by the frequent references to Freirean literacy theory—see, for example, Holzman), it has also come under attack for the same kind of coercive practices it militates against (see Ellsworth). C. H. Knoblauch suggests that for critical literacy to be workable "[t]here must be an enlightened, continuous, sometimes forceful and even raucous reappraisal of possibilities as concrete social conditions require" (138).

At the heart of many literacy discussions is the contention that certain cognitive and intellectual benefits accrue through the acquisition of print literacy. Theorists Walter Ong, Jack Goody and Ian Watt, and Eric Havelock maintain that the oral mind is quite different from the literate mind; their discussions tend to privilege the literate mind for its ability to reason, categorize, synthesize, and analyze with greater sophistication. Studies such as those by Sylvia Scribner and Michael Cole and Shirley Brice Heath suggest that school-based literacies enable students to do well at tasks required in school but don't necessarily contribute to other kinds of intellectual development.

Some definitions of literacy are more tightly wedded to print than others. Cheryl Glenn contends that one of the barriers to perceiving literacy in broader terms within the discipline of composition has to do with a preoccupation with writing. In her discussion of medieval literacy, Glenn refers to work done by Heath, Scribner and Cole, Ong, Havelock, and Hirsch to argue that:

> No matter how wide-ranging our twentieth-century views of literacy might be . . . we continue to privilege the written word. . . . Our concepts of literacy are inevitably colored by our own dependence on the physical artifact (on handwriting, on hard copy) and on our deep-seated insistence that reading and writing are inseparable arts. Thus, the text-dependency— reading books, writing books, and reading and writing about those books— in our own documentary culture and noetic world makes very difficult an accurate conception of alternative literacy practices, be they current or distant in time. (497)

Indeed, one could make the case that the focus on print literacy is what distinguishes composition studies from literacy studies. Louise Wetherbee

Phelps points out that composition is "logically subordinate" to fields like literacy "if looked at from their own altitude, which is why composition, dealing with written discourse, is so often described as a branch of rhetoric or literacy" (78).

In the future, as computer technology changes the ways texts are produced, manipulated, and regarded, scholars will be obliged to redefine "text" and textual literacy as well as reformulate what it means to be literate (see Tuman, Selfe and Hilligoss).

Darsie Bowden
DePaul University, Chicago

Works Cited

Bizzell, Patricia. 1988. "Arguing about Literacy." *College English* 50: 141–153.

Cook-Gumperz, Jenny. 1986. "Introduction: The Social Construction of Literacy." *The Social Construction of Literacy.* Ed. Jenny Cook-Gumperz. Cambridge: Cambridge University Press.

Courage, Richard. 1993. "The Interaction of Public and Private Literacies." *College Composition and Communication* 44: 484–496.

Ellsworth, Elizabeth. 1989. "Why Doesn't This Feel Empowering? Working Through the Repressive Myths of Critical Pedagogy." *Harvard Educational Review* 59.3: 297–324.

Freire, Paulo. 1982. *Education for a Critical Consciousness.* New York: Continuum.

Glenn, Cheryl. 1993. "Medieval Literacy outside the Academy: Popular Practice and Individual Technique." *College Composition and Communication* 44: 497–508.

Goody, Jack, and Ian Watt. 1968. "The Consequences of Literacy." *Literacy in Traditional Societies.* Ed. Jack Goody. Cambridge: Cambridge University Press.

Havelock, Eric Alfred. 1963. *Preface to Plato.* Cambridge: Harvard University Press.

Heath, Shirley Brice. 1984. *Ways with Words: Language, Life and Work in Communities and Classrooms.* Cambridge: Cambridge University Press.

Hirsch, E. D. 1987. *Cultural Literacy: What Every American Needs to Know.* Boston: Houghton Mifflin, 1987.

Holzman, Michael. 1988. "A Post-Freirean Model for Adult Literacy Education." *College English* 50: 177–189.

Hull, Glynda, Mike Rose, Kay Losey Fraser, and Marisa Castellano. 1991. "Remediation as Social Construct: Perspectives from an Analysis of Classroom Discourse." *College Composition and Communication* 42: 299–329.

Johnson, Michael L. 1988. "Hell is the Place We Don't Know We're in: The Control-Dictions of Cultural Literacy, Strong Reading, and Poetry." *College English* 50: 309–317.

Killingsworth, M. Jimmie. 1993. "Product and Process, Literacy and Orality: An Essay on Composition and Culture." *College Composition and Communication* 44: 26–39.

Knoblauch, C. H. 1988. "Rhetorical Constructions: Dialogue and Commitment." *College English* 50: 125–140.

Lazere, Donald. 1992. "Back to Basics: A Force for Oppression or Liberation." *College English* 54: 7–21.

Lunsford, Andrea A., Helene Moglen, and James Slevin, ed. 1990. *The Right to Literacy.* New York: The Modern Language Association of America.

Phelps, Louise Wetherbee. 1989. *Composition as a Human Science.* New York: Oxford University Press.

Ong, Walter. 1982. *Orality and Literacy: The Technologizing of the Word.* London and New York: Methuen.

Roy, Alice. 1994. "Critical Literacy, Critical Pedagogy." Rev. of *Critical Literacy: Politics, Praxis, and the Postmodern,* Ed. Colin Lankshear and Peter L. McLaren. *College English* 56: 693–702.

Scribner, Sylvia, and Michael Cole. 1981. *The Psychology of Literacy.* Cambridge: Harvard University Press.

Selfe, Cynthia L., and Susan Hilligoss, ed. 1994. *Literacy and Computers: The Complications of Teaching and Learning with Technology.* New York: The Modern Language Association of America.

Sheils, Merrill. 1978. "Why Johnny Can't Write." *Speaking of Words: A Language Reader.* Ed. James MacKillop and Donna Woolfolk Cross. New York: Holt. 2–7.

Sledd, Andrew. 1988. "Readin' not Riotin': The Politics of Literacy." *College English* 50: 495–508.

Smith, Jeff. 1994. "Against 'Illegeracy': Toward a New Pedagogy of Civic Understanding." *College Composition and Communication* 45: 200–219.

Tuman, Myron. 1994. *Word Perfect: Literacy in the Computer Age.* Pittsburgh: University of Pittsburgh Press.

Winterowd, W. Ross. 1989. *The Culture and Politics of Literacy.* Oxford: Oxford University Press.

literature

Over the past fifty years, the term *literature* has appeared in juxtaposition with the term *composition* in virtually all of our professional discussions and has been invoked variously to designate particular kinds of texts, or processes of reading and interpreting such texts, or the scholarly discipline of literary studies. Understanding how this term has been used by those in composition studies, why it continues to be paired with and against composition, and how its use has changed requires an understanding of the specialized meaning it obtained during the rise of English studies as a profession.

The etymology of *literature* reveals that its original meaning was akin to contemporary definitions of literacy (i.e., the ability to read and write) and that it referred to a wide range of imaginative and non-imaginative texts (Williams 1977). Terry Eagleton notes that it was during the Romantic period that " 'literature'—a privileged, 'creative' use of language—was . . . brought to birth, with all the resonance and panoply attendant upon traditional rhetoric, but without either its 'authoritarianism' or its audience" (107). In short, *literature* came to serve as a synecdoche for a privileged canon of imaginative texts of prose fiction, poetry, and drama. In the process, literature and literacy were bifurcated, the former coming to "refer primarily to the language" and the other "to the people" (Williams 1983, 212).

This bifurcation had an enormous impact on how English departments were structured, and led ultimately to the separation of literature and composition (Robinson). The differentiated sense of literature both as a scholarly field and as an object of study fueled vigorous debates concerning the role of literature in writing courses. On one side, those who defined literature as a particular object of study requiring a particular disciplined approach sought to protect literature against the undisciplined, and thus argued against its inclusion in a composition course (Goss). On the other side, those promoting the use of literature defined it almost solely in terms of an object of study. Some focused on its message, arguing that it provided the composition course with content, depth, and richness (Rubinstein); others on its structure, arguing that it provided useful models (Calderwood) or that it enabled students to develop a stronger and more refined sense of language (Brown); and still others on the effects of engaging with literature as an object, arguing that it enlarged students' worldly experience (Ashmead), that it had a humanizing effect (Fenstermaker), or that it developed critical thinking (Booth 1956) and critical reading skills (Fulkerson).

Despite the apparent differences among these various views, what seems to unite them is the assumption that literature represents a stable product—namely, imaginative texts—that demands a special, disciplined kind of reading. This assumption is embedded in the dominant trope invoked for literature between the early 1950s and the late 1970s. A geo-political metaphor of *place* held sway. Typical of this trope was the 1956 *CCC* symposium on the *place* of literature in first-year composition as well as in the most common title of this time, which was some form of "Literature *in* Composition" (Thorson; Hart, Stack, and Woodruff; Hayford; Stone).

Although literature was viewed by many teachers and scholars as a stable object, its pedagogical use was defined in various ways that cluster around two major views: as an object of contemplation in literature classes and as one of utility in composition classes. Leonard S. Rubinstein, for instance, warned that "at every moment the success of such a course [composition that incorporates literature] is imperiled by the teacher who forgets the difference between the use of literary material for literary purposes and the use of literary material for compositional purposes" (273). Implicit in Rubinstein's caution was the notion that literature required distinctly different treatments depending on its pedagogical location. This assumption, in part, led some to call for a ban on literature in the composition classroom. Raymond Goss, for example, argued that "students can be taught to be better writers only by writing and by talking about what *they* have written, not what someone else has written" (212; cf. Steinberg).

Not only was literature divorced from composition in terms of object and uses but reading and writing were largely viewed as discrete opposing skills (Memering). By the late 1970s and early 1980s, however, these assumptions were challenged as new theories in both literary and composition studies shifted the focus away from the products of reading and writing toward the processes of both. As a result, as Marilyn S. Sternglass pointed out, "relationships among [reading, writing, literature and literacy] have undergone shifts from being treated as parallel processes . . . , to being treated as transactive processes" (1), that is, as epistemic activities.

Viewing reading and writing as interrelated epistemic processes radically redefined literature, shifting it from a static object to a dynamic process. Anthony R. Petrosky, for instance, argued that "our comprehension of texts, whether they are literary or not, is more an act of composition—for understanding is composing—than of information retrieval" (19). Thus, for some, literature was reconceived as a tool for teaching composing processes, including strategies of invention (Peterson, L.) and revision (Burkholder). Such views paved the way for emerging efforts to draw connections between reading and writing (Newkirk; Petersen).

Throughout the 1980s, critical theories (including deconstruction, hermeneutics, feminism, neo-Marxism, postmodernism, and cultural studies) further transformed the object of literary studies by drawing attention away from seeing text, even as a process, in isolation toward seeing it as imbedded in discursive systems. Robert Scholes, for example, asserted that "a piece of writing must be understood as the product of a person or persons, at a given point in human history, in a given form of discourse, taking its meaning from the interpretive gestures of individual readers using the grammatical, semantic, and cultural codes available to them" (16). Such redefinitions of literature not only served to extend the boundaries of what could be properly conceived of as literary text but also established potential intersections between literature and composition as scholars and teachers became increasingly interested in understanding the social, political, and cultural contexts in which writing as praxis and product are embedded. Concurrently, advances in computer technology also contributed to reconceptualizing literature by drawing attention to social aspects of discourse and challenging traditional boundaries between reading and writing, and thus, between literature and composition (Moulthrop and Kaplan).

Yet despite significant transformations in literary and composition studies, Edward Rocklin has noted that, "the two realms overlap in their focus on and reconception of the *text* as both deriving from and being the source of a process; but they diverge in focusing, respectively on the *writer* and the *reader* of that text" (187). This divergence helps shed light on the tertiary use of the term *literature* in our professional discussions, namely, to designate the scholarly field of literary studies. Since the early 1980s, most of the debate on this level has centered on a perceived gap between literature and composition as fields of study (see, e.g., Booth 1981).

Disputed views of *literature* are evident in the antithetical characterizations of the relationship between composition and literary studies drawn by Winifred Bryan Horner and Jay L. Robinson. Horner argued that "in reality, literature and composition cannot be separated either in theory or in teaching practice. Composition theory and critical theory are indeed opposites of the same coin" (1). In response, Jay Robinson denied the synergy Horner described by arguing that

> in reality, or at least in the one I occupy literature and composition *are* separated, certainly in anything that can be called practice, and certainly in the ways they are regarded and supported as practices. As I read the history of critical theory in my working lifetime, critical theory and composition theory have indeed not been 'opposites of the same coin' but currencies as different as the pound and the yen. (488)

Some scholars have suggested that part of the problem may stem from the ways in which we continue to conceptualize literature. For example, Anne Ruggles Gere and Rocklin have both called attention to the problematic assumptions underlying the bridge metaphor so often used to discuss the perceived gap. Gere noted that the metaphor of the bridge "emphasizes separation and difference. . . . These two [reading literature and writing compositions] stand on opposite sides of a chasm, linked only by bridges of good will, mutual interest, or pedagogical value" (617). Rocklin similarly noted that "in speaking of 'bridging the gap' we are accepting as given a culturally created condition that is hardly inevitable, and accepting the constraints of the metaphor that may prove to be an obstacle to thinking clearly about the project we have undertaken" (178). As a remedy, he suggested reconceptualizing the relationship as one common ground rather than two whose gulf must be spanned.

Although the assumptions that led to the creation of a geo-political trope to represent the relationship between literature and composition both inside and outside the classroom have long been challenged, the trope remains firm in our discussions. Jane Peterson's challenge to the field draws attention to this very issue: "Why do we focus our discussion on the texts assigned instead of the ways we expect students to read in Freshman English?" (312); "let's admit that the original question about the *place* of literature in Freshman composition identified an inappropriate starting point" (314, italics mine). Her challenge calls for displacing the spatial metaphor so the field may be freed to think in other, more effective, ways about literature and its relationship to composition.

Maureen Daly Goggin
Arizona State University

Works Cited

Ashmead, John. 1964. "Good Writing from Great Books." *College Composition and Communication* 15: 29–33.

Booth, Wayne C. 1956. "The Place of Literature in the Freshman Course." *College Composition and Communication* 7: 35–38.

———. 1981. "The Common Aims that Divide Us; Or, Is There a 'Profession 1981'?" *ADE Bulletin* 69: 1–5.

Brown, Gladys K. 1956. "Reading for Fun at Little Rock." *College Composition and Communication* 7: 45–48.

Burkholder, Robert. 1985. "Transcendental Re-Seeing: Teaching Revision Using the Works of Emerson and Thoreau." *Teaching English in the Two-Year College* 12: 14–21.

Calderwood, Natalie. 1957. "Composition and Literature." *College Composition and Communication* 8: 201–204.

Eagleton, Terry. 1981. "A Small History of Rhetoric." In *Walter Benjamin, or Towards a Revolutionary Criticism.* London: Verso and New Left Books. 191–213.

Fenstermaker, John J. 1977. "Literature in the Composition Class." *College Composition and Communication* 28: 34–37.

Fulkerson, Richard. 1973. "Using Full-Length Books in Freshman English." *College Composition and Communication* 24: 218–220.

Gere, Anne Ruggles. 1989. "Composition and Literature: The Continuing Conversation." Review Essay. *College English* 51: 617–622.

Goss, Raymond. 1974. "Response to Richard P. Fulkerson, 'Using Full-Length Books in Freshman English'." *College Composition and Communication* 25: 212.

Hart, John A., Robert C. Stack, and Neal Woodruff Jr.. 1958. "Literature in the Composition Course." *College Composition and Communication* 9: 236–240.

Hayford, Harrison. 1956. "Literature in English A at Northwestern." *College Composition and Communication* 7: 42–45.

Horner, Winifred Bryan, ed. 1983. *Composition and Literature: Bridging the Gap.* Chicago: University of Chicago Press.

Memering, Dean. 1977. "The Reading/Writing Heresy." *College Composition and Communication* 28: 223–226.

Moulthrop, Stuart, and Nancy Kaplan. 1991. "Something to Imagine: Literature, Composition, and Interactive Fiction." *Computers and Composition* 9: 7–23.

Newkirk, Thomas, ed. 1986. *Only Connect: Uniting Reading and Writing.* Upper Montclair, NJ: Boynton/Cook.

Petersen, Bruce T., ed. 1986. *Convergences: Transactions in Reading and Writing.* Urbana, IL: National Council of Teachers of English.

Peterson, Jane. 1995. "Through the Looking-Glass: A Response." *College English* 57: 310–318.

Peterson, Linda. 1985. "Repetition and Metaphor in Early Stages of Composing." *College Composition and Communication* 36: 429–443.

Petrosky, Anthony R. 1982. "From Story to Essay: Reading and Writing." *College Composition and Communication* 33: 19–36.

Robinson, Jay L. 1985. "Literacy in the Department of English." *College English* 47: 482–498.

Rocklin, Edward. 1991. "Converging Transformations in Teaching Composition, Literature, and Drama." *College English* 53: 177–194.

Rubinstein, S. Leonard. 1966. "Composition: A Collision with Literature." *College English* 27: 273–277.

Scholes, Robert. 1982. *Semiotics and Interpretation.* New Haven: Yale University Press.

Steinberg, Erwin R. 1995. "Imaginative Literature in Composition Classrooms?" *College English* 57: 266–280.

Sternglass, Marilyn S. 1986. "Introduction." In *Convergences: Transactions in Reading and Writing,* ed. Bruce T. Petersen. Urbana, IL: National Council of Teachers of English. 1–11.

Stone, William B. 1968. "Teaching 'The Dead': Literature in the Composition Class." *College Composition and Communication* 19: 229–230.

Thorson, Gerald. 1953. "Literature in Freshman English." *College Composition and Communication* 4: 38–40.

Williams, Raymond. 1977. *Marxism and Literature.* Oxford: Oxford University Press.

———. 1983. *Writing in Society.* London: Verso.

logic

In composition studies, *logic* is a term typically associated with only one kind of discourse (argumentative writing), but whose meanings are nonetheless consistently marked by schisms and self-contradictions.

To begin with, composition studies' "transmutations of technical logic into comp-logic" are error-filled and frequently "bizarre," according to Richard Fulkerson (450; 441). In comp-logic, he says, "induction" means "going" from the particular to the general, "moving" from individual pieces of evidence to a conclusion, while "deduction" means "going" from the general to the specific, "moving" from a general statement to a conclusion about a particular case. The motion metaphor in these definitions, he contends, makes students confuse the order of presentation of an argument with the type of reasoning (437–438). But in technical logic, Fulkerson says, the difference between induction and deduction "involves neither the notion of movement nor the notion of general and specific. In technical logic, any argument in which the premises purport to prove the conclusion . . . is a deduction. And all other arguments . . . are induction" (438). The other element of comp-logic, he writes, is the teaching of a confusing list of common fallacies which "are not clearly defined and distinguished from each other," the definition of a *non sequitur*, for instance, enveloping those of *post hoc*, hasty generalization, and stereotyping (443–444).

Despite Fulkerson's critique, logic remains a central force in composition instruction because its long-standing definition as "the discipline of analyzing and evaluating argument" leads to a commonsensical conclusion that it must therefore be useful in teaching argumentative writing. In this vein, logic has long been represented as offering students organizing structures for their writing, or as Jack Pitt puts it, "valid deductive forms in accord with which paragraphs or entire essays can be organized" (89–90). It has been frequently said that by arranging their data "along a logic" (Smith 313), students can avoid writing shapeless, directionless papers. In this way, logic is also construed as a motive force or engine sequentially driving a text forward.

Another popular construction portrays logic as the study of the logical thought processes, connections, and relationships inherent in transitional words. Logic is thus represented as "a philosophical tool fit for such a practical task as the teaching of coherence in composition," as Dennis J. Packard puts it (366). In a third common version of this keyword, logic is portrayed as playing a principal role in invention. According to Nelson J. Smith III, for instance, data can consist of separate fragments of information, "but thought occurs only when these isolated bits and pieces are linked together" in logical relationships. Thus, in this construction, "logic is indispensable for rhetoric, because it aids in the production of thought" (309).

Conversely, logic is just as often represented as having scant little, if any, relevance to composition instruction. David S. Kaufer and Christine M. Neuwirth, for instance, argue that students "typically come away from their writing course with a hodgepodge of information about syllogism, Aristotelian topics, fallacy, evidence, and warrants, but they have little idea how to put this information to use when actually composing" (388). The simple reason for this, according to Fulkerson, is that logic "describes products not processes" (450). Logic and comp-logic, he says, "are tools for criticizing arguments, not for generating them" (445). This version of logic as useful "only in the analysis and arrangement of arguments, not in their discovery" (Kaufer and Neuwirth 380) thus flatly contradicts the above-mentioned conception of logic as indispensable to invention.

Furthermore, scholars in composition also figure logic as irrelevant to composition by consistently defining it in opposition to rhetoric. Logic, Charles W. Kneupper has argued, seeks formal validity, deductive certainty, and conclusive knowledge, whereas rhetoric seeks persuasion or adherence and by definition deals with probabilities and matters of uncertainty (116–117). Kaufer and Neuwirth point out that all that logic can provide, then, is formally valid arguments that are neither necessary for—nor carry any "real practical force" in—written argument (381). As Fulkerson has noted, deduction thus simply doesn't apply to "real-world discourse" (441). The "absolute nature of deduction ill suits the contingent nature of argumentative discourse," he says (450). In like manner, he argues, "Given its contingent-ness, writing has little use for the certitudes of deductive reasoning" (440). Thus, Kneupper maintains, "formal logic is the wrong place for writing teachers to go" (114), its application to the realm of rhetoric amounting to "an intrusion in a province to which it does not belong" (117).

Several other antithetical strands of meaning within *logic* should also be considered. For example, this keyword is enveloped by the "Mr. Spock" version of logic from popular culture in which logic is construed as being both a superior, self-sufficient, pure rationality unfettered by human values and emotions, and, simultaneously, a cold, mechanical, impoverished cognitive prison-house incapable of creative problem-solving. This divided portrayal is manifest in composition studies. "Subtract the sensory and affective components from any unit of thought," Albert Upton said in 1965, "and logic is what you have left." And since composition should have a deliberate, planned purpose rather than a "spontaneous, . . . impulsive or hysterical" one, he wrote, logic should "assume the dominant function" (30). In contrast, Kneupper, for example, has represented logic as a "coercive" force enacting a "tyranny . . . over judgment, human feeling and perception" (118). In this way, composition scholarship has come to equate logic both with intellectually rigorous thinking/writing and, simultaneously, with a bloodless academic discourse that imprisons writers by dismissing a host of rhetorical drives.

Similar fundamental schisms that should be noted include: the bifurcation between the Old Logic—traditional, Aristotelian, syllogistic—and the New—which "chews up prose and spits out symbols" in an entirely mathematical "propositional calculus" (Packard 367); the distinction Richard M. Coe makes between traditional logic—"a set of methods for reducing wholes into component parts"—and contemporary "eco-logic"—which "considers wholes as wholes" (232) and so emphasizes "systemic interrelations instead of analytic separations" (237); and the differentiation within classical rhetoric itself between the logic of scientific demonstration (in which the premises are taken from empirical observation and induction) and the logic of rhetoric or dialectic (in which the premises are taken from the other participant(s) in the discussion). But perhaps the single most important bifurcation is that all representations of logic in composition seem to assume (and rely upon) a fundamental disjunction between thinking and writing, with thinking coming first—an assumption obvious, for instance, in Upton's assertion that logic can help us "make a better thinker of a writer, no matter how eloquent he may be" (34).

Other constructions of logic in composition studies include logic as a source of "theory and standards of evaluation" for teachers and textbook authors (Kneupper 114), as a means to solve writing problems, as a means to make composition an intellectual discipline, and, finally, as a general term for any formalized, consciously applied thinking process.

Paul Heilker
Virginia Tech

Works Cited

Coe, Richard M. 1975. "Eco-Logic for the Composition Classroom." *College Composition and Communication* 26: 232–237.

Fulkerson, Richard. 1988. "Technical Logic, Comp-Logic, and the Teaching of Writing." *College Composition and Communication* 39: 436–452.

Kaufer, David S., and Christine M. Neuwirth. 1983. "Integrating Formal Logic and the New Rhetoric." *College English* 45: 380–389.

Kneupper, Charles W. 1984. "The Tyranny of Logic and the Freedom of Argumentation." *PRE/TEXT* 5: 113–121.

Packard, Dennis J. 1976. "From Logic to Composition and Reading." *College Composition and Communication* 27: 366–372.

Pitt, Jack. 1966. "A New Logic for Composition." *College Composition and Communication* 17: 88–94.

Smith, Nelson J. III. 1969. "Logic for the New Rhetoric." *College Composition and Communication* 20: 305–313.

Upton, Albert. 1965. "Logic, Semantics, and Composition." *College Composition and Communication* 16: 30–34.

marginalized/marginalization

The concept of *marginalization* has been defined in composition studies in various ways, depending on the positions and interests of the definers. There is general agreement on the broad idea that marginalized people, along with their languages, cultures, and ways of reasoning, are pushed to the margins of society and disenfranchised by those in the center—those with more economic, political, and social power.

Marginalization is defined in composition studies chiefly as a pedagogical challenge for both students and teachers. The presence of members of previously marginalized groups both in the student's desk and at the teacher's podium has sent compositionists in search of pedagogies based on an understanding of the language and reasoning habits of marginalized people. In this search, composition has drawn extensively on sociolinguistics, a field that defines marginalization in terms of the relative statuses assigned to various languages and dialects. The work of Basil Bernstein, especially *Class, Codes, and Control*, is widely cited. In his theory of "restricted" and "elaborated" codes, Bernstein sees marginalization in terms of the relationship between dominant and subordinate discourses and educational styles. Myron C. Tuman extends Bernstein's definition in emphasizing "a correlation between the social and economic background of our students and the kind of writing curriculum they are conditioned to respond to" (45). Lucille M. Schultz, Chester H. Laine, and Mary C. Savage cite Bernstein in support of a definition of marginalized students as those who may not simply fail to "respond" to pedagogical styles from the "advanced levels" of elite schools, but may actually reject them (148).

Beyond this shared basic definition, however, compositionists interpret the meaning of marginalization in many different, and sometimes incompatible, ways. The differences in the definitions depend on whether the writing teacher views marginalization as either a negative or a positive quality, or defines the margin as either a position of weakness or a position of strength.

No issue crystallizes the distance between these definitions like that of the teaching of academic discourse, a dialect of linguistic conventions and ideological assumptions alien to members of marginalized groups. Among those who define marginalization as a negative quality, there are those who believe that the teaching of academic discourse can be a way to bring marginalized voices into the process of producing the academic knowledge of the center. Peter Elbow, for example, while conceding that the practice may still exclude some students, still sees marginalization as a problem to solve through the teaching of academic discourse. Mike Rose sees marginalization as perpetuated by misguided attempts at liberation which encourage students to "use their own languages" (329), and emphasizes the importance of academic discourse as a worthwhile "conversation" which can counter student marginalization. David Bartholomae is even stronger in asserting that marginalization is reinforced by denying students the opportunity to master academic discourse, arguing that certain valuable forms of knowledge are inaccessible or literally unthinkable without academic discourse (142–143). Patricia Bizzell defines marginalization in terms of marginalized students' " 'outlandishness'—their appearance to many teachers and to themselves as the students who are most alien in the college community" (294) and insists that marginalized students must be immersed in academic discourse to join that community.

Other compositionists, by contrast, define marginalized languages and habits of thought as sources of strength and worthy of inclusion, and argue against the teaching of academic discourse as a solution to marginalization. Olivia Frey, for instance, sees marginalization as reinforced by academic discourse rather than solved by it, arguing that "the profession by and large values conventions of literary critical discourse that may not fit the values, the perceptual frameworks, and the ways of writing of many women in English departments across the country" (507–508). She and other feminist compositionists speak from the margins to reconceive academic discourse so that it includes previously marginalized forms such as personal narrative.

In their redefinition of the margin as a place of potential strength, feminist compositionists frequently cite the work of Carol Gilligan and Mary Field Belenky *et al.* These writers define marginalization in terms of gender, associating it with a dominant masculine discourse that marginalizes feminine ways of reasoning and constructing knowledge, and calling for recognition of previously marginalized feminine discourses. Some feminist compositionists extend the notion of marginalization as a feminine space to other forms of marginalization. Marilyn M. Cooper and Cynthia L. Selfe, for example, point to Gilligan's idea of the "different" but valuable truths inherent in the experiences of women and, by extension, all marginalized people (858), while Karyn L. Hollis similarly extends the work of Gilligan and Belenky *et al.* on marginalized feminine epistemology to "other silenced groups" (341) such as racial minorities and those with working-class origins.

Compositionists who define the margin as a place of strength often cite Gloria Anzaldúa and bell hooks. Anzaldúa's *Borderlands/La Frontera* has been especially influential on redefinitions of the margin as a valorized position with the potential to transform the center. Anzaldúa's ideas are integral, for example, to Min-zhan Lu's view of marginalization in the basic writing classroom as an aid to the development of a "new consciousness" that can conceive of positive social change (888). Similarly, bell hooks argues for a definition of the margin not as "a sign marking . . . despair," but as "position and place of resistance" (1990, 150). As such, the margin is "a central location for the production of a counter-hegemonic discourse that is not just found in words but in habits of being and the way one lives" (1990, 149). She defines the view from the margin as essential to a complete conception of intellectual life for both herself and her students, asserting that the margin is a site of class awareness and enrichment: "Maintaining awareness of class differences, nurturing ties with the poor and working-class people who are our most intimate kin, our comrades in struggle, transforms and enriches our intellectual experience" (1989, 83).

It should be noted that many compositionists apply the concept of marginalization to the status of composition studies itself relative to, most often, literary studies (Friend; Hatlen; Woods). The debate over this issue parallels that over the definition of marginalization as a positive or negative quality. Christy Friend, seeing marginalization as negative, finds in the marginalization of composition a challenge for departmental restructuring and suggests that composition should be redefined as more central to English Departments. Belenky (in Ashton-Jones and Thomas) emphasizes the positive aspects of marginality, asserting that composition's marginalization is a source of strength: "You're on the cutting edge. . . . It is certainly not high status to be at the margins[,] . . . but anybody who is involved in working across disciplines is much more likely to have a lively mind and a lively life. You may not get as many brownie points, but in the long run you probably make a better contribution" (292).

Clyde Moneyhun
New Mexico Highlands University
Guanjun Cai
University of Arizona

Works Cited

Anzaldúa, Gloria. 1987. *Borderlands/La Frontera.* San Francisco: Aunt Lute Books.

Ashton-Jones, Evelyn, and Dene Kay Thomas. 1990. "Composition, Collaboration, and Women's Ways of Knowing: A Conversation with Mary Belenky." *Journal of Advanced Composition* 10: 275–292.

Bartholomae, David. 1985. "Inventing the University." *When a Writer Can't Write.* Ed. Mike Rose. New York: Guilford. 134–165.

Belenky, Mary Field, Blythe McVicker Clinchy, Nancy Rule Goldberger, and Jill Mattuck Tarule. 1986. *Women's Ways of Knowing: The Development of Self, Voice, and Mind.* New York: Basic Books.

Bernstein, Basil. 1975. *Class, Codes, and Control.* London: Routledge.

Bizzell, Patricia. 1986. "What Happens When Basic Writers Come to College?" *College Composition and Communication* 37: 294–301.

Cooper, Marilyn M., and Cynthia L. Selfe. 1990. "Computer Conferences and Learning: Authority, Resistance, and Internally Persuasive Discourse." *College English* 52: 847–869.

Elbow, Peter. 1991. "Reflections on Academic Discourse." *College English* 53: 136–155.

Friend, Christy. 1992. "The Excluded Conflict: The Marginalization of Composition and Rhetoric Studies in Graff's *Professing Literature.*" *College English* 54: 276–285.

Frey, Olivia. 1990. "Beyond Literary Darwinism: Women's Voices and Critical Discourse." *College English* 52: 507–526.

Gilligan, Carol. 1982. *In a Different Voice.* Cambridge, Mass.: Harvard University Press.

Hatlen, Berton. 1988. "Michel Foucault and the Discourse[s] of English." *College English* 50: 786–801.

Hollis, Karyn L. 1992. "Feminism in Writing Workshops: A New Pedagogy." *College Composition and Communication* 43: 340–348.

hooks, bell. 1989. "Keeping Close to Home: Class and Education." *Talking Back: Thinking Feminist, Thinking Black.* Boston: South End. 73–83.

———. 1990. "Choosing the Margin." *Yearning: Race, Gender, and Cultural Politics.* Boston: South End. 145–153.

Lu, Min-zhan. 1992. "Conflict and Struggle: The Enemies or Preconditions of Basic Writing?" *College English* 54: 887–913.

Rose, Mike. 1988. "Remedial Writing Course: A Critique and a Proposal." *The Writing Teacher's Sourcebook.* Second edit. Ed. Gary Tate and Edward P. J. Corbett. New York: Oxford. 318–337.

Schultz, Lucille M., Chester H. Laine, and Mary C. Savage. 1988. "Interaction Among School and College Writing Teachers: Toward Recognizing and Remaking Old Patterns." *College Composition and Communication* 39: 139–153.

Tuman, Myron C. 1988. "Class, Codes, and Composition: Basil Bernstein and the Critique of Pedagogy." *College Composition and Communication* 39: 42–51.

Woods, Marjorie Curry. 1992. "Among Men—Not Boys: Histories of Rhetoric and the Exclusion of Pedagogy." *Rhetoric Society Quarterly* 22: 18–26.

multiculturalism

Multiculturalism refers to the inclusion in the educational mainstream of texts, theories, and questions by and about previously marginalized groups. It is part of a larger concern about diversity and difference in the humanities which gained force in the 1980s from sources such as civil rights, feminism, French post-structuralist theory, a concern about political correctness, changes in U.S. demographics, and the move toward a global economy. Most conceptions of multiculturalism focus primarily on race and ethnicity, though its definition is often extended to gender, class, sexual orientation, and religion.

Michael Geyer claims that multiculturalism in general education is "not a body of academic thought but a contested politics of social and cultural transformation in which academics participate" (513). Debate over multiculturalism is in part a function of the diverse definitions of the term, definitions which are, in part, determined by ideological positions occupied by participants in the discussion.

Some conceptions of multiculturalism, implicit in the work of radical educators such as James A. Banks, Wahneema Lubiano, and William G. Tierney, stress educational and social transformation. They maintain that an effective multicultural education questions existing power structures and addresses the social and political contexts of education. Lubiano defines what she calls "radical" or "strong" multiculturalism as a way to reconstitute academic knowledge and academia itself: a "system for reconceptualizing education and its relation to power" which "aims at critical engagement with the entire process of information creation as well as political, economic, and social decision-making" (11; 19).

Self-proclaimed radical criticisms of some multicultural approaches reveal the tensions between different proponents' definitions of multiculturalism. Implicit in these criticisms are an insistence on political awareness and social transformation absent from less overtly political versions of multiculturalism. Lubiano distinguishes "strong" multiculturalism from some multiculturalists' attempts to " 'manage' diverse student populations and curricula" and from the reduction of multiculturalism to "cultural relativism, to an empty and non-critical pluralism" with slogans such as " 'different strokes for different folks' " and concepts such as a "national 'melting pot' " which ignore issues of power relations among diverse groups (11–13). Tierney also criticizes definitions of multiculturalism which avoid political questions about "how power and knowledge function to create socially created categories" (4). Geyer calls such versions of multiculturalism "signs of a distinct turn to a plural middle ground" which support a merely symbolic inclusion of marginalized groups and ignore social injustices (516). Banks criticizes what he terms the "contributions approach," the "heroes and holidays approach," and the "ethnic additive approach" for leaving the mainstream curriculum unaltered, ignoring important cultural contexts, and reinforcing stereotypes and misconceptions (192–195). Banks defines effective multiculturalism as a "transformation approach" that changes basic curricular goals and assumptions, enabling students to view concepts, issues, themes, and problems from several ethnic perspectives (196).

Other definitions of multiculturalism also stress the political nature of the term, but these frame the politicization of education as inappropriate and dangerous. Roger Kimball links multiculturalism with political correctness and considers them manifestations of higher education's "ideological indoctrination" that constitute an "assault on free speech" and "an abridgment of fundamental liberal principles in the name of 'diversity,' 'difference,' and 'pluralism' " (10). Dinesh D'Souza defines multiculturalism and political correctness as a " 'victim's revolution on campus' " leading toward " 'an education in closed-mindedness and intolerance' " (qtd. in Kimball 7).

Furthermore, both radicals and conservatives see multiculturalism as affecting not only curriculum and classroom practice but university policies such as investments, research, hiring, and promotion. Radicals see this as a necessary and desirable goal (Lubiano 15), while conservatives oppose these changes, labeling them "affirmative-action thinking" with lowered standards in order to fulfill quotas (Kimball 9).

Some definitions of multiculturalism in composition are based on the relation(s) between language and culture. Lillian Bridwell-Bowles argues that the multicultural composition classroom is one way to change society, that multiculturalism entails a consideration of social and political contexts in approaching language and texts:

> if we are to invent a truly pluralistic society, we must envision a socially and politically situated view of language and the creation of texts—one that takes into account gender, race, class, sexual preference, and a host of issues that are implied by these and other cultural differences. (349)

Implicit in some compositionists' discussions of multiculturalism is a definition of the term as a cultural negotiation between students and teachers, as a bridge between home and academic cultures created by multiculturalist course content. Terry Dean, for example, stresses that "teachers need to structure learning experiences that both help students write their way into the university and help teachers learn their way into student cultures" (23).

Other compositionists define multiculturalism as a way of perceiving student texts in terms of conflict rather than mediation. For Min-zhan Lu, a multicultural pedagogy involves considering the composition classroom as a manifestation of Mary Louise Pratt's "contact zone" and "explicitly foregrounding the category of 'resistance' and 'change' " when approaching student writing (447). Lu applies this version of multiculturalism to a consideration of student texts, developing a "multicultural approach to style, particularly those styles of student writing which appear to be ridden with 'errors' " (442).

Inherent to most pedagogical discussions of multiculturalism is its definition as a problem in teacher training. For many radical multiculturalists such as Lubiano, current concepts of teacher authority contradict the goal of multicultural education; power dynamics in the traditional classroom must be reconceived to meet the goal of institutional transformation through multiculturalism. Harvey Wiener defines multicultural teacher training in composition and other fields not as a problem of negotiating power but of gaining knowledge about their students' cultures. He urges that teachers acquire general "multicultural literacy," which he describes as "acknowledg[ing] . . . the cultural equipment students bring to the classroom and to the collegiate society at large," learning and interacting with diverse styles students bring from other backgrounds (101–102).

Some compositionists agree with abstract goals such as inclusion and diversity, but define multiculturalism as an overly political practice which is pedagogically unsound and unnecessary. For example, Maxine Hairston sees multiculturalism as a counterproductive intrusion of politics in the classroom, a practice which constrains both students and teachers. She implicitly defines multiculturalism as creating a "high-risk" environment and requiring writing topics that students "perceive as politically charged and about which they feel uninformed" (189). Hairston describes multiculturalism as "too complex and diverse" to be dealt with in writing courses, especially first-year composition courses, and as fostering "stereotyping and superficial thinking" (190). She maintains that multiculturalism is unnecessary: insisting that a student-centered writing classroom is inherently culturally inclusive, she seeks to "promote genuine diversity in our classes" while keeping "students' own writing [at] the center of the course" and writing teachers "within our area of professional expertise" (186).

Nancy Buffington
Guanjun Cai
University of Arizona

Works Cited

Banks, James A. 1989. "Integrating the Curriculum with Ethnic Content: Approaches and Guidelines." *Multicultural Education: Issues and Perspectives.* Ed. Cherry M. and James A. Banks. Boston: Allyn and Bacon. 189–207.

Bridwell-Bowles, Lillian. 1992. "Discourse and Diversity: Experimental Writing within the Academy." *College Composition and Communication* 43: 349–368.

Dean, Terry. 1989. "Multicultural Classrooms, Monocultural Teachers." *College Composition and Communication* 40: 23–37.

Geyer, Michael. 1993. "Multiculturalism and the Politics of General Education." *Critical Inquiry* 19: 499–533.

Hairston, Maxine. 1992. "Diversity, Ideology, and Teaching Writing." *College Composition and Communication* 43: 179–193.

Kimball, Roger. 1991. "Moral Homicide: Illiberal Education in America." *The New Criterion* 9.8: 5–11.

Lu, Min-zhan. 1994. "Professing Multiculturalism: The Politics of Style in the Contact Zone." *College Composition and Communication* 45: 442–458.

Lubiano, Wahneema. 1992. "Multiculturalism: Negotiating Politics and Knowledge." *Concerns* 22: 11–21.

Tierney, William G. 1994. *Multiculturalism in Higher Education: An Organizational Framework for Analysis.* Center for the Study of Higher Education. Project R117G10037 CFDA 84.117G.

Weiner, Harvey S. 1985. "Multicultural Literacy for Faculty: Accommodating Non-native Speakers of English in Content Courses." *Rhetoric Review* 4: 100–107.

paradigm

Paradigm entered the field of composition studies by way of Thomas S. Kuhn's analysis of the history of the physical sciences. In composition studies, where it proved both fertile conceptually and valuable politically, it became a buzzword in the 1980s and was often associated with what were taken to be the competing paradigms of current-traditional rhetoric and process theory. By the 1990s, the boundaries of the term had been stretched so far that it could be used to signify any theoretical, methodological or conceptual model a particular writer might happen either to advocate or oppose.

A paradigm, as Kuhn initially defines the term in *The Structure of Scientific Revolutions*, is a scientific achievement that shares two essential characteristics: first, it must be "sufficiently unprecedented to attract an enduring group of adherents away from competing modes of scientific activity"; second, it must be "sufficiently open-ended to leave all sorts of problems for the redefined group of practitioners to resolve" (10). In a postscript added to the second edition of the book, however, Kuhn acknowledged that a critic of the first edition found that within its pages, the term was used "in at least twenty-two different ways" (181). Two of the senses in which the term was used, Kuhn added, needed especially to be distinguished. On the one hand, he explained, a paradigm is a "disciplinary matrix," or "the entire constellation of beliefs, values, techniques, and so on shared by the members of a given community." On the other, paradigms are "exemplars," or "the concrete puzzle-solutions which, employed as models or examples, can replace explicit rules as a basis for the solution of the remaining puzzles of normal science" (175, 182, 187).

Richard E. Young in 1978 was the first to apply Kuhn's concepts and terminology to the field of composition studies. Young acknowledged that "Kuhn's work is an effort to account for deep and rapid changes in the sciences" and that "there is some question whether it is legitimate to apply it to other disciplines," but Young concluded that there were sufficient similarities between scientific disciplines and composition studies to warrant his undertaking (29n). He defined a paradigm as that which "determines, among other things, what is included in the discipline and what is excluded from it, what is taught and not taught, what problems are regarded as important and unimportant, and, by implication, what research is regarded as valuable in developing the discipline" (29). He also defined a paradigm as "an eye to see with" (30). The first of these definitions indicates that for Young, a paradigm is what Kuhn calls a "disciplinary matrix." The second indicates that, since an eye perceives selectively, a paradigm operates as what Kenneth Burke calls a "terministic screen." Young argued that one paradigm (which he called the "current-traditional" paradigm but which has subsequently also been called the product-centered paradigm) had guided the teaching of writing since the beginning of the century. Its features, which Young said were "obvious enough," included

> the emphasis on the composed product rather than the composing process; the analysis of discourse into words, sentences, and paragraphs; the classification of discourse into description, narration, exposition, and argument; the strong concern with usage (syntax, spelling, punctuation) and with style (economy, clarity, emphasis); the preoccupation with the informal essay and the research paper; and so on. (31)

One of the chief faults of the current-traditional paradigm and a chief reason why it did not provide an adequate model for teaching or research, in Young's view, was its failure to include invention within the province of rhetoric (33). Young concluded that the current-traditional paradigm was no longer viable and that a new, process-centered paradigm, based on new theories of invention, was emerging in its place (35).

Four years after Young's article appeared, Maxine Hairston joined him in using Kuhnian concepts to explain developments in composition studies. In particular, she appropriated Kuhn's notion of the "paradigm shift," defining it as the "replacement of one conceptual model by another" and arguing that "our profession is probably in the first stages of a paradigm shift" (77). To Young's list of the features of the current-traditional paradigm, Hairston added the following three: "its adherents believe that competent writers know what they are going to say before they begin to write[,] . . . that the composing process is linear, . . . [and] that teaching editing is teaching writing" (78). Hairston then listed twelve features of the emerging, process-centered paradigm for the teaching of writing. The new paradigm was rhetorically based, it was informed by other disciplines, notably by linguistics and by cognitive psychology, and it was grounded in empirical research into the writing process. Any instructor who subscribed to the new paradigm would view writing as a recursive process. She would value expressive as well as expository writing. She would intervene in the actual writing of her students and then evaluate what they wrote in accordance with how well it fulfilled their intentions (86).

Louise Wetherbee Phelps, however, argued in 1988 that the "reorientation of composition from product to process" did not constitute a "paradigmatic change" (135). She conceded that contemporary composition theory was dominated by the opposition of process and product and that this opposition had "succeeded in reversing the value structure of composition pedagogy and, by opening a new field of questions and topics, in reconstituting the field as a research discipline" (132). But she argued that the "process/product opposition is itself compartmentalizing, in that it separates the text from the historical process of production, and writing from reading" (135). She concluded that composition studies was currently in "a transitional stage leading to a genuinely new paradigm as yet only dimly perceived." This new paradigm, when at last it did emerge, would be recognized "by its power to reintegrate texts into a dynamic of discourse." Phelps acknowledged, however, that since paradigms as she was defining them "are made up of precisely those assumptions that remain tacit, unrecognized, and unexamined," recognizing the new paradigm would require special powers of perception (136).

Susan Miller's answer, in 1991, to the "question of whether a paradigm shift has actually occurred," was "[N]ot quite." Miller argues that "process theory has not yet provided an accurate or even a very historically different theory of contemporary writing, even if we grant it partial paradigmatic status" (108). She concedes it has been politically useful for composition studies to claim to possess "a 'paradigm' like those that centralize the activities of other professional groups and well-established disciplines" (105). She also concedes that "the process model has, as New Criticism did for literature, stabilized a field that originally was a loosely connected set of untheorized practices" (115). According to Miller, however, " 'Current-traditional' or 'product' theory appears to have been created at the same time that process theory was, to help explain process as a theory pitted against old practices," and both theories "share underlying assumptions about the 'problem' that each approach to teaching has addressed" (110–111). The creation of the bipolar opposition between the theories, Miller argues, was a politically diversionary tactic which worked to "sustain what is in fact a single paradigm for the field" (10). She suggests, moreover, that the term *paradigm* is overused, pointing out that "[j]ust as the telescope and the microscope have been credited with paradigm shifts in science, so too have cheap paper, ballpoint pens, word processors, and disposable textbooks created a new situation in which writing can be reconceived" (107).

Robert J. Connors observed in 1983 that composition scholars were using Kuhnian terminology in two primary ways. The first, of which Connors said the Young and Hairston analyses were the most popular examples, "involves the assumption that the field of composition studies already has a paradigm and either is or should be in the midst of shifting to another paradigm." The second "consists in the assumption that the field is in a preparadigmatic stage" (4–5). Connors noted that the use of the term *paradigm* amounted to a claim that "composition studies should be a scientific or prescientific discipline" (5). He criticized Young and Hairston for having failed to distinguish between different senses of *paradigm*, noting that for Kuhn the term had signified both "disciplinary matrix" and "exemplar." Composition studies, according to Connors, possessed an understructure of values and beliefs but lacked exemplars. This lack of models upon which to base the solution to problems was due, Connors explained, "to our not having very much agreement on what are to be the methodology and conditions for puzzle-solving within our field" (9).

Stephen M. North has observed that the paradigm-shift account of developments in composition studies is more remarkable for "what it tries to do" than "for what it says." He suggests it should be read as a sort of "power play" whereby Young and other advocates of change have attempted to set new agendas for composition research. According to North, Young's claim that composition was guided by a paradigm (albeit a "current-traditional" paradigm) at the turn of the century amounts to a claim that composition has had the coherence of a discipline since the century began. North observes, moreover, that Young's characterization of composition studies as a field governed by a paradigm does not square with the eclecticism of his (Young's) research agenda. Nor does it square with what North calls the "methodological pluralism" of composition teaching and research (318–321).

Competing methodologies, of course, can be said to grow out of different research paradigms. Susan H. McLeod, for example, describes quantitative and qualitative research methods in this way. After noting that she is using the term paradigm "in the Kuhnian sense of a system of shared beliefs or a world view," she argues that quantitative methods grow out of a positivist research tradition (374). Qualitative methods, on the other hand, are the product of a "new paradigm, which has been described not only as post-positivist but also 'hermeneutical' " (375). McLeod argues that the two paradigms "need not be incompatible." Instead, she says, they represent "different ways of looking at the world, different stances, different lenses through which we may examine phenomena." McLeod concludes that "[a]s long as we are aware of the paradigms, we can choose our methods carefully and wisely, according to how well they fit what we and others need to know" (379).

Robin Varnum
American International College

Works Cited

Burke, Kenneth. 1966. *Language as Symbolic Action: Essays on Life, Literature, and Method.* Berkeley: University of California Press.

Connors, Robert J. 1983. "Composition Studies and Science." *College English* 45: 1–20.

Hairston, Maxine. 1982. "The Winds of Change: Thomas Kuhn and the Revolution in the Teaching of Writing." *College Composition and Communication* 33: 76–88.

Kuhn, Thomas S. 1962; 2nd ed. 1970. *The Structure of Scientific Revolutions.* Chicago: University of Chicago Press.

McLeod, Susan H. 1992. "Evaluating Writing Programs: Paradigms, Problems, Possibilities." *Journal of Advanced Composition* 12: 373–382.

Miller, Susan. 1991. *Textual Carnivals: The Politics of Composition.* Carbondale, IL: Southern Illinois University Press.

North, Stephen M. 1987. *The Making of Knowledge in Composition: Portrait of an Emerging Field.* Upper Montclair, NJ: Boynton/Cook.

Phelps, Louise Wetherbee. 1988. *Composition as a Human Science: Contributions to the Self-Understanding of a Discipline.* New York: Oxford University Press.

Young, Richard E. 1978. "Paradigms and Problems: Needed Research in Rhetorical Invention." *Research on Composing: Points of Departure.* Ed. Charles R. Cooper and Lee Odell. Urbana, IL: NCTE.

pedagogy

In general academic usage, *pedagogy* has been a term of ignominy for centuries. *The Oxford English Dictionary* describes it as "the function, profession, or practice of a pedagogue," which carries "a more or less contemptuous or hostile sense, with implication of pedantry, dogmatism, or severity." Or as Jane Tompkins puts it, "[w]e have been indoctrinated from the very start . . . to look down on pedagogy. . . . [T]eaching was exactly like sex for me—something you weren't supposed to talk about or focus on in any way but that you were supposed to be able to do properly when the time came" (655).

Pedagogy—with no adjective—became (retrospectively at least) current-traditional pedagogy, then process pedagogy (composed of diverse forms of teaching undergirded by broadly ranging assumptions) and finally critical pedagogy. That pedagogy entered composition studies not routinely linked with an adjective suggests it was then assumed to be self-evident, separable from theory. Richard Fulkerson argues that, as a general rule, theory and practice began to be conflated in pedagogy only in the 1980s; before that, it was accepted teacherly practice to discuss the characteristics of good writing without also imagining how writers might write or how teachers might enable writers (410–411).

Four who figured prominently in the early 1980s' project of theorizing process pedagogy were Maxine Hairston, Ann E. Berthoff, C. H. Knoblauch and Lil Brannon. However, as Steven Lynn concludes from Hairston's "The Winds of Change," Berthoff's *Forming Thinking Writing: The Composing Imagination*, and Knoblauch and Brannon's *Rhetorical Traditions and the Teaching of Writing*, these conceptions of process pedagogy were more diverse than similar. For instance, pedagogy for Hairston is an interventionist procedure in which the teacher conveys information, rehearses strategies, and renders accepted models of thought (903). Knoblauch and Brannon, on the other hand, consider pedagogy to be less a matter of providing students with patterns and more an attempt at motivating students to create their own "personal world of meaning" (908). Unlike Hairston, Knoblauch and Brannon see the teacher's role as auxiliary to the process of writing rather than central to it. And finally, to Berthoff pedagogy is a hybrid of these distinct orientations: teaching is interventionist up to a point, motivational beyond that (909).

The significant differences between Hairston's and Knoblauch and Brannon's configurations of process pedagogy might also be viewed as the differences between a discipline-centered approach and a student-centered one, two perspectives which William F. Woods argues dominated composition texts from 1960 to 1980. Woods writes that the discipline-centered see pedagogy as a civilizing influence; it offers values, skills, and precepts to primitive beings, whereas proponents of a student-centered pedagogy perceive themselves as giving voice to (inherently good) humanity (395–396).

Divergent as these perspectives are, they hold in common at least one trait: their localized focus on individual teachers and individual students. Process pedagogy is secure in its nonpartisanship. However, it eventually came under fire for this very serenity in the midst of conflict, or as Linda Brodkey writes in the late 1980s, for preserving the fiction of "universal education," in which "teachers and students relate to one another undistracted by the classism, racism, and sexism that rage outside the classroom" (139).

Paulo Freire's call in 1982 for "education as the practice of freedom" (6) was strongly influential in ushering in the contemporary era of critical, sometimes called "oppositional" or "radical," pedagogy. Freire juxtaposes two forms of pedagogy:

> Banking education (for obvious reasons) attempts, by mythicizing reality, to conceal certain facts which explain the way men exist in the world; problem-posing education sets itself the task of demythologizing. Banking education resists dialogue; problem-posing education regards dialogue as indispensable. . . . Banking education treats students as objects of assistance; problem-posing education makes them critical thinkers. Banking education inhibits creativity and domesticates. . . . Problem-posing education bases itself on creativity and stimulates true reflection and action upon reality. (71)

To many, it was immediately obvious that choosing one or the other of these pedagogies would result in radically different people, schools, and societies. Freire's primary contribution was in revealing the interactions between education and society, thus elevating pedagogy to its prominent contemporary position as an agent for social change.

However, for many in the discipline, this viewpoint equating education with "liberation" compromises ideals of objectivity and the possibility that education might be a wholesome, virtuous endeavor. Hairston argues that the classroom is not the place to confront political forces or to address social wrongs, declaring that "[a]s educators of good will, we shouldn't even have to mention our anger about racism and sexism in our society—that's a given" (187). For her as for many others, pedagogy is decidedly not linked in any essential ways to the ills of society; rather it is an ideal form of interaction among dedicated teachers and diligent students occurring within the politically neutral space of the classroom.

The view of pedagogy from the political left, as expressed by James Berlin, is that "a way of teaching is never innocent. Every pedagogy is imbricated in ideology, in a set of tacit assumptions about what is real, what is good, what is possible, and how power ought to be distributed" (492). Within this framework, pedagogy has been assigned sharply conflicting tasks: to help students understand themselves better, to impress on students the radically communal nature of writing, to urge learners to resist inequity in its many guises. Lou Kelly, for example, reflects the late 1960s slogan of "power to the people" when he articulates the expressivist assumption that truth resides in the individual: "the student's own language and the experiences . . . that he wishes to share make the best content for composition" (3). Cynthia L. Caywood and Gillian R. Overing maintain that pedagogy, by facilitating and legitimizing students' and women's voices, can restructure patriarchal ways of being (xii). Elizabeth Flynn argues that, by replacing the "figure of the authoritative father with an image of a nurturing mother," pedagogy has reconstructed learning itself as a collaborative and cooperative, rather than competitive and autonomous, undertaking (423).

But to those for whom writing is a social rather than an individual act, pedagogies of self-discovery have too little to say about resisting the totalizing impact of mainstream culture. As Susan C. Jarratt (1991) puts it, "affirming the voice of a white, middle- or upper-middle-class student often involves teachers in . . . endorsing the cliches of competitive self-interest that perpetuate a system of racism, sexism, and classism" (109). Donald Lazere rues "the present, generally unquestioned (and even unconscious) imposition of capitalist, white-male, heterosexual ideology that pervades American education" (190) and describes a pedagogy that offers "systematic exposure to a full spectrum of ideologies" present in the rhetoric of political speeches, news reporting, and journals of opinion (191). Dale M. Bauer contends that pedagogy should prepare women and men for responsible citizenship by modeling a range of behaviors including "how to belong, how to identify, as well as how to resist" (391).

And finally, pedagogy is sometimes defined as vigilance against the coercion of pedagogy itself. To Greg Myers, collaborative learning and peer evaluation encourage unthinking conformity and the failure of skepticism needed if, for instance, students are to identify their interests as different from their employers' (170). Alan W. France contends that pedagogies of expressivism and textual criticism are internally contradictory, claiming empowerment for students but actually, by alienating them from public discourse, bringing them "to terms" with the social inequities of commodity capitalism (602).

Composition's interest in pedagogy and our claims for and about it, although disparate and conflicting, have been fairly intense. Jarratt (1995) strikes a proprietary note in her response to Tompkins's extensively-debated "Pedagogy of the Distressed," contending: "Here was Tompkins, a person with a major reputation in literary criticism and theory who had seemingly just discovered the concept of pedagogy, coming to lecture a group of people many of whom had spent their professional lives working on pedagogy." Jarratt writes: "I'm glad she discovered pedagogy, writing, and the West. But, curiously, I find myself already in those places she discovered, a native in habitats stumbled upon by an anthropologist" (351).

Karen Fitts
Loyola College in Maryland

Works Cited

Bauer, Dale M. 1990. "The Other 'F' Word: The Feminist in the Classroom." *College English* 52: 385–396.

Berlin, James. 1988. "Rhetoric and Ideology in the Writing Class." *College English* 50: 477–94.

Brodkey, Linda. 1989. "On the Subjects of Class and Gender in 'The Literacy Letters'." *College English* 51: 125–141.

Caywood, Cynthia L., and Gillian R. Overing, ed. 1987. *Teaching Writing: Pedagogy, Gender, and Equity.* Albany: SUNY Press.

Flynn, Elizabeth A. 1988. "Composing as a Woman." *College Composition and Communication* 39: 423–435.

France, Alan W. 1993. "Assigning Places: The Function of Introductory Composition as a Cultural Discourse." *College English* 55: 593–609.

Freire, Paulo. 1982. *Pedagogy of the Oppressed.* Trans. Myra Bergman Ramos. New York: Continuum.

Fulkerson, Richard. 1990. "Composition Theory in the Eighties: Axiological Consensus and Paradigmatic Diversity." *College Composition and Communication* 41: 409–429.

Hairston, Maxine. 1992. "Diversity, Ideology, and Teaching Writing." *College Composition and Communication* 43: 179–193.

Jarratt, Susan C. 1991. "Feminism and Composition: The Case for Conflict." *Contending with Words: Composition and Rhetoric in a Postmodern Age.* Ed. Patricia Harkin and John Schilb. New York: MLA. 105–123.

———. 1995. "Encounters with Jane Tompkins." *JAC: A Journal of Composition Theory* 15: 351–356.

Kelly, Lou. 1973. "Toward Competence and Creativity in an Open Class." *College English* 34. Rpt. in *Ideas for English 101: Teaching Writing in College.* Ed. Richard Ohmann and W. B. Coley. Urbana: NCTE, 1975. 2–18.

Lazere, Donald. 1995. "Teaching the Conflicts about Wealth and Poverty." *Left Margins: Cultural Studies and Composition Pedagogy.* Ed. Karen Fitts and Alan W. France. Albany: SUNY Press. 189–205.

Lynn, Steven. 1987. "Reading the Writing Process: Toward a Theory of Current Pedagogies." *College English* 49: 902–910.

Myers, Greg. 1986. "Reality, Consensus, and Reform in the Rhetoric of Composition Teaching." *College English* 48: 154–174.

Tompkins, Jane. 1990. "Pedagogy of the Distressed." *College English* 52: 653–660.

Woods, William F. 1981. "Composition Textbooks and Pedagogical Theory 1960–1980." *College English* 43: 393–409.

peer evaluation

The term peer evaluation enjoys widespread, often casual, use in composition studies, and yet the meanings assigned to it are as diverse and mutable as the field itself. The activity of evaluation is equated with sharing, editing, reviewing, responding, empathizing, sympathizing, inquiring, helping, critiquing, criticizing, tutoring, describing, writing, correcting, fixing, and facilitating. Peers have been variously represented as, among other things, fellow writers, surrogate teachers, members of a general audience, members of a specific discourse community, critical readers, sympathetic responders, apprentices, and masters.

In its most practical terms, peer evaluation is a pragmatic time saver affording instructors a way to "get the job done" that conserves time and energy while also effectively serving students. This "works good" reasoning has, according to Karen Spear, resulted in "[o]ne of the most perplexing gaps between theory and practice in teaching writing," the use of peer response groups (i). Located within the space of this gap, however, is a diverse body of publication made coherent by its persistent attention to the relationships of writers, readers, teachers, texts, and institutions as they are manifested in discussions of production, authenticity, ownership, community, authority, and meaning.

In many classrooms, peer evaluation is a way to teach standards of productivity and correctness traditionally associated with essay literacy. In Alan Cooper's "group correction," students "strenuously confine themselves to the features at issue: no correcting spelling or agreement during a session on FRAG's, R-O's and c.s.'s" (347). Through the process of writing and editing, "the student learns about his own susceptibility to committing these basic errors, and about his ability to detect them in the writing of his classmates" (347). In his discussion of the limitations of peer evaluation, Michael Graner identifies his and others' concern that peer evaluation is often nothing more than "small talk or social chit-chat," (41) or a case of "the blind leading the blind with unskilled editors guiding inexperienced writers in a process neither understands well" (40). Alternatively, he presents peer evaluation as a "revision workshop" that does not require teachers to "surrender any classroom control" and allows them to "supervise the group and ensure that the task is being completed" (43).

Issues of authority and control have been addressed very differently by others who see peer evaluation as generative of an egalitarian community of writers within the existing academic structure. Donald Murray presents peer evaluation as a way to develop critical thinking in "a community where apprentices and masters work side by side in the practice of their craft" (187). As writers "struggle to make their meanings clear to others" by "put[ting] on the skins of particular readers" they "find out what [they] mean" (189). Additionally, Murray represents peer evaluation as a means of diminishing the authority of the teacher and encouraging students "to learn to appeal to many individual readers and to handle their contradictory responses" (190) in order to "develop their own meanings and their own voices" (187). Murray's position is slightly modified in Peter Elbow's "teacherless classroom," where peer evaluation is a way to foster learning without teaching. Elbow's goal is to enable "the writer to come as close as possible to being able to see and experience his own words *through* seven or more people. That's all" (77). This experience allows the material in the writer's head "to be restructured by what the other person says" (50) in an effort to produce ideas or points of view unavailable to the writer before peer evaluation.

James Moffett views the term classroom learning as an oxymoron, describing peer evaluation as an opportunity to provide instruction that is "individual, relevant, and timely" by engaging students in "authentic kinds of discourse such as exist outside of school" (193). Moffett presents peers as a "natural audience," in contrast to the instructor, whose often authoritarian role is "potent enough to distort the writer-audience relationship" (193), the effect of which is "to dissociate writing from real intent and pervert the rhetorical process into a weird irony" (194). Within Ken Macrorie's "helping circle," peer evaluation is a means of promoting self-sufficiency within individual writers by training them to develop an internal critic. While Macrorie shares with Murray, Elbow, and Moffett a concern for the development of writers' critical faculties, his understanding of how these faculties are generated differs from their positions in an important way. While the others emphasize the active and continuous role authentic readers and their responses play in peer evaluation, Macrorie presents the dialogue of writers and readers as being important only to the extent that it promotes a sensitivity to, rather than a dependence on, responses from readers. Evaluative standards established by the interaction of writers and readers are then to be internalized by the writers so that they "can be better critics of their own work when they are alone with it" (88). Macrorie is careful to emphasize that the writer, whether assisted by others or not, is "ultimately responsible for his sentences" (88).

Others have challenged the notion that peer evaluation should emphasize authentic, uncritical, responses to student writing. Many who are committed to the use of peer evaluation as a way to familiarize writers with audience expectations are, nonetheless, suspicious of what they perceive to be excessively sympathetic reading practices. Asserting that students too often create "coherence out of incoherence" in the writing of their peers (124), Elizabeth Flynn presents peer evaluation as an activity that "necessitates sophisticated reading skills, the ability not only to comprehend but also to critically assess writing that is frequently incoherent, unfocused" (126). Critical assessment, Flynn points out, is often lacking in students whose authentic responses frequently defer to the authority of the text. Peer readers, therefore, "must be trained to recognize incoherence, and the training must be rigorous enough to counter their conditioned expectations about the nature of written texts" (127). Joan Wauters also promotes a more critical approach, presenting "nonconfrontational critique" as a form of peer evaluation that addresses some of the problems she identifies in authentic response centered approaches. In Wauters's practice, "editing teams" respond to a writer's draft without the writer being present, which "allows [the editing teams] adequate privacy for more deliberate responses" (160).

Further complicating issues of authenticity and authority in peer evaluation are theories of collaborative learning and social construction that represent writing as a primarily social act involving not just the immediate classroom communities formed by individual writers and their peer readers but a much broader and larger community. Kenneth Bruffee, whose *A Short Course in Writing* was the first influential composition textbook based on collaborative learning, cites peer evaluation as a type of collaborative learning situation in which, "students learn to describe the organizational structure of a peer's paper, paraphrase it, and comment both on what seems well done and what the author might do to improve the work" (1984, 637–638). Such an exercise "makes students aware that writing is a social artifact, like the thought that produces it" and "provides a social context in which students can experience and practice the kinds of conversation valued by college teachers" within "a community of status equals: peers" (642). According to Bruffee (1993), "[l]earning to make sound evaluative judgments about each other's writing and explain them effectively is what peer review is all about" (170).

In affirming the power of social construction and collaborative learning theories, John Trimbur returns to issues of student-teacher authority, once again presenting peer evaluation as a means of redistributing what he believe to be an uneven distribution of power and authority in the classroom. Rather than returning to individual autonomy as a means of restructuring classroom authority, Trimbur asserts that "consensus need not inevitably result in accommodation" (603). He asserts that a "fear of consensus often betrays fear of peer group influence—a fear that students will keep their own records, work out collective norms, and take action" and that such a position is "implicitly teacher-centered and authoritarian" (604). "A rehabilitated notion of consensus in collaborative learning," he writes, "can provide students with exemplary motives to imagine alternative worlds and transformations of social life and labor. In its deferred and utopian form, consensus offers a way to orchestrate dissensus and to turn the conversation in the collaborative classroom into a heterotopia of voices" (615).

Carrie Shively Leverenz, however, questions Trimbur's assertion that students can escape the normalizing function of consensus by "agreeing to disagree." She suggests that the traditional authoritative and hierarchical structures of academic culture represented in peer evaluation are so pervasive that true peer relationships among students may not be possible (271). Paul Heilker's Foucauldian analysis of writing groups more fully radicalizes the position held by Leverenz, describing the innocent circle of desks often accompanying peer evaluation as "the collaborative composition cell" (5). According to Heilker, peer evaluation is a practice that "actually disempowers students and does so in an especially efficient and ingenious manner: by having them do the work of making each other yet even more visible" (9).

Despite (or, in many cases, as a result of) the application of theory to practice, it seems the use of peer evaluation in teaching writing remains a "perplexing gap" in composition studies. While some may fret over the patchwork of (not always new) terms, practices and theories that constitute the meanings of peer evaluation, the resulting state of indeterminacy will continue to serve the field well in animating practitioners, theorists and researchers to construct even more meanings for an exigent element in the theory-practice of our field.

Kurt P. Kearcher
The University of Toledo

Works Cited

Bruffee, Kenneth. 1984. "Collaborative Learning and the 'Conversation of Mankind.' " *College English* 46: 635–652.

———. 1993. *A Short Course in Writing*. 4th ed. New York: Harper Collins College Publishers.

Cooper, Alan. 1986. "Daily Writing for Peer Response." *College Composition and Communication* 37: 346–348.

Elbow, Peter. 1973. *Writing without Teachers*. New York: Oxford University Press.

Flynn, Elizabeth A. 1984. "Students as Readers of Their Classmates' Writing: Some Implications for Peer Critiquing." *The Writing Instructor* 3: 120–128.

Graner, Michael H. 1987. "Revision Workshops: An Alternative to Peer Editing Groups." *English Journal* 76: 40–45.

Heilker, Paul. 1994. *"Discipline and Punish* and Process and Paradigms" (or Foucault, Visibility, (Dis)Empowerment, and the Construction of Composition Studies). *Composition Studies* 22: 4–13.

Leverenz, Carrie Shively. 1994. "Peer Response in the Multicultural Classroom: Dissensus—A Dream (Deferred)." *Composition Theory for the Postmodern Classroom.* Ed. Gary A. Olson and Sidney I. Dobrin. Albany, NY: State University of New York Press. 254–273.

Macrorie, Ken. 1968. *Writing to be Read.* New York: Hayden.

Moffett, James. 1968. *Teaching the Universe of Discourse.* Boston: Houghton Mifflin.

Murray, Donald M. 1985. *A Writer Teaches Writing.* 2nd ed. Boston: Houghton Mifflin,

Spear, Karen. 1988. *Sharing Writing: Peer Response Groups in English Classes.* Portsmouth, NH: Heinemann, Boynton/Cook.

Trimbur, John. 1989. "Consensus and Difference in Collaborative Learning." *College English* 51: 602–616.

Wauters, Joan K. 1988. "Non-Confrontational Critiquing Pairs: An Alternative to Verbal Peer Response Groups." *The Writing Instructor* 7: 156–166.

portfolio

While "portfolios have dominated discussion about writing assessment and classroom evaluation" since 1989 (Black *et al.* 1), Patricia Belanoff and Marcia Dickson emphasize that the nature of portfolios is local and situated: "The very creation of a portfolio system, embedded as it inevitably is within the academic context of a unique institution ensures its individual character" (xix). Hence, according to Kathleen Blake Yancey (1992b), portfolios can operate "as cultural artifacts, as collection devices, as instruments of process, as assessment tools, as means of education reform, as resources for teachers, as pictures of and guides for curriculum" (12).

Portfolios serve as collection sites for student work, but they are not merely static depositories. Catherine D'Aoust depicts the "artistic writing portfolio" as "a collection of writing samples, garnered over time, illustrating exemplary student writing" (40). The "process writing portfolio" contains "completed works, unfinished work, successful texts, texts that were abandoned, ideas for writing" (41).

In 1978, James E. Ford and Gregory Larkin depict portfolios as a programmatic remedy for the symptom of grade inflation. Portfolios "cure" the "problem of the rogue teacher" who does not teach the required material, and they "protect the integrity of letter grades" (954). Later, Peter Elbow and Belanoff (1991) temper Ford and Larkin's medical rhetoric with a rhetoric of pragmatic problem-solving and improved assessment methods. Portfolios at SUNY-Stony Brook serve as a "substitute" for single-sample writing proficiency exams. Replacing proficiency exams with portfolios, they argue, enables teachers to implement a kind of "quality control" without sacrificing process-based principles of revision and reflection (5). In addition, portfolios offer "an antidote" to teacher isolation and promote "community and collaboration" among teachers and students (Belanoff and Elbow 31; 27).

The community fostered by portfolios has sometimes been represented as an industrial or contentious space. Peter Elbow refers to portfolios "as a mechanism for teachers to work together on evaluating student writing in order to hammer out some communal agreements or community standards" (xi). In addition, the group portfolio process helps teachers openly acknowledge the previously hidden chaos and tension that accompanies evaluation: "It's a relief for us to see all this disparity of judgment out on the floor as interaction between people—as heads butting against other heads" (Elbow and Belanoff 1986, 338).

Furthermore, portfolios are consistently portrayed as being powerfully transformative. Portfolios alter traditional pedagogical authority relations, encouraging the teacher to occupy "the role he or she actually fulfills, the friend and mentor who has a great stake in preparing the student to pass the portfolio" (Ford and Larkin 952). Portfolios transform evaluation in the basic writing classroom as well, Irwin Weiser concludes, because they remove "the often punitive element that comes from grading work before students have practice and begin to master the composing process" (100). Moreover, portfolios, Roberta Camp asserts, encourage reflection and metacognition and empower teachers and peers "to look back at their writing and to discover what they see and what they value in it" (78).

Indeed, the metaphor of "change" appears repeatedly in the discourse on portfolios. Portfolios, Kathleen Blake Yancey (1992a) asserts, enable teachers to become agents of change because they open up "new ways to learn to write; new ways to think about the teaching of writing; new ways to read and understand our students, ourselves, and our curricula; and new ways to describe and then report on what we find" (vii). Portfolios "are about changing what teachers and students learn from classroom writing," writes Catherine Lucas, since they profoundly shift teachers' and students' attitudes toward evaluation. Lucas further claims portfolios are nothing short of revolutionary: "nothing since the advent of small-group collaborative learning has carried such potential to revolutionize the teaching and assessment of writing" (1). Carl R. Lovitt and Art Young similarly find that portfolios in a writing across the disciplines program can be "subversive" since they "fundamentally challenge the way teachers customarily do business" (339). In short, portfolios challenge the individualistic, product-oriented paradigm that drives educational culture and create an "authentic" and direct means of writing assessment (Wiggins 703–704).

Portfolios also serve as faculty development tools, creating spaces for teacher development, allowing new teachers "room to breathe and grow" (Burnham 125–126). Wendy Bishop contends that portfolios may prove interesting to teacher-trainers "because they promise an evaluation method consistent with process-teaching practices" (216). Nevertheless, portfolios have been portrayed as being potentially disorienting for inexperienced teachers. Bishop, for instance, says that new teachers' unfamiliarity with portfolios may cause them to feel they are " 'going up the creek without a canoe' " (226). Like Bishop, Yancey (1994) warns against "a hasty approach to portfolios" by new teaching assistants, arguing that if "portfolios are to 'work,' certain kinds of support are required: adequate time for preparation; resources; and guidance" (216).

In addition, some advocates of portfolio assessment warn that widespread enthusiasm for the concept may inevitably be its downfall. Marjorie Roemer, Lucille M. Schultz, and Russell K. Durst argue that portfolios are best suited to a "personal, local, small-scale" situation that involves small groups or team negotiations. They warn that "[w]hen such designs are 'adopted' by larger bodies (school districts, university programs, whole systems, state or provincial school boards), they become monolithically imposed, and while the forms may be enacted, the cooperative spirit of the idea may be lost" (457). Edward Kearns has critically analyzed what he calls the "portfolio bandwagon," which he claims "got underway at Stony Brook in 1986" (50). Kearns wishes to remain on the "running board of the portfolio bandwagon" because he believes that it "got started on spurious grounds, namely a series of unexamined assertions against existing practices [impromptu writing exams]" (56). Suspicious of the "portfolio parade," Kearns questions the "reliability" of portfolios (50), a concern Edward White shares as well. White sees portfolios as "a collection concept that only appears to be a measurement concept" (538) and calls for portfolio advocates to find ways to make portfolio assessment "reliable and valid enough so that the measurement result can become part of the national assessment agenda, can yield usable data, can connect with and challenge traditional testing theory, can help writing programs demonstrate their value in more than anecdotal ways" (539). Portfolio practitioners, he warns, must pay more attention to reliability or else portfolios will be no "more than a passing fad, attractive and responsive to process theories, but too expensive and unreliable to be depended upon for serious decisions" (539). Because portfolios have become so popular, they risk becoming commodified, pre-packaged into "dumbed-down" kits. Hence, Liz Hamp-Lyons and William Condon caution that a portfolio assessment system must be critically self-aware, "must continually be questioned" by "1) prompting readers to be aware of the process they are going through; 2) gathering appropriate data about that process; and 3) making the changes or accommodations which each new iteration shows are necessary" (177).

In sum, portfolios appear to be presently caught in a growing tension between practitioners concerned with the classroom, students, and practices, and writing programs and assessment specialists who focus on the overarching problems of measurement and meaningful data. Only the test of time will tell if portfolio as an all-purpose assessment tool will be relegated to the institutional closet or will remain a vital part of the everyday business of teaching and assessing writing.

Eileen E. Schell
Syracuse University

Works Cited

Belanoff, Patricia, and Marcia Dickson, ed. 1991. *Portfolios: Process and Product.* Portsmouth, NH: Boynton/Cook.

Belanoff, Patricia, and Peter Elbow. 1986. "Using Portfolios to Increase Collaboration and Community in a Writing Program." *WPA: Journal of Writing Program Administration* 9: 27–40.

Bishop, Wendy. 1991. "Going up the Creek without a Canoe: Using Portfolios to Train New Teachers of College Writing." In Belanoff and Dickson. 215–228.

Black, Laurel, Donald Daiker, Jeffrey Sommers, and Gail Stygall, ed. 1994. *New Directions in Portfolio Assessment: Reflective Practice, Critical Theory, and Large-Scale Scoring.* Portsmouth, NH: Boynton/Cook.

Burnham, Christopher. 1986. "Portfolio Evaluation: Room to Breathe and Grow." *Training the New Teacher of College Composition.* Ed. Charles Bridge. Urbana, IL: NCTE. 125–138.

Camp, Roberta. 1992. "Portfolio Reflections in Middle and Secondary Classrooms." In Yancey 1992a. 61–79.

D'Aoust, Catherine. 1992. "Portfolios: Process for Students and Teachers." In Yancey 1992a. 39–48.

Elbow, Peter. 1991. "Foreword." In Belanoff and Dickson. ix–xvi.

Elbow, Peter, and Pat Belanoff. 1986. "Portfolios as a Substitute for Proficiency Examinations." *College Composition and Communication* 37: 336–339.

———. 1991. "State University of New York at Stony Brook Portfolio-based Evaluation Program." In Belanoff and Dickson. 3–16.

Ford, James E., and Gregory Larkin. 1978. "The Portfolio System: An End to Backsliding Writing Standards." *College English* 39: 950–955.

Hamp-Lyons, Liz, and William Condon. 1993. "Questioning Assumptions about Portfolio-Based Assessment." *College Composition and Communication* 44: 176–190.

Kearns, Edward. 1993. "On the Running Board of the Portfolio Bandwagon." *WPA: Journal of Writing Program Administration* 16: 50–58.

Lovitt, Carl R., and Art Young. 1994. "Portfolios in the Disciplines: Sharing Knowledge in the Contact Zone." In Black *et al.* 334–346.

Lucas, Catherine. 1992. "Introduction: Writing Portfolios-Changes and Challenges." In Yancey 1992a. 1–12.

Roemer, Marjorie, Lucille M. Schultz, and Russel K. Durst. 1991. "Portfolios and the Process of Change." *College Composition and Communication* 42: 455–469.

Weiser, Irwin. 1992. "Portfolio Practice and Assessment for Collegiate Basic Writers." In Yancey 1992a. 89–102.

Wiggins, Grant. 1989. "A True Test: Toward More Authentic and Equitable Assessment." *Phi Delta Kappan* 70: 703–713.

White, Edward M. 1992. Review of *Portfolios: Process and Product*, by Patricia Belanoff and Marcia Dickson, ed. *College Composition and Communication* 43: 537–539.

Yancey, Kathleen Blake, ed. 1992a. *Portfolios in the Writing Classroom.* Urbana, IL: NCTE.

———. 1992b. "Teacher's Stories: Notes toward a Portfolio Pedagogy." In Yancey 1992a. 12–19.

———. 1994. "Make Haste Slowly: Graduate Teaching Assistants and Portfolios." In Black *et al.* 210–218.

power

The term *power* is highly visible in the title of Peter Elbow's *Writing with Power.* Elbow theorizes that power in writing occurs when "[t]he words so well embody what they express that when readers encounter the words they feel they are encountering the objects or ideas themselves, not words" (280). For Elbow, then, power manifests itself in an objective relationship between words and the "non-linguistic reality" those words represent (94).

More frequently, though, *power* is defined as a feature of social relations, one often construed in terms of "empowerment." Carolyn Matalene defines the act of "empowering" a student writer as "valuing her and her experience" (258). Students are said to gain "satisfaction and power" from "shar[ing] experience of some importance" (Dixon 6) or from "[s]haping personal knowledge for public communication" (Matalene 260).

Conscious of the imbalance of power between student and teacher in any classroom, many critics have spoken out against the notion of "empowerment." For instance, Lester Faigley, in "Judging Writing, Judging Selves," argues that the idea of empowerment "avoids the question of how exactly teachers are to give students power" (410). Because "talk of empowerment" relies upon an outmoded notion of the self as "a developing rational consciousness" rather than the prevailing notion of the self as "discursively produced and discursively bounded," Faigley says, "power" is mistakenly seen as something that teachers can "confer . . . as an essential quality of [students'] makeup" (411). Instead, he insists, we should see power as being "exercised in a network of social relations and reconstituted in each act of communicating" (411).

This view of power as a systemic force has made its way into composition studies with the influx of poststructuralist thought, mainly via the works of French philosopher Michel Foucault, who defines power as "a mode of action which does not act directly and immediately on others." Rather, "power" is capable of "guiding the possibility of conduct and putting in order the possible outcome" (219–221). One may analyze power relationships,

Foucault says, by concentrating on carefully defined institutions and the system of social networks within them. "Power" thus exerts an ineluctable hold or influence upon the thoughts and actions of those within any institution (broadly defined). Robert Scholes has this sense of power in mind when he argues that the aim of English studies should be to "help students recognize the power texts have over them" (39). According to Scholes, though, power can reside not only in texts but also in individuals who are able to produce effective texts. Scholes says that "we move from a submission of textual authority in reading, through a sharing of textual power in interpretation, toward an assertion of power through opposition in criticism [i.e., writing]" (39). Scholes' notion of power is consistent with that of Steven Mailloux, who notes that "power is not simply a negative force, obstructing, suppressing, canceling the energy of action. It also functions in a positive way, creating, enabling, energizing various sociopolitical activities" (59–60). That this Foucauldian notion of "power" is not merely a negative force is asserted, as well, by Faigley in *Fragments of Rationality*, where he states that "[i]ndividuals are not so much 'repressed' as they are 'shaped' by the technologies of power" (145).

As this sense of the term has been adopted by compositionists, power has come to be constructed as a cultural force whose precise definition is conflated with those of other terms. The index of Patricia Donahue and Ellen Quandahl's collection *Reclaiming Pedagogy*, for example, cross-lists "Power" with "Culture," "Ideology," and "Politics" (177), and in Carolyn Hill's *Writing from the Margins*, under "Power" we are told to see also "Political action" and "Politics" (282). This broad-based notion of power is also apparent in James Berlin's "Rhetoric and Ideology in the Writing Class." According to Berlin, the term *ideology* necessarily "includes conceptions of how power should ... be distributed in society. Power here means political force but covers as well social forces in everyday contacts. Power is an intrinsic part of ideology, defined and reinforced by it, determining ... who can act and what can be accomplished" (479). For Berlin, as well as for Hill and for Donahue and Quandahl, then, "power" is a cultural force, but its precise definition is caught up in and mingled with such terms as "ideology" and "politics."

The most notable analyses of power relationships in the classroom have been undertaken by feminists scholars and by followers of Brazilian educator Paulo Freire. Freire's notion of a "liberatory" or "critical" pedagogy (employed by Ira Shor, Henry Giroux, bell hooks, and others) is defined by Patricia Bizzell as a Marxist-influenced theory of education that seeks "both to delegitimate forms of pedagogy that imitate and generate unjust social power relations, and to delineate [those] that imitate and generate egalitarian social power relations" (55). But, like most who address power in the classroom, Bizzell is aware of "a theoretical impasse" that arises: "[W]e want to serve the common good with the power we possess by virtue of our position as teachers, and yet we are deeply suspicious of any exercise of power in the classroom" (54). Bizzell's use of "power" here is roughly synonymous with "authority"; it is a quality that inheres in the role of the teacher and which hinders true collaboration (58–59).

This Marxist-influenced concept of power has also been assumed by feminist compositionists. In referring to the commonalities between Marxist and feminist thought, Elizabeth A. Flynn believes that attempts by instructors "to bring about the conditions to promote powerful writing by women students" are often hindered by such societal conditions as "patriarchal oppression" (148–149). Flynn suggests that if female students are ever going to be able "[t]o write with power and authority," then a necessary "change in the social order, a shift in the balance of power" must first occur (149). Flynn's notion of "power," which at first seems merely synonymous with "authority," also encompasses cultural and political "forces beyond the class-room." On the level of classroom practices aimed at promoting this transfor-mation of the social order, Catherine E. Lamb proposes "a feminist theory of power" for the composition classroom. By placing "an emphasis on cooperation, collaboration, shared leadership, and integration of the cognitive and affective which is characteristic of feminist pedagogy," Lamb is respond-ing to the privileged place of "monologic argument" in the composition curriculum (11–15). Her theory of power provides "a feminist response to conflict"—an alternative to the "adversarial method" of conflict resolution—that stresses mediation and negotiation (13). Power, for Lamb, is not some-thing possessed by an individual; rather, it emerges from the social interactions of individuals; it "maintains [the] space in which people act and speak" (15–21) and is, as Susan M. Hubbuch explains, "a 'neutral fact' of any and all social actions" (43).

According to Susan C. Jarratt, "[t]hough educational institutions enforce the power and control of the existing social order, they also allow students and teachers to challenge, oppose, and resist those forces" (118). Power, thus, is inscribed as an inevitable problematic in composition studies.

Donald E. Bushman
University of North Carolina at Wilmington

Works Cited

Berlin, James. 1988. "Rhetoric and Ideology in the Writing Class." *College English* 50: 477–494.

Bizzell, Patricia. 1991. "Power, Authority, and Critical Pedagogy." *Journal of Basic Writing* 10: 54–70.

Dixon, John L. 1975. *Growth through English: A Report Based on the Dartmouth Seminar 1966.* 3rd edit. Oxford: Oxford University Press.

Donahue, Patricia, and Ellen Quandahl, ed. 1989. *Reclaiming Pedagogy: The Rhetoric of the Classroom.* Carbondale: Southern Illinois University Press.

Elbow, Peter. 1981. *Writing with Power: Techniques for Mastering the Writing Process.* Oxford: Oxford University Press.

Faigley, Lester. 1989. "Judging Writing, Judging Selves." *College Composition and Communication* 40: 395–412.

———. 1992. *Fragments of Rationality: Postmodernity and the Subject of Composition.* Pittsburgh: University of Pittsburgh Press.

Flynn, Elizabeth A. 1991. "Composition Studies from a Feminist Perspective." *The Politics of Writing Instruction: Postsecondary.* Ed. Richard Bullock and John Trimbur. Portsmouth, NH: Boynton/Cook. 137–154.

Foucault, Michel. 1983. "Afterword: The Subject and Power." *Michel Foucault: Beyond Structuralism and Hermeneutics.* Ed. Hubert L. Dreyfus and Paul Rabinow. 2nd edit. Chicago: University of Chicago Press. 208–226.

Hill, Carolyn Ericksen. 1990. *Writing from the Margins: Power and Pedagogy for Teachers of Composition.* New York: Oxford University Press.

Hubbuch, Susan M. 1989–90. "Confronting the Power in Empowering Students." *The Writing Instructor* 9: 35–44.

Jarratt, Susan C. 1991. "Feminism and Composition: The Case for Conflict." *Contending with Words: Composition and Rhetoric in a Postmodern Age.* Ed. Patricia Harkin and John Schilb. New York: Modern Language Association. 105–123.

Lamb, Catherine E. 1991. "Beyond Argument in Feminist Composition." *College Composition and Communication* 42: 11–24.

Mailloux, Steven. 1989. *Rhetorical Power.* Ithaca: Cornell University Press.

Matalene, Carolyn. 1992. "Experience as Evidence: Teaching Students to Write Honestly and Knowledgeably about Public Issues." *Rhetoric Review* 10: 252–265.

Scholes, Robert. 1985. *Textual Power: Literary Theory and the Teaching of English.* New Haven: Yale University Press.

practice/praxis

In composition studies, practice is often joined with theory in a hierarchal binary in which theory informs practice but practice doesn't inform theory. According to Alice Roy, this view of practice as handmaiden to theory is often characterized by theory that privileges "the study and interpretation of texts . . . over the production of texts or the study of the language in which texts are produced" and by a particular set of practices: "skills-based, handbook-driven writing courses, . . . or modes-and-structures syllabuses, or literature-based 'writing courses' " (694–695). In his study of the discourse(s) of English, Burton Hatlen defines writing and teaching writing as practices largely marginalized by departmental focus on the study of a limited set of classic texts (796). Stephen M. North, too, contends that routine practice—an "ancient . . . hard-won" body of knowledge (16) that matches "standard problems . . . with standard sets of solutions" (40)—began to be devalued when composition became "Composition"—academic field, capital "C" (9): "[practice's] credibility, its power vis-a-vis other kinds of knowledge, has gradually, steadily, diminished" (22).

In opposition to this view of practice as subordinate to theory, many have constructed it as a form of inquiry. North, for example, argues that practice, or practitioners' lore, becomes inquiry by "produc[ing] 'new' knowledge": trying a new approach because the problem is unusual, or because the problem is standard but the usual solution is perceived to be inadequate, or because both the situation and the proposed solution are new (33). Recognizing practice as a mode of inquiry contributes to new understandings of knowledge making. "The irregular, ad hoc procedures of lore" are valuable, Patricia Harkin contends, because of their postdisciplinary "willingness to use, but refusal to be constrained by, existing institutional rules of knowledge production." Lore can subvert the tendency of disciplines to "look at what they recognize or, more precisely, see only what they recognize no matter where they look" (130–131). Ruth E. Ray argues that the new discourse of teacher research, by challenging the positivist research paradigm (53) and empowering teachers and students through collaboration (65), "illustrates a political reality: most significant changes in education occur not from the top down . . . but from the bottom up through the questioning and experimenting of teachers attempting to solve real problems in their own classrooms" (71).

Viewed from this perspective, changes in practice must change theory. According to James Berlin, solutions to the "most pressing issues facing us in English studies today" are being "situat[ed] . . . within the context of the classroom. . . . [T]his means that theory is something that teachers and students do, not something done *to* them" (vii–viii). This was not the case, though, in the 1970s when many took a consciously theoretical interest in the writing of students. Janet Emig's ground-breaking work in 1971 shifted attention from written products to the processes of writing, thus bringing teaching practices into sharper focus and clearing the way for later practitioner-theorists such as Sondra Perl and Nancy Sommers. These and other researchers, by redefining writing as a recursive and collaborative rather than linear and solitary process, created multiple opportunities for the teacher's intervention and guidance.

As Susan Miller has argued, however, new practices did not bring about new theory. In her view, " 'product' and 'process' share underlying assumptions about the 'problem' that each approach to teaching has addressed: student (and other) writers" (110–111). While "current-traditional" teaching practices were "basically corrective [and] remedial," designed for the "winnowing and indoctrination" of students (63), process-oriented practices— "multiple revisions, group work, and personal interactions"—reflect the existence of "cheap paper, ballpoint pens, word processors, and disposable textbooks" more than they reflect "a revolutionary idea that sets a new set of problems for the field" (106–107).

A "new set of problems" did arrive, however, in the 1990s when, as Patricia A. Sullivan and Donna J. Qualley point out, teachers found themselves in "an age of politics," with heightened interest in social contexts (rather than individual processes) of writing (viii). Patricia Bizzell's position is representative: "my postmodern conviction that value-neutral teaching is not possible . . . combine[s] with my ethical conviction . . . that value-neutral teaching is not desirable" (195). Her "pedagogy of persuasion, not coercion," she writes, consists of "modeling the practices of a participatory democracy, fostering civic virtue" (198).

A decisive contribution to the contemporary age of politics was Paulo Freire's introduction of *praxis* to composition studies in the early 1980s. For while practice almost inevitably is set off against theory, praxis erases this polarity through the means of dialectics. Raymond Williams contends that in its modern sense, developed in Hegelian and Marxist thought, "*praxis* is *practice* informed by *theory* and . . . less emphatically, *theory* informed by *practice*." Praxis thus restores theory and practice to one another, describing "a whole mode of activity in which, by analysis but only by analysis, *theoretical* and *practical* elements can be distinguished, but which is always a whole activity, to be judged as such" (318). The dialectic of theory and practice brought together as praxis—in David Kaufer and Gary Waller's inimitable formulation, "To read is to write is to read is to write is to read. Right?" (91)—is considered particularly powerful. According to Freire: "There is no true word that is not at the same time a praxis. Thus, to speak a true word is to transform the world" (75).

In the 1980s and 1990s the political left has argued that education is a powerful social institution which, if not a challenge to mainstream culture and ideology, will instead reproduce it. As Robert Con Davis has pointed out, the goal of those on the left is "to theorize but also to initiate radical social change through pedagogy, through what students are taught and how they are taught it." Those on the right, Davis continues, revile such practices as "exploiting a privileged position to satisfy ulterior (political) motives: [they reveal] the teacher-as-political-deviant" (249). In any case, the commitment to greater social and political equity through classroom practices is especially characteristic of feminists, marxists, multiculturalists, and other oppositional pedagogues.

Notice, for example, the focus on revolutionary activity in Adalaide Morris's description of feminist practice. It is, she writes, "founded in opposition to existing social relations and fueled in equal parts by anger and exhilaration." Feminists encourage students to "ask embarrassing questions" and "resist, refuse, and/or try to renegotiate given cultural definitions and values" (465). The desire to bring about social change through pedagogy is also reflected in Peter F. Murphy's definition of cultural studies, a Marxist scholarly method favoring an "intrinsically practice-oriented approach to knowledge." Cultural studies, he contends, "embraces history from the bottom up and celebrates the struggles embodied in those who organize against domination in its many forms" (37). Or, consider Gregory S. Jay's plan for breaking down, through multicultural and dialogical practices in teaching writing, our "oppressive nationalist ideology which is the nightmare side of the 'American dream'" (264). These oppositional pedagogues exemplify some of the more combative and challenging uses of practice in the current composition and rhetoric scene.

Practice has been defined in composition studies according to a range of uses and meanings. Writing in 1991, Sharon Crowley attributes many of the skirmishes between old and new practice(s), conservative and radical, to conflicting assumptions of modernism and postmodernism. In the previous decade, she argues, the scene of teaching writing was imagined as harmonious and communal, taking place in "an isolated, insulated classroom containing a teacher who administered and graded writing assignments and a group of students who carried out the assignments." By contrast, postmodernists construct classrooms populated by persons who "inevitably bring with them the patriarchal, racist, or classist discourses of the dominant culture."

Postmodernism's refigured classrooms and people have created new theories and practices, ones that "tolerate ambiguity, variety, and conflict instead of valuing clarity, identity, and harmony" (190–191).

Karen Fitts
Loyola College in Maryland

Works Cited

Berlin, James A. 1994. "Foreword." Downing vii–xii.

Bizzell, Patricia. 1994. "The Teacher's Authority: Negotiating Difference in the Classroom." Downing 194–201.

Crowley, Sharon. 1991. "Reimagining the Writing Scene: Curmudgeonly Remarks about *Contending with Words.*" Harkin and Schilb 189–197.

Davis, Robert Con. 1990. "A Manifesto for Oppositional Pedagogy: Freire, Bourdieu, Merod, and Graff." *Reorientations: Critical Theories and Pedagogies.* Ed. Bruce Henricksen and Thais E. Morgan. Urbana: University of Illinois Press. 248–267.

Downing, David B., ed. 1994. *Changing Classroom Practices: Resources for Literary and Cultural Studies.* Urbana: NCTE.

Emig, Janet. 1971. *The Composing Processes of Twelfth-Graders.* NCTE Research Report No. 13. Urbana: NCTE.

Freire, Paulo. 1982. *Pedagogy of the Oppressed.* Trans. Myra Bergman Ramos. New York: Continuum.

Harkin, Patricia. 1991. "The Postdisciplinary Politics of Lore." Harkin and Schilb 124–138.

Harkin, Patricia, and John Schilb, ed. 1991. *Contending with Words: Composition and Rhetoric in a Postmodern Age.* New York: MLA.

Hatlen, Burton. 1988. "Michel Foucault and the Discourse(s) of English." *College English* 50: 786–801.

Jay, Gregory S. 1991. "The End of 'American' Literature: Toward a Multicultural Practice." *College English* 53: 264–281.

Kaufer, David, and Gary Waller. 1985. "To Write Is to Read Is to Write, Right?" *Writing and Reading Differently: Deconstruction and the Teaching of Composition and Literature.* Ed. C. Douglas Atkins and Michael Johnson. Lawrence: University Press of Kansas. 66–92.

Miller, Susan. 1991. *Textual Carnivals: The Politics of Composition.* Carbondale: Southern Illinois University Press.

Morris, Adalaide. 1987. "Review: Locutions and Locations: More Feminist Theory and Practice, 1985." *College English* 49 (1987): 465–475.

Murphy, Peter F. 1992. "Cultural Studies as Praxis: A Working Paper." *College Literature* 19: 31–43.

North, Stephen M. 1987. *The Making of Knowledge in Composition: Portrait of an Emerging Field.* Upper Montclair, NJ: Boynton/Cook.

Perl, Sondra. 1980. "Understanding Composing." *College Composition and Communication* 31: 363–369. Rpt. Tate and Corbett 113–118.

Ray, Ruth E. 1993. *The Practice of Theory: Teacher Research in Composition.* Urbana: NCTE.

Roy, Alice. 1994. "Critical Literacy, Critical Pedagogy." *College English* 56: 693–702.

Sommers, Nancy. 1980. "Revision Strategies of Student Writers and Experienced Adult Writers." *College Composition and Communication* 31: 378–388. Rpt. Tate and Corbett 119–127.

Sullivan, Patricia A., and Donna J. Qualley, ed. 1994. *Pedagogy in the Age of Politics: Writing and Reading (in) the Academy.* Urbana: NCTE.

Tate, Gary, and Edward P. J. Corbett, ed. 1988. *The Writing Teacher's Sourcebook.* 2nd ed. New York: Oxford University Press.

Williams, Raymond. 1983. *Keywords: A Vocabulary of Culture and Society.* Rev. ed. New York: Oxford University Press.

process

Process entered into the lexicon of composition studies in the late 1960s and early 1970s as a method of writing instruction that relied heavily upon invention strategies. The process method developed in contrast to "current-traditional rhetoric," which tended to emphasize the correctness of the writer's text as a "product" and to disregard the creative and intellectual processes of the individual writer who created the text (Crowley). Consequently, process quickly came to mean "a critique (or even outright rejection) of traditional, product-driven, rules-based, correctness-obsessed writing instruction" (Tobin 5) that generated formulaic student papers. Process rebelled against this "feel-nothing, say-nothing language" (Macrorie 18) by focusing on the cultivation of the student's "authentic voice" (Stewart). As a result, "the focus in the teaching of writing" shifted from "a product-oriented, content-conscious. point of view to a process-oriented, holistic point of view" (Pianko 275).

Beyond such general methodological contours, early attempts to define process took place in a "terminological thicket" (Sommers 209). Theorists sought to define *the* composing process as an unvarying pattern rather than to examine the processes of individual writers. However, they were largely unsuccessful in their efforts because they used the same nomenclature to describe process as to describe product; they were able to identify stages of the product but not the operations of the process; and they failed to develop "the necessary vocabulary to adequately discuss the psychological and intellectual operations of the composing process" (Sommers 209–210). Their efforts demonstrated the need for a research model that would raise important questions about writers' composing processes and that would lead theorists "to ask basic ontological questions of how the process differs from the product" (Sommers 211).

Expressivists like William Coles, Peter Elbow, Ken Macrorie, Donald Murray, and Donald Stewart argued for a definitional model that associated process with a writer's effort "to discover meaning in experience and communicate it" (Murray 21). Exploration of the self through language was the central goal of any writer's composing process (Murray 26), and this process of self-discovery was revealed in the development of the writer's personal ability to create meaningful relationships among the ideas presented within the writer's text (Gorrell). One consequence of this perspective is that process pedagogy and personal writing often came to be linked "in practice and perception" (Tobin 6).

The importing of ideas from cognitive and developmental psychology into composition studies during the 1970s eventually moved the expressive model from the realm of personal explorations and self-discovery to a consideration of the thought processes underlying all creative activities. Thus, process became associated with an effort to understand metacognition. A leading advocate of this approach was Janet Emig, who used a process model based on case-study methods and think-aloud protocols to examine how writers actually composed. By far, the most extensive influence on the cognitive model of process emerged from the work of Linda Flower and John R. Hayes, who sought to examine "writing behaviors and concomitant mental activities" (Pianko 277). Flower and Hayes discussed ways of combining problem- solving strategies with critical inquiry strategies as a means for students to coordinate and carry out the act of composition. Frank D'Angelo presented a similar perspective by transforming *topoi* into cognitive strategies. The underlying assumption was that cognitive structures and conceptual processes are related (Stallard).

The cognitive model gave a scientific base to composition studies (Voss 279), but it was criticized for oversimplifying the dynamics of the writing process. Further, both the cognitive and the expressive models came under fire for focusing on the composing processes of individual writers while ignoring the social and cultural influences shaping those writers' identities. Theorists such as David Bartholomae, James Berlin, Patricia Bizzell, Kenneth Bruffee, and Marilyn Cooper advocated a social view of the writing process that reflected a postmodern sense of multicultural influences and of anti-foundational epistemologies. This perspective, generally called social con-structionism or social-epistemic rhetoric, maintains that knowledge and all meaning-making activities are the product of social interaction. As a conse-quence, the social-epistemic model of process introduces the writer to a dialogic pedagogy based on discourse communities and the construction of knowledge within those groups. In social constructionism, writers come to understand the writing process through group interactions, consensus build-ing, and collaborative learning, but some theorists, such as Paolo Freire, Ivan Illich, Stanley Aronowitz, and Henry Giroux, argue that this pedagogical approach merely replicates existing power structures and encourages social elitism and accommodation to the existing order (Ryan). For these theorists, often identified with the concept of "liberatory" or "radical" pedagogy (Ward 91), instruction in writing as a process should be based on "dialogic methods that attempt to subvert the traditional form of education as a 'depositing' of information in students" (Ward 91). In a liberatory pedagogy, the social process model of writing instruction works toward encouraging the student to examine and ultimately transform the social structures, "including the social structure of schooling" (Ward 95), that are oppressive in enforcing conformity and hegemony.

Irene Ward states that the expressivist, social-epistemic, and liberatory perspectives "often assume varying and sometimes contradictory notions," yet "all of these perspectives are considered part of composition's 'process' paradigm" (129).

Recently, reevaluations of the "process paradigm" have been undertaken by theorists seeking to understand and evaluate the legacy of this influential concept. Charles Bazerman questions whether the process movement was ever truly successful in addressing the ontological question of how process differs from product. As he states, "The distinction and/or relation between process and content of writing is as slippery and dangerous as that other ancient binary chestnut of the arts of representation: form and content" (140). Gregory Ulmer, William A. Covino, and Thomas Kent have applied poststructuralist and deconstructionist ideas to composition pedagogy "to devise a postprocess, postmodern theory for composition studies" (Ward 130). The effort is to redefine earlier models of epistemology, language, and communication in light of poststructuralist theories. Kent, for example, argues that "many of our most influential theories of discourse production and analysis can explain satisfactorily neither the nature of language nor how the effects of language are produced" (505). Lad Tobin contends that the process movement opened up for investigation and critique many of the concepts central to poststructural theorists in the 1990s. Without the process movement, issues of the decentering of teacher authority, the hegemony of social conventions, and the social aims of discourse would not be as accessible to contemporary theorists. In recontextualizing process within the poststructural 1990s, when "the writing process movement has begun to get squeezed by the past and the future, by the right and the left" (5), Tobin considers its legacy an essential defining element within newer theories of the postmodern era. In a practical vein, Tobin argues, too, that many of the fundamental beliefs of the writing process movement—"that writing should be taught as a process, that writing can generate as well as record thought, that students write best when they care about and choose their topics, that good writing is strongly voiced, that a premature emphasis on correctness can be counterproductive"—"continue to hold power for most writing teachers and students" (7). The result is "an odd though not unusual discontinuity between theory and practice" in which "the writing process movement, and particularly its emphasis in expressivism, is frequently dismissed in contemporary scholarly books, journal articles, and conference papers, while it is still embraced by huge numbers of classroom teachers" (7).

Christina Murphy
Texas Christian University

Works Cited

Bazerman, Charles. 1994. *Constructing Experience.* Carbondale: Southern Illinois University Press.

Crowley, Sharon. 1977. "Components of the Composing Process." *College Composition and Communication* 28: 166–169.

D'Angelo, Frank. 1975. *A Conceptual Theory of Rhetoric.* Cambridge: Winthrop Publishers.

Emig, Janet. 1971. *The Composing Processes of Twelfth Graders.* NCTE Research Report No. 13. Urbana: National Council of Teachers of English.

Flower, Linda, and John R. Hayes. 1980. "A Cognitive Process Theory of Writing." *College Composition and Communication* 31: 365–387.

Gorrell, Robert M. 1983. "How to Make Mulligan Stew: Process and Product Again." *College Composition and Communication* 34: 272–277.

Kent, Thomas. 1989. "Beyond System: The Rhetoric of Paralogy." *College English* 51: 492–507.

Macrorie, Ken. 1970. *Uptaught.* New York: Hayden.

Murray, Donald M. 1970. "The Interior View: One Writer's Philosophy of Composition." *College Composition and Communication* 16: 21–26.

Pianko, Sharon. 1979. "Reflection: A Critical Component of the Composing Process." *College Composition and Communication* 30: 275–278.

Ryan, Howard. 1991. "The Whys of Teaching Composition: Social Visions." *Freshman English News* 19.3: 9–17.

Sommers, Nancy. 1978. "Response to Sharon Crowley." *College Composition and Communication* 29: 209–211.

Stallard, Charles. 1976. "Composing: A Cognitive Process Theory." *College Composition and Communication* 27: 181–184.

Stewart, Donald C. 1972. *The Authentic Voice: A Pre-Writing Approach to Student Writing.* Dubuque: Brown.

Tobin, Lad. 1994. "Introduction: How the Writing Process Was Born—And Other Conversion Narratives." *Taking Stock: The Writing Process Movement in the '90s.* Ed. Lad Tobin and Thomas Newkirk. Portsmouth: Boynton/Cook Heinemann. 1–14.

Tobin, Lad, and Thomas Newkirk, ed. 1994. *Taking Stock: The Writing Process Movement in the '90s.* Portsmouth: Boynton/Cook Heinemann.

Voss, Ralph. 1983. "Janet Emig's *The Composing Processes of Twelfth Graders*: A Reassessment." *College Composition and Communication* 34: 278–283.

Ward, Irene. 1994. *Literacy, Ideology, and Dialogue.* Albany: State University of New York Press.

reading

Within composition scholarship, reading has been represented as (1) a skill necessary to the writing process, (2) an epistemic act, (3) a writing strategy for generating further texts, (4) a social act, and (5) a deconstructive act. The complex interactions between reading and writing that manifest themselves in the act of composing can be seen in the wide range of implied definitions of the term.

Many studies of composing processes imply that reading is a necessary skill used by writers in evaluating how well their own texts realize an intention, or as a way to edit for error or mistranscription (Perl, Pianko, and Bridwell). These studies define reading (within the writing process) as an important orienting function; as Margaret Atwell explains, reading during writing enables writers to adhere to global text plans resulting in organized and coherent prose. Likewise, Donald Murray defines reading as a kind of generative writing strategy, noting that writers act as their own "first readers," reading and re-reading their own prose to evaluate the content, form, and language of the material they produce. These researchers define reading and writing as undeniably connected, interdependent processes.

Reading is also defined in composition literature as a process for "creating new meanings" by engaging with texts, "meanings that did not exist independently before either in the mind of the author or of the reader" (Sternglass 151). Christina Haas defines reading in terms of constructing meaning out of language—the construction of "complex understandings woven out of textual cues, prior knowledge, social convention, and cultural expectations" (21). This definition of reading builds on reading-to-write tasks described by Linda Flower *et al.*—tasks that are familiar to academic settings and require incorporating existing texts into a novel contribution to (what Charles Bazerman, and Kaufer and Geisler describe as) an existing textual or scholarly "conversation." Flower and Hayes define reading as a decision-making act whereby readers make choices—"what features of texts to attend to, what knowledge and strategies to bring to bear, and how to judge the claims of an author—which determine the richness and depth of their constructed meaning for texts" (22–23). Similarly, Peter Elbow says that reading "serves" writing by acting as a springboard; writers use reading "as something to reply to, bounce off of, or borrow from." Writers "misread or misuse or distort the works of others as a way to enable" their own writing (21). As Patricia Bizzell explains, "[T]he reader does not simply take ideas up out of the words; rather, he generates his own version of the text through the process of reading. Both writing and reading are meaning-making processes" (176).

"Transactional models" of reading/writing suggest that reading is constructive and rhetorical, and that it often involves conscious decisions and choices on the part of the reader. For example, David Bartholomae portrays reading as the way people further their own rhetorical intentions as writers and define a position from which they might speak. Stuart Greene suggests that "reading is a strategic process that entails reconstructing some of the choices and decisions writers make in a given situation" (33). And Maxine Hairston represents reading as a rhetorical act, whereby we "focus simultaneously on the content of an essay and on the process by which it was written" (181).

Reader-response critics, such as Louise Rosenblatt and Wolfgang Iser, have provided composition theorists who examine what Patricia Bizzell labels "the cultural situation of writing" another way of representing reading (177). Rosenblatt defines reading as a "transaction" between reader and text in which neither claims total ascendance. Her distinction between efferent reading—in which the reader's attention is focused on the information he or she takes away from the reading—and aesthetic reading—in which the reader focuses on what happens during the reading, "*on what he is living through during his relationship with that particular text*" (25), has been appropriated by composition theorists in examining the generative nature of reading during writing. Nancy Shanklin, for example, suggests "that a writer, like Louise Rosenblatt's reader, enters into a 'transactional' relationship with his or her developing text. During the process the text activates relevant schemata—that is, anticipatory knowledge structures—in the writers' mind that promote the generation of further text" (qtd. in Brandt 116).

Christina Haas and Linda Flower incorporate literary theorists' definitions of reading into their reading/writing model. As Haas notes, "Reader-response theories of literary criticism have been quite powerful and influential in helping us understand how readers, in dynamic relationship both with written texts and with authors, produce meaning" (21). Deborah Brandt claims that "much current research in composition," influenced by "much contemporary literary theory," now defines reading as "going off alone with language" to sustain "what Barry Kroll has called 'the autonomous production of texts' to be weaned away from interpretive dependence on situational context and learn to make meaning solely out of the semantic resources and logical relationships of written language" (115). Mariolina Salvatori's definition of reading also invokes reader response criticism. She constructs reading as "an extremely complicated activity in which the mind is at one and the same time relaxed and alert, expanding meanings as it selects and modifies them, confronting the blanks and filling them with constantly modifiable projections produced by inter-textual and intra-textual connections." She claims that "because of the nature of the reading process, each reading remains as 'indeterminate' as the text that it is a response to" (661). Although Salvatori agrees with other composition scholars that reading and writing are interconnected, she believes that "the activity of reading seems to subsume the activity of writing" (666).

Poststructuralist thinking and theory—questioning as it does the meaning of texts, the nature of reality, and the notion of the integrated self—has exercised increasing influence over representations of reading within composition scholarship. Jack Blum asserts that "through its focus upon textuality, poststructuralism reinstates a strong emphasis upon reading as a central commitment of the composition classroom" (94). He defines poststructural reading as reading against the text, questioning its assumptions and identifying what Barbara Johnson has termed the text's "warring forces of signification" (5). The poststructuralist definition of reading assumes, according to Kaufer and Waller, "that reading and writing serve one another *asymmetrically*. Reading is the way in which we evaluate (not develop or complete) writing skill" (71). Paul Northam views reading in the poststructuralist composition classroom "not only as a tool of analysis but also as an attitude towards the texts surrounding us" (126). He defines reading in terms of affective benefits for readers: "[Reading] provides powerful incentives to inspiration, . . . leads students to the cultivation of a sense of playful intellectual joy in interpretation, . . . and produce[s] the conviction in students that their perspectives of topics—be they literary, social, academic, aesthetic, political, or whatever—are original and insightful" (126). And J. Hillis Miller (1983) says that reading in the poststructuralist composition classroom is "not rhetoric as putting together, composition, but rhetoric as taking apart, decomposition." However, Miller acknowledges "that no skillful composition is possible without that prior act of decomposition practiced through reading models of composition by others" (43).

Elsewhere, Miller (1993) represents reading as an unnatural cultural and social act associated with "appropriation, accommodation, or socialization" within a cultural ideology (312). This construction of reading stresses the relationship between community-governed reading strategies and self-advancement and preservation of the community. Finally, Eileen Bularzik portrays reading as fundamental to academic success and to civic responsibility, suggesting that reading is a culturally constructed, class-marked activity.

Lynée Lewis Gaillet
Georgia State University

Works Cited

Atkins, G. Douglas, and Michael J. Johnson, ed. 1985. *Writing and Reading Differently: Deconstruction and the Teaching of Composition and Literature.* Lawrence, KS: University Press of Kansas.

Atwell, Margaret. 1980. "The Evolution of Text: The Interrelationship of Reading and Writing in the Composing Process." Ph.D. Dissertation. Indiana University.

Bartholomae, David. 1985. "Inventing the University." *When a Writer Can't Write.* Ed. Mike Rose. New York: Guilford. 134–165.

Bartholomae, David, and Anthony Petrosky. 1986. *Facts, Artifacts, and Counterfacts: Theory and Method for a Writing Course.* Upper Montclair, NJ: Boynton.

Bazerman, Charles. 1980. "A Relationship between Reading and Writing: The Conversational Model." *College English* 41: 656–661.

Bereiter, Carl, and Marlene Scardamalia. 1984. "Learning about Writing from Reading." *Written Communication* 1: 163–188.

Bizzell, Patricia. 1986. "On the Possibility of a Unified Theory of Composition and Literature." *Rhetoric Review* 4: 174–180.

Blum, Jack. 1994. "Poststructural Theories and the Postmodern Attitude in Contemporary Composition." *Composition in the Rhetorical Tradition.* Ed. Ross Winterowd. Urbana: NCTE. 92–111.

Brandt, Deborah. 1986. "Social Foundations of Reading and Writing." *Convergences: Transactions in Reading and Writing.* Urbana: NCTE. 115–126.

Bridwell, Lillian. 1980. "Revising Strategies in Twelfth Grade Students' Transactional Writing." *Research in the Teaching of English* 14: 192–222.

Bularzik, Eileen M. 1991. "Reading Processes: Responding to Discourse Community Constraints." Paper presented at the Conference on College Composition and Communication. Boston, MA, 22 March.

Elbow, Peter. 1993. "The War between Reading and Writing and How to End It." *Rhetoric Review* 12: 5–24.

Flower, Linda. 1988. "The Construction of Purpose in Reading and Writing." *College English* 50 (1988): 528–550.

Flower, Linda, *et al.* 1990. *Reading to Write: Exploring a Cognitive and Social Process.* New York: Oxford University Press.

Greene, Stuart. 1993. "Exploring the Relationship Between Authorship and Reading." *Hearing Ourselves Think.* Ed. Ann Penrose and Barbara Sitko. New York: Oxford University Press. 33–51.

Haas, Christina. 1993. "Beyond 'Just the Facts': Reading as Rhetorical Action." *Hearing Ourselves Think.* Ed. Ann Penrose and Barbara Sitko. New York: Oxford University Press. 19–32.

Haas, Christina, and Linda Flower. 1988. "Rhetorical Reading Strategies and the Construction of Meaning." *College Composition and Communication* 39: 167–184.

Hairston, Maxine. 1986. "Using Nonfiction Literature in the Composition Classroom." *Convergences: Transactions in Reading and Writing.* Ed. Bruce Petersen. Urbana: NCTE. 179–188.

Horner, Winifred. 1983. *Composition and Literature: Bridging the Gap*. Chicago: University of Chicago Press.

Johnson, Barbara. 1980. *The Critical Difference*. Baltimore: Johns Hopkins University Press.

Kaufer, David, and Cheryl Geisler. 1989. "Novelty in Academic Writing." *Written Communication* 6: 286–311.

Kaufer, David, and Gary Waller. 1985. "To Write Is to Read Is to Write, Right?" *Reading and Writing Differently*. Ed. G. Douglas Atkins and Michael L. Johnson. Lawrence: Kansas University Press. 66–92.

Kroll, Barry. 1985. "Social-Cognitive Ability and Writing Performance: How Are They Related?" *Written Communication* 2: 293–305.

Miller, J. Hillis. 1983. "Composition and Decomposition: Deconstruction and the Teaching of Writing." *Composition and Literature: Bridging the Gap*. Ed. Winifred B. Horner. Chicago: Chicago University Press. 38–56.

———. 1993. "Nietzsche in Basel: Writing Reading." *Journal of Advanced Composition* 13.2: 311–328.

Murray, Donald M. 1982. "Teaching the Other Self: The Writer's First Reader." *College Composition and Communication* 33: 140–147.

Northam, Paul. 1985. "Heuristics and Beyond: Deconstruction/Inspiration and the Teaching of Writing Invention." *Reading and Writing Differently*. Ed. G. Douglas Atkins and Michael L. Johnson. Lawrence: Kansas University Press. 115–128.

Perl, Sondra. 1979. "The Composing Processes of Unskilled College Writers." *Research in the Teaching of English* 13: 317–336.

Petersen, Bruce T., ed. 1986. *Convergences: Transactions in Reading and Writing*. Urbana: NCTE.

Pianko, Sharon. 1979. "A Description of the Composition Processes of College Freshman Writers." *Research in the Teaching of English* 13: 5–22.

Rosenblatt, Louise. 1978. *The Reader, The Text, The Poem*. Carbondale: Southern Illinois University Press.

Salvatori, Mariolina. 1983. "Reading and Writing a Text: Correlations Between Reading and Writing Patterns." *College English* 45: 657–666.

Shanklin, Nancy. 1980. "Relating Reading and Writing: Developing a Transactional Theory of the Writing Process." Ph.D. Dissertation. Indiana University.

Sternglass, Marilyn. 1986. "Writing Based on Reading." *Convergences: Transactions in Reading and Writing*. Ed. Bruce Petersen. Urbana: NCTE. 151–162.

Winterowd, Ross, and Jack Blum, ed. 1994. *Composition in the Rhetorical Context*. Urbana: NCTE.

research

What research means in a given rhetorical situation depends partly on the type of research in question and partly on the synonyms invoked to stand in for this keyword. Metaphorical constructions, of course, also shape the meaning of the term in particular contexts. The interdisciplinary array of research types identified in composition is impressive, at times redundant, and revealing of the agonistic and semantic diversity in the field—what Anne Gere calls a "charged space in which multiple 'sites' of interaction appear" (4). The major research aims and methods writers have variously classified in composition include "quantative" and "qualitative" (Bridwell-Bowles); experimental, clinical, formal, and ethnographic (North); empirical-experimental, phenomenological-ethnographic, and philosophical-historical (Brannon). Sandra Stotsky and Cindy Mall break these general classifications down into even more specific categories, including positivistic, scientific, hypothesis-testing and holistic, phenomenological, hypothesis-generating, participant-observational, ethnographic, humanistic, naturalistic, interpretive, and hermeneutical. Synonyms for research most frequently invoked within these classifications include investigation, inquiry, analysis, description, study, and experiment. Thus, depending on the context, research might mean philosophical inquiry, or ethnographic description, or scientific experimentation, or clinical study, and so on.

In their efforts to define valid research in composition as scientific investigation, Braddock, Lloyd-Jones, and Shoer, throwing down the gauntlet for all future composition specialists with empirical inclinations, distinguished between research that was "inconclusive or trivial"—that is, bad science—and research that was "substantial"—that is, good science (29). Research, thus, was taken as a means to make substantial that which otherwise lacked substance in the form of scientific credibility. Picking up the gauntlet in 1986, George Hillocks assures the reader that "we have the power to teach and to continue to research well beyond the stage of alchemy" (to which Braddock *et al.* had likened composition research prior to their own scientific intervention). Hillocks frequently employs "study"—in the scientific sense—as a synonym for research, as for example when he notes that "while many studies included in the bibliography of this report suffer from similar flaws [e.g., uncontrolled or undescribed variables], there are also many studies which are, I believe, exemplary and which contribute to our knowledge of composition" (xvi).

In sharp contrast to Hillocks' exclusive embrace of research as empirical study, Ben McClelland and Timothy Donovan swing toward a more inclusive definition of research in composition when they say of the writers included in their *Perspectives on Research and Scholarship in Composition*:

> the authors describe research and scholarship that repudiates the ignominy that composition studies once suffered within English departments. Their work recognizes the significant evolution of both literary and composition studies, rejects the isolated positions of narrow specialists, and calls for a reexamination of the disciplinary boundaries of English studies. (viii)

Research as a diverse phenomenon is thus figured as an arbiter, even a hero, of near-mythic proportions, ready and able to repudiate past ignominy. Implicit in this, as in other constructions of research in composition, is the meaning of research as institutional power—as the ways and means of attaining and maintaining power in the academy.

In her edited anthology, however, Anne Gere explicitly disavows the institutional meaning of research-as-power as means to disciplinary legitimacy. "Questions about the status of composition," she writes, "whether it possesses the features of a discipline, whether it merits a place in the 'disciplined' academy—give way, in these essays, to new ways of talking about composition" (3). In his contribution to this ostensibly "deconstructive" collection, for instance, David Bleich wants to reject what he calls the "masculine" scientific meanings assigned to research by Braddock *et al.*, Hillocks, and other empiricists in favor of "socially generous research." Rather than aiming exclusively to bolster the status of the researcher and/or his field, socially generous research, deriving from feminist ethnographic principles as articulated, for instance, by Frances E. Mascia-Lees, Patricia Sharpe, and Colleen Ballerino Cohen, "contributes to the empowerment of the subject community . . . and the research community" by " 'framing research questions according to the desires of the oppressed group' and 'choosing to do work that "others" want and need' " (qtd. in Bleich 178). In this context—linked explicitly to its socio-political value—research means something like the pursuit of social justice through mutual inquiry into the dynamic conditions and problems of a given culture and/or community.

Lynn Worsham conceives of research in the form of hermeneutic inquiry as a remedy or counter-balance to what she sees, in part, as composition's complicity in the kind of "conflation of invention and technology [or science]" that strives for the "total utilization of all beings and the efficient arrangement of human potential" (201–202). Perhaps as a challenge to the scientific meanings variously assigned to research in composition (Braddock *et al.*, Hillocks, Lauer and Asher, etc.), Worsham assigns "researchers" and research qua inquiry the moral task of asking—in addition to all the research questions one might pursue—"how we are to feel at home in a world rendered bloodless by technological thinking" (202). Thus, Worsham might find the following definition of empirical research preferred by Lauer and Asher inadequate for its lack of epistemological self-reflexivity, assuming as it does an unproblematic stance toward "systematized knowledge": "Empirical research is the process of developing systematized knowledge gained from observations that are formulated to support insights and generalizations about the phenomena under study" (7). For Lauer and Asher, research embraces systematized knowledge; for Worsham, research-as-inquiry should keep systematized knowledge at arms length. For both, research signifies a specific relationship to knowledge and culture.

Like Worsham, Thomas Newkirk views "traditional research"—i.e., research posited on the scientific method or, perhaps, on some variant of Taylorism—as a menacing reduction of teachers' lived experience and the authority they gain from their "intimate knowledge of the classroom and students, from intuitions honed by making thousands of judgments and observations of student work" (133). Research as naturalistic "observation," on the other hand, promises to keep teachers in touch with the "source of their strength," which includes both their intellectual and emotional ("intuitive") ties to students. Thus, in the feminist ethnographic tradition, Newkirk includes "the narrative, the immediate, the empathetic, and the subjective" as indispensable parts of meaningful research in composition (132). In her survey of the first twenty years of research published in *Research in the Teaching of English*, Anne Herrington notes the emergence of such qualitative research along with a plea to all researchers to "keep an open mind so we can have some chance of understanding the contributions each of us can make from our various standpoints, a willingness to participate in open deliberations over differences, and a recognition that we share common interests in writing, learning, and teaching" (134).

Ruth Ray draws on feminist theory in her elaboration of "teacher research" which is "based on the premise that theory comes from many places, including the classroom, and that theory is generated by many people, including teachers in collaboration with students and other teachers" (xi). A "bridge [over] the widening gap between theory and practice," research is figured by teacher researchers as both a political and intellectual site of mediation between different and often competing institutional interests and activities, whether of a personal or institutional character (159). If de-contextualized forms of research teach graduate students to see " 'research' as another opportunity for faculty to judge and critique them," teacher research, emphasizing as it does local context, knowledge, and personal experience, becomes a "means of personal inquiry" (110), thereby linking public and private discourses. According to Ray, such "integration of the public and the private make both discourses better—more accountable to their various constituencies" (39).

Finally, most writing instructors and composition specialists have at one time or another affixed "research" to "paper" in the form of an adjective, a construction that Richard Larson, for one, has found profoundly lacking in substance. "If research can refer to almost any process by which data outside the immediate and purely personal experiences of the writer are gathered, then I suggest that just as the so-called 'research paper' has no conceptual or substantive identity, neither does it have a procedural identity; the term does not necessarily designate any particular kind of data nor any preferred procedure for gathering data" (182). Research, in this light, is figured as an empty signifier, a "generic" term that means everything and nothing at once (185).

As Richard Larson suggests, "we would all agree . . . I think, that research is an activity in which one engages" (181), but what that activity is and how one engages in it in a particular rhetorical situation depends, as we have seen here, on a host of variable factors.

Thomas C. Kerr
Virginia Tech

Works Cited

Bleich, David. 1993. "Ethnography and the Study of Literacy: Prospects for Socially Generous Research." *Into the Field: Sites of Composition Studies.* Ed. Anne Ruggles Gere. New York: The Modern Language Association of America.

Braddock, Richard *et al.* 1963. *Research in Written Composition.* Champaign: National Council of Teachers of English.

Brannon, Lil. 1985. "Toward a Theory of Composition." *Perspectives on Research and Scholarship in Composition.* Ed. Ben W. McClelland and Timothy R. Donovan. New York: The Modern Language Association of America.

Bridwell-Bowles, Lillian. 1991. "Research in Composition: Issues and Methods." *An Introduction to Composition Studies.* Ed. Erika Lindemann and Gary Tate. New York: Oxford University Press.

Gere, Anne Ruggles. 1993. Introduction. *Into the Field: Sites of Composition Studies.* Ed. Anne Ruggles Gere. New York: The Modern Language Association of America.

Herrington, Anne J. 1989. "The First Twenty Years of *Research in the Teaching of English* and the Growth of a Research Community in Composition Studies." *Research in the Teaching of English* 23: 117–138.

Hillocks, George Jr. 1986. *Research on Written Composition: New Directions for Teaching.* Urbana: ERIC and NCTE.

Larson, Richard. 1994. "The 'Research Paper' in the Writing Course: A Non-Form of Writing." *The Writing Teacher's Sourcebook.* 3rd ed. Ed. Gary Tate *et al.* New York: Oxford University Press.

Lauer, Janice M., and J. William Asher. 1988. *Composition Research: Empirical Designs.* New York: Oxford University Press.

McClelland, Ben, and Timothy Donovan. 1985. "Where are English Departments Going?" *Perspectives on Research and Scholarship in Composition.* Ed. Ben W. McClelland and Timothy R. Donovan. New York: The Modern Language Association of America.

Newkirk, Thomas. 1991. "The Politics of Composition Research: The Conspiracy Against Experience." *The Politics of Writing Instruction: Postsecondary.* Ed. Richard Bullock and John Trimbur. General ed. Charles Schuster. Portsmouth: Boynton/Cook-Heinemann.

North, Stephen M. 1987. *The Making of Knowledge in Composition: Portrait of an Emerging Field.* Portsmouth, NH: Boynton/Cook Publishers.

Ray, Ruth E. 1993. *The Practice of Theory: Teacher Research in Composition.* Urbana: NCTE.

Stotsky, Sandra, and Cindy Mall. 1990. "Understanding Research on Teaching the English Language Arts: An Introduction." *Handbook of Research on Teaching the English Language Arts.* Ed. James Flood *et al.* New York: Macmillan.

Worsham, Lynn. 1987. "The Question Concerning Invention: Hermeneutics and the Genesis of Writing." *PRE/TEXT* 8: 197–244.

resistance

The term *resistance* in composition studies most commonly refers to a general opposition to authority, a student's opposition to pedagogical authority and, especially, a writer's opposition to discursive conventions. Thus, the term's connotation depends on an author's stance toward classroom politics (for a range of positions, see Hurlbert and Blitz). Most often, resistance is considered a positive good, a signifier of student agency (Ewald and Wallace) or of democratic defiance of elitist practices (Stygall). In composition studies, "resistance" is almost always an activity of students, its connotation determined by the instructor's stance toward the specific power relationships of a pedagogical situation.

As a structuring concept of contemporary composition theory, "resistance" was introduced by Geoffrey Chase's 1988 essay in *College Composition and Communication*. Chase borrowed the conceptual apparatus of his argument from Henry Giroux (1983). Following Giroux, Chase divides student response to pedagogical authority into three categories: accommodation, opposition, and resistance. Accommodation is the "process by which students learn to accept conventions" of discourse communities (14). Opposition and resistance are both means by which the relatively powerless contest authority (or "domination" in Giroux's Gramscian lexicon). For Giroux, opposition refers to disruptive behavior that is likely to be reactionary: the "appropriation and display of power," which, like sexist or racist insults, is "fueled by and reproduces the most powerful grammar of domination" (103). Because Chase is concerned only with college writing instruction, he limits opposition to students' failure "to learn the patterns and conventions of a particular discourse community" (15).

More interesting is the way Chase applies Giroux's concept of "resistance." Giroux draws his Gramscian theory of hegemony and resistance from British cultural studies, especially the work of Paul Willis (98–107). He writes that resistance "must have a revealing function, one that contains a critique of domination and provides theoretical opportunities for self-reflection and for struggle in the interest of self-emancipation and social emancipation"

(109). Chase also observes that resistance "is a behavior that actively works against the dominant ideology" (15), but he is more concerned with the individual student's emancipation, a sense perhaps closer to that designated as "empowerment."

While he quotes Giroux's Gramscian formulation of resistance approvingly—"resistance must have a revealing function, one that contains a critique of domination"—Chase restricts the concept to the personal experience and perspective of individual students: "Resistance . . . refers to a student's refusal to learn in those cases in which the refusal grows out of a larger sense of the individual's relationship to liberation" (15). From the beginning, therefore, Chase gave Giroux's formulation of resistance a personal, experiential cast, making it a micropolitical picture of the individual student's interface with institutional authority.

But what happens when students resist not the status quo but the leftist composition instructor? Resistance can become affirmation of authority rather than its interrogation. Students are thus seen as representatives of rather than allies against cultural conservatism. In other words, while Chase's view allies instructors and students in resistance to the status quo, the leftist perspective (often designated "advocacy") places instructors in resistance to a status quo that includes their students. Christopher Wise, for example, writes of his student's resistance to Freud's ideologically repugnant concept of childhood sexuality. Dale Bauer explores student resistance in the form of antipathy to feminist teachers and their practices. In an attempt to better understand this process, Karen Fitts and Alan France have studied the rhetorical strategies students use to resist "oppositional" pedagogy.

Some scholars, however, worry that teacher-advocacy (i.e., the instructor's open identification with a political position) will silence student resistance rather than appropriating it for effective writing pedagogy. Maxine Hairston has argued that resistance—in the form of socio-political conflict between instructor and students—will result in "intellectual intimidation" rather than fruitful dialogue because of the instructor's power and students' apprehension about their grades. Pedagogical conflict and resistance thus force students into a "fake discourse" of vacuous generality, hypocrisy, and political correctness (188–189). A similar concern has been recognized on the left by Donald Lazere, and Carl Herndl observes that "[politically] confrontational pedagogy is more likely to produce opposition among students, than to encourage cultural resistance" (359).

In the years since Chase introduced "resistance" as a means for students to challenge demands that their writing reproduce the conventions of academic discourse, scholars have continued to broaden the concept in their examination of the individual-institutional interface. Min-zhan Lu provides a recent example, arguing that grammatical error and "inappropriate" usage are often best seen as student resistance (rather than ignorance and insensitivity) to discursive authority (448). Lu asks us to consider the writing classroom as a multicultural "contact zone" and to reconceptualize "deviations from the official codes of academic discourses" (448). Instructors might then teach "a range of choices and options" that would include "ways of resisting the unifying force of 'official' discourse" (455–456).

Lu's concept of resistance reflects the dominant contemporary usage of the term. It preserves Giroux's Gramscian "critique of domination" while maintaining Chase's primary emphasis on enabling individual students to negotiate their own positions "in the context of . . . socio-political power relationships" (448). While the cultural politics of this usage remains implicit, its Gramscian origin can be perceived in Lu's professed multicultural objectives: to understand students' difficulties with official discourses as "the refusal of 'real' writers to reproduce the hegemonic conventions of written English" (447). In composition studies, as throughout American culture, it seems the exercise of power (including resistance to it) is seen from the individual's perspective.

Alan W. France
West Chester University

Works Cited

Chase, Geoffrey. 1988. "Accommodation, Resistance and the Politics of Student Writing." *College Composition and Communication* 39: 13–22.

Ewald, Helen Rothschild, and David C. Wallace. 1994. "Exploring Agency in Classroom Discourse or, Should David Have Told His Story?" *College Composition and Communication* 45: 342–368.

Fitts, Karen, and Alan W. France. 1994. "Advocacy and Resistance in the Writing Class: Working toward Stasis." *Pedagogy in the Age of Politics: Writing and Reading (in) the Academy.* Ed. Patricia A. Sullivan and Donna J. Qualley. Urbana: NCTE. 13–24.

Giroux, Henry A. 1983. *Theory and Resistance in Education: A Pedagogy for the Opposition.* South Hadley, MA: Bergin & Garvey.

Hairston, Maxine. 1992. "Diversity, Ideology, and Teaching Writing." *College Composition and Communication* 43: 179–193.

Herndl, Carl G. 1993. "Teaching Discourse and Reproducing Culture: A Critique of Research and Pedagogy in Professional and Non-Academic Writing." *College Composition and Communication* 44: 349–363.

Hurlbert, C. Mark, and Michael Blitz, ed. 1991. *Composition and Resistance.* Portsmouth, NH: Boynton Cook.

Lazere, Donald. 1995. "Teaching the Political Conflicts: A Rhetorical Schema." *College Composition and Communication* 43: 194–213.

Lu, Min-zhan. 1994. "Professing Multiculturalism: The Politics of Style in the Contact Zone." *College Composition and Communication* 45: 442–458.

Stygall, Gail. 1994. "Resisting Privilege: Basic Writing and Foucault's Author Function." *College Composition and Communication* 45: 320–341.

Wise, Christopher. 1995. "Pee-Wee, Penley, and Pedagogy, or Hands-on Feminism in the Writing Class." *Left Margins: Cultural Studies and Composition Pedagogy.* Ed. Karen Fitts and Alan W. France. Albany: SUNY Press. 129–137.

revision

Although revision is regarded as an essential component of writing, researchers and practitioners disagree upon a definition of the term. Revision has been represented as a quick form of editing—the act of finding errors and polishing sentences at the end of the writing process, as an epistemic act, as a way for the writer to make a written piece conform to readers' expectations, and as an embedded subprocess within other subprocesses of writing.

The definition of *revision* as error correction within a linear model—prewriting, writing, and postwriting (Britton, Burgess, Rohman)—prevailed until the early 1970s. In 1978, Donald Murray, perhaps the first to pointedly study revision, renamed the linear stages in the writing process "prevision," "vision," and "revision." He defined revision or "seeing again" as "what the writer does after a draft is completed to understand and communicate what has begun to appear on the page" (87). Murray makes a distinction between internal revision, "everything writers do to discover and develop what they have to say," and external revision, "what writers do to communicate what they have to say" (87). Although Murray's work was embedded within a linear stage model of writing, his view of writing marks a transition in writing theory.

By the late 1970s, revision is given theoretical attention within a process-oriented rather than product-focused conception of writing, and is no longer defined simply as the act of making editorial changes. At this point, researchers began supporting a dynamic hierarchical cognitive theory of writing, involving planning, transcribing, and reviewing. The new model emphasized the recursive nature of writing as exemplified in the work of Linda Flower and John Hayes, who define revision, or "reviewing," as a goal-directed process that can take precedence over and interrupt all other writing processes at any time. Sondra Perl defines revision similarly as the way a writer looks forward and backward as he or she writes—backward to what is written, forward to what will be read. She suggests that writers are guided by a subjective "felt sense," which she defines as the "internal criterion writers seem to use to guide them when they are planning, drafting, and revising" (367). These definitions of revision as a process embedded within other subprocesses of writing expanded earlier conceptions of the term, which defined revision as editorial proofreading performed as the last stage of a linear writing process.

As interest in the process of revision increased, it became increasingly more difficult to define the term. Researchers of the early 1980s seem to disagree whether the term means changes that are made to the final product, or the process authors go through in their minds when they write, or both. Beach's problem-solving model and Bridwell's model of revision appear to include both the mental process and the actual changes made. Scardamalia and Bereiter preferred to separate revision process and products, explaining that their model of the process of making textual changes was not called a model of revision because revision refers to something that happens to a text. More recently, Scardamalia and Bereiter coined the term "reprocessing" to refer to the mental aspects of revision, saying that "reprocessing is a more suitable theoretical term than revision because it refers to what goes on mentally rather than being tied to differences in surface behavior." Reprocessing "spans everything from editing for mistakes to reformulating goals. Revision is a special case of reprocessing, applied to actual text" (790).

Regardless of their conceptualization of the term revision, most researchers who define revision—implicitly or explicitly—do take into account rhetorical elements affecting the final written product. In 1980, for example, Nancy Sommers examines how authors consider their readers' expectations and particular occasions for writing. She defines revision, or "re-seeing," as a recursive rather than linear process guided by "a sequence of changes in a composition—changes which are initiated by cues and occur continually throughout the writing of a work" (380). Sommers describes the act of revision as analogous to both reading and writing, and so weaves "changes" and "cues" into a process of revision around a text that involves both "re-creating" and "de-creating" a text. Likewise, Carol Berkenkotter views revision in terms of audience awareness. She defines revision as the way skilled writers "automatically internalize their audiences" and then use this sensed audience and their relationship to it to help them modify assigned writing tasks, select appropriate types of discourse, and make a wide range of "rhetorical, organizational, and stylistic decisions" while they write. And Faigley and Witte—in opposing implicit constructions of what revision has meant to some researchers in the field—define revision not as "the number of changes a writer makes," but rather changes that "bring a text closer to fitting the demands of the situation" (411).

Other definitions of revision suggest that it is performed not only in a rhetorical context but in what Kenneth Dowst terms an epistemic context—as a means for generating knowledge. For example, Sommers defines the revision of mature writers as part of the ongoing process of invention, as a technique for producing meaning. Faigley and Witte define revision in terms of discovering what "exactly" one has to say (107). And Bartholomae and

Petrosky define revision as "stages in the ongoing process of working out what we know and what we can say about the subject that engages us" (168).

Despite the attention revision has received in the last twenty years (both theoretical and pedagogical), Nancy Sommers (1992) suggests that still "left unexamined [is] the most important fact of all: revision does not always guarantee improvement; successive drafts do not always lead to clearer vision. You can't just change the words around and get the ideas right" (26). Likewise, Jeffrey Carroll asserts that "revision in itself has little value to the composer beyond privileging a mode of writing that emphasizes variation, repetition, and a sense of process. Revision does not guarantee progress or success or quality in writing, and in fact can work against it" (69). While revision may be largely prescriptive, Carroll argues that "it must also be subordinate to the intentions and expectations of writer and reader, and to the intertext which defines them" (72). He suggests that "a recognition and exploitation of this intertextual web . . . may lead to a more practical and profitable view of revision as *ongoing* and *summative*, not mechanistic and microstructural" (70). Carroll (re)constructs revision as "dipping into the intertext—the internalized sum of texts that readers and writers draw upon—a nonquantifiable act that occurs as a natural part of our reading and writing" (69).

Lynée Lewis Gaillet
Georgia State University

Works Cited

Bartholomae, David, and Anthony Petrosky. 1986. *Facts, Artifacts, and Counterfacts: Theory and Method for a Reading and Writing Course.* Upper Montclair: Boynton/Cook.

Beach, Richard, and Sara Eaton. 1984. "Factors Influencing Self Assessing and Revising by College Freshmen." *New Directions in Composition Research.* Ed. Richard Beach and Lillian Bridwell. New York: Guilford. 149–170.

Bereiter, Carl, and Marlena Scardamalia. 1983. "Levels of Inquiry in Writing Research." *Research on Writing: Principles and Methods.* Ed. Peter Mosenthal *et al.* New York: Longman. 3–25.

Bridwell, Lillian. 1980. "Revising Strategies in Twelfth Grade Students' Transactional Writing." *Research in the Teaching of English* 14: 197–222.

Britton, James, *et al.* 1975. *The Development of Writing Abilities.* London: Macmillan Education. 11–18.

Carrol, Jeffrey. 1989. "Disabling Fictions: Institutionalized Delimitations of Rhetoric." *Rhetoric Review* 8: 62–72.

Dowst, Kenneth. 1980. "The Epistemic Approach: Writing, Knowing, and Learning." *Eight Approaches to Teaching Composition.* Ed. Timothy Donovan and Ben W. McClelland. Urbana: NCTE. 65–85.

Faigley, Lester, and Stephen Witte. 1981. "Analyzing Revision." *College Composition and Communication* 32: 400–414.

———. 1984. "Measuring the Effects of Revision on Text Structure." *New Directions in Composition Research*. Ed. Richard Beach and Lillian Bridwell. New York: Guilford. 95–108.

Flower, Linda, *et al.* 1986. "Detection, Diagnosis, and the Strategies of Revision." *College Composition and Communication* 37: 16–55.

Flower, Linda, and John R. Hayes. 1981. "A Cognitive Process Theory of Writing." *College Composition and Communication* 32: 365–387.

Murray, Donald. 1978a. "Internal Revision: A Process of Discovery." *Research on Composing: Points of Departure*. Ed. Charles Cooper and Lee Odell. Urbana: NCTE. 85–103.

———. 1978b. "Teach the Motivating Force of Revision." *English Journal* 67: 56–60.

Perl, Sondra. 1980. "Understanding Composing." *College Composition and Communication* 31: 363–369.

Rohman, D. Gordon. 1965. "Pre-writing: The Stages of Discovery in the Writing Process." *College Composition and Communication* 16: 106–112.

Scardamalia, Marlena, and Carl Bereiter. 1986. "Research on Written Composition." *Handbook of Research on Teaching*. Ed. Merlin C. Wittrock. New York: Macmillan. 778–803.

Sommers, Nancy. 1992. "Between the Drafts." *College Composition and Communication* 43: 23–31.

———. 1980. "Revision Strategies of Student Writers and Experienced Adult Writers." *College Composition and Communication* 31: 378–388.

rhetoric

Rhetoric is buffeted by storms of signification coming from two directions. From one direction comes the general public's perception, reinforced by the popular media, of rhetoric as bombast, figurative language designed to cover up either deception or shallow substance. Some compositionists distance themselves from this meaning (see, for example, Erika Lindemann's dismissal of it as a "fraudulent practice" [35]), yet one finds in some corners of composition studies a fascination, kindled by French deconstructionists, with the figurative nature of language. J. Hillis Miller (1985), for example, proposes that "rhetoric [as] knowledge of the intricacies of the tropes should be taught in courses in composition, along with grammar and rhetoric in the sense of persuasion" (101). From another direction comes the implied meaning, embraced within most academic circles, of rhetoric as the subject matter that gets taught in composition courses. Embodying a definition of composition as applied, "taught" rhetoric are collections of essays for writing teachers and scholars—for example, Richard Graves' 1976 *Rhetoric and Composition: A Sourcebook for Teachers* and Patricia Harkin and John Schilb's 1991 volume, *Contending with Words: Composition and Rhetoric in a Postmodern Age*. This definition leads authors to refer to composition textbooks as rhetorics; consider, for example, Richard M. Coe's *Process, Form, and Substance: A Rhetoric for Advanced Writers*.

For most of this century, rhetoric, supported by a tradition of philosophical/theoretical scholarship, has been invoked to rescue composition from its seemingly anti-intellectual baggage of word-, sentence-, and paragraph-level pedantry. As early as 1936, I. A. Richards proposed that his *Philosophy of Rhetoric*, "a study of misunderstanding and its remedies," should offer an antidote to traditional rhetoric, which represented "the dreariest and least profitable part of the waste that the unfortunate travel through in Freshman English" (3). In the 1960s, two versions of the term came to the fore. The first considers the degree to which any piece of written discourse—a theme, a novel or story, an advertisement, an editorial, and so on—embodies an implied "speaker," a writer attempting to shape a message that she hopes will be effective for a certain "audience" of readers. The major spokesperson for rhetoric was Wayne Booth, whose 1963 essay defines "The Rhetorical Stance" as the "common ingredient that I find in all of the writing I admire":

> a stance which depends on discovering and maintaining in any writing situation a proper balance among the three elements that are at work in any communicative effort: the available arguments about the subject itself, the interests and particularities of the audience, and the voice, the implied character of the speaker. (141)

In a later article, Booth makes it clear that rhetoric should be couched in the current times: "[I]t would be naive to think that reviving Aristotle or Quintilian or Campbell or Whately could solve our problems. . . . The revival must do more than echo the past" (11). The second 1960s' conception of rhetoric, however, was boldly historical. It aims to find sources for contemporary composition pedagogy in the pre-Socratic sophists, Plato, Aristotle, Cicero, Quintilian, and their successors. Leading the cause in the 1960s for rhetoric in composition was Edward P. J. Corbett. In a 1963 essay, "The Usefulness of Classical Rhetoric," Corbett explains the concepts of rhetorical appeals, audience, status theory, arrangement, imitation, and style developed by Aristotle, Cicero, and Quintilian and suggests their application in contemporary composition classes. His 1965 textbook, *Classical Rhetoric for the Modern Student*, embodies Corbett's belief that "the elaborate system of the ancients, which taught the student how to find something to say, how to select and organize his material, and how to phrase it in the best possible way, is still useful and effective—perhaps more useful and effective than the various courses of study that replaced it" (ix).

While these 1960s-inspired significations are still frequently invoked when *rhetoric* is used without an article, a vast array of different theories of speaking and writing employ the term either preceded by the indefinite article and followed by a prepositional phrase or preceded by a specific adjective. The only characteristic these theories share is that their proponents seem to envision their rhetoric as being able either to explain how speakers and writers behave in certain situations or to direct speakers and writers to generate language that has certain, presumably effective, characteristics. In 1963, for example, Francis Christensen promulgated "A Generative Rhetoric of the Sentence" comprised of a series of syntactic strategies—primarily addition and movement of modifying phrases in sentence-final positions—that would add "texture" to prose (8).

In 1965, Richard Young and Alton Becker offered an essay, "Toward a Modern Theory of Rhetoric: A Tagmemic Contribution." Young and Becker based their work on Kenneth Pike's linguistic theory of tagmemics, holding that "any linguistic unit is assumed to be well defined only when three aspects of the unit are specified: its contrastive features, its range of variation, and its distribution in sequence and ordered classes" (456). Arguing that "the procedures the linguist uses in analyzing and describing a language are in some important ways like the procedures a writers uses in planning and writing a composition" (457), Young and Becker developed "an epistemological heuristic" based on the tagmemic triad of contrast, variation, and distribution. Young and Becker, thus, saw their tagmemic rhetoric as primarily a tool for invention, leading the writer not to overpower and subdue the belief systems of the reader; instead, "the writer must seek to have his readers identify his message with their emic system" (94).

In the 1980s, James Berlin held a strong brief for what he termed epistemic rhetoric, in which "truths arise out of dialectic, out of the interaction of individuals in discourse communities" (17). Berlin explained further:

> Truth is never simply "out there" in the material world or the social realm, or simply "in there" in the private and personal world. It emerges only as the three—the material, the social, and the personal—interact, and the agent of mediation is language. (17)

To Berlin, thus, epistemic rhetoric represented primarily an attitude toward language use that sees all elements of a communicative transaction—"interlocutor, audience, material world"—as "verbal constructs" (16).

In her 1991 book, Susan Jarratt envisions a feminist rhetoric derived from the philosophical, linguistic, and social theories of the pre-Socratic sophists. Acknowledging the basic sophistic belief in the anti-foundationalism of knowledge, feminist rhetoric, according to Jarratt, places an emphasis on "habit and practice, on historical contingency [of truth claims], and the rejection of essence" (70). Sophistic rhetoric enables a feminist reading/writing practice of breaking into the "received histories" of the discourse of man (78). For Jarratt, then, feminist rhetoric encourages writers to accept openly the "positionality" of their claims and to situate their claims in ways that will give voice to women's ideas that have long been marginalized by male-centered discourses.

Finally, extending her research on writing and cognition in the 1970s and 1980s, Linda Flower has recently proposed the existence of cognitive rhetoric, which, she notes, "locates its inquiry in a fine-grained analysis of individual minds, in action, in problematic rhetorical situations" (172). According to Flower, cognitive rhetoric asks whether "this constructive, interpretive, knowledge-forming process" operates

> for everyone alike[,] . . . for the politically conscious as it does for the naive, for the educated as it does for the illiterate, for a student before and the same student after a composition course? . . . Cognitive rhetoric, then, works by building observation-based theory; it pursues the concerns of rhetoric with the exploratory methods of the social sciences, which can uncover revealing comparisons. (172)

To Flower, then, cognitive rhetoric represents a set of principles and methods for studying how situated writers construe their tasks, their personae, their readers, and their texts.

David A. Jolliffe
DePaul University
William A. Covino
University of Illinois at Chicago

Works Cited

Berlin, James A. 1987. *Rhetoric and Reality: Writing Instruction in American Colleges, 1900–1985.* Carbondale, IL: Southern Illinois University Press.

Booth, Wayne C. 1963. "The Rhetorical Stance." *College Composition and Communication* 14: 139–145.

———. 1965. "The Revival of Rhetoric." *PMLA* 80: 8–12.

Christensen, Francis. 1963. "A Generative Rhetoric of the Sentence." Reprinted in *Notes Toward a New Rhetoric: Six Essays for Teachers.* 1967. New York: Harper and Row.

Coe, Richard M. 1990. *Process, Form, and Substance: A Rhetoric for Advanced Writers.* Englewood Cliffs, NJ: Prentice-Hall.

Corbett, Edward P. J. 1963. "The Usefulness of Classical Rhetoric." *College Composition and Communication* 14: 162–164.

———. 1965. *Classical Rhetoric for the Modern Student.* New York: Oxford University Press.

Flower, Linda. 1993. "Cognitive Rhetoric: Inquiry into the Art of Inquiry." *Defining the New Rhetorics.* Ed. Theresa Enos and Stuart C. Brown. Newbury Park, CA: Sage.

Graves, Richard L., ed. 1976. *Rhetoric and Composition: A Sourcebook for Writing Teachers.* Rochelle Park, NJ: Hayden.

Harkin, Patricia, and John Schilb, ed. 1991. *Contending with Words: Composition and Rhetoric in a Postmodern Age.* New York: Modern Language Association.

Jarratt, Susan C. 1991. *Rereading the Sophists: Classical Rhetoric Refigured.* Carbondale, IL: Southern Illinois University Press.

Lindemann, Erika. 1987. *A Rhetoric for Writing Teachers.* 2nd edition. New York: Oxford University Press.

Miller, J. Hillis. 1983. "Composition and Decomposition: Deconstruction and the Teaching of Writing." In *Composition and Literature: Bridging the Gap.* Ed. Winifred Bryan Horner. Chicago: University of Chicago Press.

———. 1985. "The Two Rhetorics: George Eliot's Bestiary." *Writing and Reading Differently.* Ed. G. Douglas Atkins and Michael C. Johnson. Lawrence, KS: University of Kansas Press.

Richards, I. A. 1936. *The Philosophy of Rhetoric.* Oxford: Oxford University Press.

Young, Richard E., and Alton L. Becker. 1965. "Toward a Modern Theory of Rhetoric: A Tagmemic Contribution." *Harvard Educational Review* 35: 450–468.

self/the subject

The terms *self* and *subject* are often used interchangeably in composition studies, so much so that definitions of the terms may seem indistinguishable. Nevertheless, a closer look at how compositionists employ them yields a number of useful distinctions in addition to a noticeable shift from the use of *self* to the use of *the subject* to define the writer, or the writing *self/subject*. These terms fluctuate in meaning due to the necessity to borrow from debates in philosophy, social science, psychology, political science, and rhetoric as compositionists struggle "over the meaning and status of the writer, or the writing subject" (Clifford 39).

During the 1970s, the self was generally defined by scholars like William E. Coles, Jr., Donald Murray, and Peter Elbow as a romanticist, personal, core, self uninfluenced by social forces or historical context. James A. Berlin (who labels this expressivism) attributes this portrayal to the Platonic belief in the soul whose truth is discovered "through an internal apprehension, a private vision of a world that transcends the physical" (1982, 771). For example, Coles makes a distinction between the "literary self . . . construable from the way words fall on a page" and the "other self, the identity of a student," a self that is a mystery, one with which a teacher "can have nothing to do" (12). In a similar vein, Murray teaches that writing is a process of listening to one's self. He tells students, "[p]ay close attention to your own self, learn from your own learning" (xi). One metaphor associated with this kind of central, personal self is voice, and both Murray and Elbow utilize voice as a way to explain what they mean by self. As Murray puts it: "Voice is the writer revealed" (144). Elbow varies this only slightly when he notes (see Berlin 1988, 486) that the "main source [of his theory of writing] is my own experience" (16). Experience, voice, and that "other identity" sound the defining bell of an essential, core self.

Berlin's definition of the self, a central tenet in his theory of social-epistemic rhetoric, departs radically from the expressivist conceptions of self described above. According to Berlin, "[t]here is no universal, eternal, and

authentic self that beneath all appearances is at one with all other selves"
(1988, 489). In social-epistemic rhetoric, "the subject is itself a social
construct that emerges through the linguistically-circumscribed interaction of
the individual, the community, and the material world" (489). Berlin's subject
may be caught in a web of "socially-devised definitions" (489), but this does
not mean, he argues, that individuals can never act to change their social
conditions. Blending the terms *self* and *subject*, Berlin's construction marks
the turning point in composition in the late 1980s when *the subject* becomes
a political and linguistic term for defining the self.

According to Richard Lanham, the history of Western education has been
an "uneasy combination of the two basic concepts of the self, central and
social, of the two complementary basic conceptions of society, of language
as transmission and language as creation, of thought as rule-governed and
thought as coaxing chance" (147). Lanham envisions the self as a *process* of
oscillating between the poles. In other words, for Lanham, the self is situated
in a matrix of consciousness (14) within which it alternates between the
extreme poles of "central and social, sincere and hypocritical, philosophical
and rhetorical" (25). Indeed, Lanham goes so far as to say that the whole of
humanities teaching sustains that "bi-stable oscillation which forms the heart
of the Western self" (25).

From the late 1970s to the late 1980s, resistance to either the central or
the socially defined self grew, fueled by a surge in composition's alliance
with postmodern theory. Several recent critiques focus on deconstructive,
psychoanalytic, and discursive definitions of *the subject* in composition
studies. After Jacques Derrida claimed, "the subject of writing [is] . . . a
system of relations between strata: The Mystic [Writing] Pad, the psyche,
society, the world" (227), some compositionists began to adopt deconstructive
approaches to writing instruction. Sharon Crowley, for instance, writes that
Derrida's deconstruction of a sovereign self means that "the scene of writing
thus mandates the writer's pluralization" (34). Not only is the "subject"
enmeshed in multiple relations, but when writing, "writer becomes audience"
as well (34). In short, a plurality occurs in the "subject" in at least two ways:
as part of a plural system of relations and as a movement between plural
roles (as between writer and reader) (see also Neel 122–123).

In 1987, *College English* devoted two special issues to psychoanalysis
and the problem of the "subject" in composition pedagogy (see Davis).
Gregory S. Jay follows Jacques Lacan in defining *the subject* as "a phenomenon of language," as an entity "that comes into being through the assumption
of positions offered to it by cultural discourses" (790). Not long afterward,
Susan Miller published the first full treatment of the subject in composition:
Rescuing the Subject. She calls for retheorizing a *writing* subject "quite
different from the unitary speaking subject whom both modern philosophy
and oral rhetoric have imagined" (4). Unwilling to completely deny a central
self, and yet also unable to continue to argue for the unitary speaking subject,

Miller situates the writing self in the inescapable middle terrain. Adopting a Nietzschean perspective, Miller argues (with Paul deMan) that the human subject has no privileged viewpoint, that such a perspective " 'is a mere metaphor' " (deMan 109; qtd. in Miller 25). In short, she maintains that this "metaphoric construction of a self, which I have placed in the space a theorized writer occupies, substitutes a 'human-centered' meaning for the possibility of cosmic insignificance" (25). Lester Faigley shares the ambivalent middle terrain between modernity and postmodernity with Miller when he portrays the subject as a "momentarily situated" and "metropolitan" subject capable of "both crossing social divisions" and "negotiating among many competing discourses" (239). Leaning toward the postmodern, however, Faigley agrees with Jean-François Lyotard that "subjects are like nodes in networks of discourses," moving in and out of heterogeneous subject positions and "contingent discourses" (218; 227).

To conclude, the *self* and *subject* are terms with complex histories and diverse definitions that can occupy extreme poles of oppositional meaning. From Elbow, who posits a central, core self to Victor Vitanza who counters that "when the Subject writes, or chooses, the Subject is always already written, or chosen" (398), the self and subject occupy the center of a dialectical tension in composition studies that continues to provoke critical and productive discourse.

Cynthia Haynes
University of Texas at Dallas

Works Cited

Berlin, James A. 1982. "Contemporary Composition: The Major Pedagogical Theories." *College English* 44: 765–777.

———. 1988. "Rhetoric and Ideology in the Writing Class." *College English* 50: 477–494.

Clifford, John. 1991. "The Subject in Discourse." *Contending with Words: Composition and Rhetoric in a Postmodern Age.* New York: MLA. 38–51.

Coles, Jr. William E. 1978. *The Plural I: The Teaching of Writing.* New York: Holt, Rinehart and Winston.

Crowley, Sharon. 1989. *A Teacher's Introduction to Deconstruction.* Urbana, IL: NCTE.

Davis, Robert Con. 1987. "Freud's Resistance to Reading and Teaching." *College English* 49: 621–627.

DeMan, Paul. 1979. *Allegories of Reading: Figural Language in Rousseau, Nietzsche, Rilke, and Proust.* New Haven: Yale University Press.

Derrida, Jacques. 1978. "Freud and the Scene of Writing." *Writing and Difference.* Trans. Alan Bass. Chicago: University of Chicago Press. 196–231.

Elbow, Peter. 1973. *Writing without Teachers.* Oxford: Oxford University Press.

Faigley, Lester. 1992. *Fragments of Rationality: Postmodernity and the Subject of Composition.* Pittsburgh: University of Pittsburgh Press.

Jay, Gregory S. 1987. "The Subject of Pedagogy: Lessons in Psychoanalysis and Politics." *College English* 49: 785–800.

Lanham, Richard A. 1993. *The Electronic Word: Democracy, Technology, and the Arts.* Chicago: University of Chicago Press.

Miller, Susan. 1989. *Rescuing the Subject: A Critical Introduction to Rhetoric and the Writer.* Carbondale: Southern Illinois University Press.

Murray, Donald. 1984. *Write to Learn.* New York: Holt, Rinehart and Winston.

Neel, Jasper. 1988. *Plato, Derrida, and Writing.* Carbondale, IL: Southern Illinois University Press.

Vitanza, Victor J. 1994. "Concerning a Postclassical *Ethos* as Para/Rhetorical Ethics, the 'Selphs,' and The Excluded Third" in *Ethos: New Essays in Rhetorical and Critical Theory.* Ed. James S. Baumlin and Tita French Baumlin. Dallas: Southern Methodist University Press. 389–431.

social construction

Generally speaking, the interpretive turn in composition to social construction represents a new paradigm for understanding how meaning is made, how knowledge is constructed, and how the self is constructed. To say, however, that social construction is a recent phenomenon is to ignore the meanings that allowed it to gain such prominence in our field and the meanings that threaten its current status.

Social construction is the result of efforts that were underway shortly after the turn of this century with the onset of progressive education. So writes James A. Berlin: "Even before 1930, attempts had been made to shift the attention of the writing classroom away from expressionism on the one hand and current-traditional rhetoric on the other" (82). Mara Holt agrees and claims that composition articles from that period attest to this shift. According to Holt, "articles on pedagogy in the 1930s begin by offering a social approach to teaching English as part of a national economic remedy" (542). Thus, early portrayals of social construction are those of "social approaches" to writing instruction linked to hard times and progressive democratic education.

Most composition scholars, however, cite key texts from the 1960s and 1970s when drawing the map of social construction and its culmination in the 1980s within composition studies: Thomas S. Kuhn's *Structure of Scientific Revolutions*, Peter L. Berger and Thomas Luckmann's *The Social Construction of Reality*, Richard Rorty's *Philosophy and the Mirror of Nature*, and Clifford Geertz's *Local Knowledge* (see Bruffee, LeFevre, and Faigley). As the titles suggest, these authors radically reconceive how reality and knowledge are constructed. Of interest to composition, and absent from this list, is a representation of social construction as "rhetorical in nature" (Faigley 15). According to Lester Faigley, due to poststructuralist critiques of modernist notions "that language provides an unproblematic access to reality" (8), rhetorical views of language have redefined how the self and knowledge are constructed. Faigley calls his approach a "social view" (similar to Berlin's "social-epistemic" category of rhetoric). That is, "an individual writer [is] a constituent of culture" (17).

Given the convergence of modern and postmodern discourses within a number of disciplines, there seems to be no argument that *social construction* is a broad term for a new philosophy of knowledge and reality. For example, Kenneth A. Bruffee (1986) claims that a social constructionist position "assumes that entities we normally call reality, knowledge, thought, facts, texts, selves, and so on are constructs generated by communities of like-minded peers" (774). From this view compositionists derived consensus-oriented models of learning likewise being developed in other fields, but largely the result of higher education open admissions policies in the early 1970s (Bruffee 1984, 637). That is, due to larger and larger classes, teachers had to turn to having students teach each other. Using social constructionist theories, teachers advocated collaborative learning as alternatives to teacher-centered authoritarian models of learning. In Bruffee's view, since knowledge is a "social artifact," this challenges the "traditional basis of the authority of those who teach" (648; 649). In other words, for Bruffee *social construction* means a consensus-oriented pedagogical theory that restructures traditional classroom hierarchies.

The questions that seems to occupy current debates about social construction include: "Who (or what) does the constructing? Who gets included? What are the effects?" Thus, recent contested meanings of *social construction* are a series of differing views about the ideologies it harbors. By the late 1980s, leftist critiques of social constructionist pedagogy began to coalesce. John Trimbur, for instance, refers to scholars, like David Foster, who worry that "the use of consensus in collaborative learning is an inherently dangerous and potentially totalitarian practice that stifles individual voice and creativity, suppresses differences, and enforces conformity" (602). Citing Foster's notion that collaborative learning is based on an "epistemological mistake," Trimbur reports that, for Foster, social construction means indoctrination and the loss of individual autonomy. In addition, Trimbur suggests, leftist critics like Greg Myers worry "that Bruffee's social constructionist pedagogy runs the risk of limiting its focus to the internal workings of discourse communities and of overlooking the wider social forces that structure the production of knowledge." In Myer's opinion, Trimbur says, knowledge and reality are indeed socially constructed, but social construction also encompasses the "wider social forces" outside knowledge communities (603). Thus, by the early 1990s, composition scholars had alternately embraced and rejected social construction (see Faigley 15, 31–35).

While some define it as a new method of invention—assigning articles about social construction as a heuristic to show students how they are socially constructed (Rouster)—others say social constructionists do not see beyond its methodological value. That is, some say they do not go far enough in questioning the theoretical bases in which the methods are grounded. Victor

J. Vitanza, for example, explains that when compositionists (using recent work by Patricia Bizzell, David Bartholomae, John Trimbur, and Karen Burke LeFevre) shifted "the conceptual starting place for a theory of composition from the self as inventor (or *ethos* or the cognitive perspective) to the community as inventor (or *pathos* or the social perspective)[,] . . . they neglect[ed] to point out similarly that the social (or *pathos* or consensus) is itself previously (and insidiously and invidiously) constructed" (157). For Vitanza, *social construction* means that the social itself is constructed, it doesn't *do* the constructing. These critics contend that social construction should be understood as both a philosophy and a practice/method of displacing previous epistemologies and models of learning that privilege individuals, authors, the teacher, and in some instances, the social itself.

In summary, most definitions of *social construction* prompt compositionists to agree that it has radically altered conceptions of knowledge, reality, the self, and writing. How it has been deployed and to what ends is another matter. As Christina Murphy points out, on the one hand, social construction is a force that has fostered new attitudes toward diverse student populations (multicultural voices) and helped usher in diverse perspectives (feminism, Marxism, deconstructionism, social science/communication interests) (33). On the other hand, social construction is a pedagogical theory that can stifle dissent and ignore different learning styles (27–28). It represents a highly restricted view of the self, a style of teaching that deemphasizes the emotions, and a utilitarian approach that identifies with the more conservative views of education that seek to educate students for the workforce (31–32). As it currently stands, the contestations over social construction lead Murphy to issue precautions when embracing or rejecting its principles:

> Social constructionism provides us with a paradigm that explains a number of aspects of writing instruction; however, to argue that it provides all the answers, or even answers sufficient to warrant the devaluing of other theories and philosophies of education . . . seems unwise. (36)

Whether it is a new paradigm or a panacea that elides other valuable theories, Murphy sounds the call for continued inquiry into this term and its representations, avoiding what Carole Blair calls the search for a "meta-ideology" (qtd. in Murphy 36) so that rhetoric and composition may not close down the question of social construction, but seek ways to sustain the tension among the different philosophical and pedagogical meanings of the term.

Cynthia Haynes
University of Texas at Dallas

Works Cited

Bartholomae, David. 1985. "Inventing the University." *When a Writer Can't Write: Studies in Writer's Block and Other Composing Problems.* Ed. Mike Rose. NY: Guilford. 134–165.

Berger, Peter L., and Thomas Luckmann. 1967. *The Social Construction of Reality: A Treatise in the Sociology of Knowledge.* New York: Anchor Books.

Berlin, James A. 1987. *Rhetoric and Reality: Writing Instruction in American Colleges, 1900–1985.* Carbondale, IL: Southern Illinois University Press.

Bizzell, Patricia. 1986. "Foundationalism and Anti-Foundationalism in Composition Studies." *Pre/Text* 7: 37–56.

Bruffee, Kenneth A. 1984. "Collaborative Learning and the 'Conversation of Mankind'." *College English* 46: 635–652.

———. 1986. "Social Construction, Language, and the Authority of Knowledge: A Bibliographical Essay." *College English* 48: 773–790.

Faigley, Lester. 1992. *Fragments of Rationality: Postmodernity and the Subject of Composition.* Pittsburgh: University of Pittsburgh Press.

Geertz, Clifford. 1983. *Local Knowledge.* NY: Basic.

Holt, Mara. 1993. "Knowledge, Social Relations, and Authority in Collaborative Practices of the 1930s and the 1950s." *College Composition and Communication* 44: 538–555.

Kuhn, Thomas S. 1970. *The Structure of Scientific Revolutions.* 2nd ed. Chicago: University of Chicago Press.

LeFevre, Karen Burke. 1987. *Invention as a Social Act.* Carbondale, IL: Southern Illinois University Press.

Murphy, Christina. 1994. "The Writing Center and Social Constructionist Theory." *Intersections: Theory-Practice in the Writing Center.* Ed. Joan A. Mullin and Ray Wallace. Urbana, IL: NCTE. 25–38.

Rorty, Richard. 1979. *Philosophy and the Mirror of Nature.* Princeton: Princeton University Press.

Rouster, William J. 1992. "Social Construction, the Dominant Classes, and Cultural Criticism." *Pre/Text* 13: 117–130.

Trimbur, John. 1989. "Consensus and Difference in Collaborative Learning." *College English* 51: 602–616.

Vitanza, Victor J. 1991. "Three Countertheses: Or, A Critical In(ter)vention into Composition Theories and Pedagogies." *Contending with Words: Composition and Rhetoric in a Postmodern Age.* Ed. Patricia Harkin and John Schilb. New York: MLA. 139–172.

students

Students is an omnipresent term in composition studies and a contested keyword in a number of ways. First and foremost, Andrea Lunsford has said that those working in the field should not use the term at all because it is misleading, because it habitually blinds those who invoke such a reductive, homogenizing, generic categorical referent, and that teachers and scholars need instead to start speaking and writing about the individuals that populate writing classrooms in terms of their idiosyncratic matrices of age, race, gender, class, sexual orientation, and so on. Similarly, Sharon Crowley has argued that composition teachers need to relinquish their common, debilitating conception and representation of students as people with no locations, no histories, and no politics.

Lunsford's and Crowley's arguments notwithstanding, the disciplinary language of composition studies has constructed the people referred to by this signifier in diverse, highly contested, often contradictory ways over the last three decades. Many of these historical representations have had remarkable staying power and exist today as sometimes obscured yet ever-present strands of the meaning of *students* in composition studies. In 1966, for instance, W. L. Garner characterized students as "late adolescents," as "self-centered, restless, striving, discontented, driven by glands, hedonistic, insecure, volatile, idealistic, scatter-brained, emotional, seething, imbalanced, [and] unpredictable" (228–229). In a similar vein, three years later, Steven Carter typified students as passive, apathetic, and resigned. Students are also, he said, "a wall of clichés," dogma, and homily, and have no true ideas of their own because their minds are "abstracted," "uncreated," and characterized by their "formlessness" (40–42). Writing at the same time, Donald M. Murray portrayed students as a group whose power comes from "a rhetoric that is crude, vigorous, usually uninformed, frequently obscene, and often threatening" (118), while Robert Zoellner nearly equated students with lab rats or pigeons in Skinner boxes in his behaviorist pedagogy, and Jerry Farber imagined *The Student as Nigger*, asserting that students have a "slave mentality: obliging and ingratiating on the surface, but hostile and resistant underneath" (93). More recently, we have witnessed: Allan Bloom's conception of students as people with savage minds that need to be enlightened and elevated; Mary Rose O'Reilley's portrayal of students as a "glowering . . . implacable force brooding over an inscrutable intention" (142); Gerald Graff's construction of students as people estranged from and hungry for the culture of intellectual argument, as people eager to engage in cultural conflicts; Patricia Harkin's understanding of students as driven, scheming, and savvy consumers of knowledge commodities; and Lester Faigley's representation of students as people with fragmented rationalities and multiple postmodern subjectivities. We must likewise consider Susan Miller's observations that writing students are treated "finally . . . as emerging, or as failed, but never as actually responsible 'authors' " and that "students in those freshman courses taken to be at the center of composition studies are socially and politically imagined as children whose Victorian innocence retains a tainted need for 'civilizing' " (196). Moreover, as Marguerite Helmers has documented in one strand of our disciplinary discourse, scholarship in composition consistently constructs students as people who suffer from some essential deficiency or lack—or, conversely, as people who suffer from bestial, alien excesses of some kind—but in either event, as people who thus always stand in opposition to the instructor's aims.

Furthermore, for a full rendering of this keyword, we must also begin excavating the more commonly invoked but far more implicit versions of the people referred to in informal uses of the word *students*. In the discussion sessions following papers presented at the 1994 Conference on College Composition and Composition convention, for instance, the term was used to represent the people who populate composition classes as, among other things, nascent rhetor/citizens, apprentices who learn the trade by imitating the work processes of their masters, novitiates undergoing rites of passage to enter a hallowed and cloistered community, angry and alienated persons susceptible to conservative propaganda, disempowered and helpless people unaware that they are being sucked into white, male, heterosexual, able-bodied, capitalistic, corporate drone-ism, and as heroes who struggle valorously to resist this same co-optation. These discussions also imagined students as egocentric, ignorant, unprepared, lost, and fearful people with low self-esteem who need nurturing, guidance, and survival skills, as people unconscious of their own lives and in danger of losing their own lives as they move into and across the university, as uncultured, uncouth, irresponsible, immature, and television-addled ingrates and illiterates who are not serious about their studies, as people who expect to fail, as problems to be fixed, as spaces to be colonized, as texts to be read, as stories to be rewritten, as clients, and as products. But always, it seems, the disciplinary language of composition studies constructs students as Others, as people (or things) that are fundamentally quite different from their teachers.

Paul Heilker
Virginia Tech

Works Cited

Bloom, Allan. 1987. *The Closing of the American Mind.* New York: Touchstone.

Carter, Steven. 1969. "Freshman English and the Art of Empathy." *College Composition and Communication* 20: 39–42.

Crowley, Sharon. 1995. "Teaching in the Field of Dreams." Paper presented at the annual convention of the Conference on College Composition and Communication, Washington, D.C., 24 March.

Farber, Jerry. 1970. *The Student as Nigger.* New York: Simon and Schuster.

Faigley, Lester. 1992. *Fragments of Rationality: Postmodernity and the Subject of Composition.* Pittsburgh: University of Pittsburgh Press.

Garner, W. L. 1966. "The Dilemmas of Programming." *College Composition and Communication* 17: 227–232.

Graff, Gerald. 1992. *Beyond the Culture Wars: How Teaching the Conflicts Can Revitalize American Education.* New York: Norton.

Harkin, Patricia. 1993. "Teaching the Commodities." Paper presented at the annual convention of the Modern Language Association, Toronto, Ontario, Canada, 29 December.

Helmers, Marguerite. 1994. *Writing Students: Composition Testimonials and Representations of Students.* Albany: State University of New York Press.

Lunsford, Andrea. 1992. "Race, Class, Gender." Paper presented at the University of New Hampshire Fifth Biennial Conference on Writing, Durham, New Hampshire, October.

Miller, Susan. 1991. *Textual Carnivals: The Politics of Composition.* Carbondale: Southern Illinois University Press.

Murray, Donald M. 1969. "Finding Your Own Voice: Teaching Composition in an Age of Dissent." *College Composition and Communication* 20: 118–123.

O'Reilley, Mary Rose. 1989. " 'Exterminate . . . the Brutes'—And Other Things that Go Wrong in Student-Centered Teaching." *College English* 51: 142–146.

Zoellner, Robert. 1969. "Talk-Write: A Behavioral Pedagogy for Composition." *College English* 30: 267–320.

style

The "word 'style' has been a source of particular confusion," Seymour Chatman has said, because its multiple "senses compete in a peculiarly obfuscating way" (72). Louis T. Milic (1966) likewise observed that a "slipshod kind of definition" has reduced the term to "expressing a mere *je-ne-suis-quoi* of distinctiveness" (125). Hence, the meanings of style within composition studies are complex and contradictory. Chatman, citing John Middleton Murry, posits four definitions of style: " 'personal idiosyncrasy of expression, . . . the power of lucid exposition, . . . the complete realization of a universal significance in a personal and particular expression, . . . and ornamentation' " (72–73). And Frank D'Angelo imagines style in both organic and economic terms. There are "embryonic phases" that characterize "an evolving style," he says. Yet, students should also "assimilat[e] the best features of a writer's style" to better stock their "meager store[s] of stylistic resources" (283).

Style has also long been invoked as a quantifiable object. In 1966, Milic contended that style "must be described in concrete and verifiable terms, which finally means, in quantitative terms" (126). Similarly, style has often been represented as something divisible into its constituent parts. William Strunk and E. B. White discuss *The Elements of Style*, for example, with White defining style as "the rules of usage and principles of composition" (xii). A similar perspective is apparent in Joseph M. Williams's well-known book, in which style—defined as "clarity and grace" in one's written expression—is considered in ten lessons.

While Richard Lanham has argued that "[s]tyle must be taught for and as what it is—a pleasure, a grace, a joy, a delight" (20), Winston Weathers has suggested that many students "think of style as a kind of aesthetic luxury" (144), as a "dainty humanistic pastime" (145). To better interest students in style, he said, teachers should "say that style is the proof of a human being's individuality[,] . . . is a gesture of personal freedom against inflexible states of mind" (144). In contrast, Gary Sloan contends that the "pervasive view that styles are myriad and strikingly diverse, inescapable marks of self, probably stems from the illusion that we have recognized characteristic style when what we have really recognized is characteristic subject matter" (507). Like Sloan, Tim Shopen argues that styles do not vary "without limit from individual to individual" (777). Rather, Shopen imagines "style as a set of criteria" (776), contextually- and culturally-determined criteria that writers use to choose the most effective utterances from the among the possible utterances generated by their grammars (777).

Richard Ohmann has emphasized that style, as it is represented in most textbooks, is an ideological force pushing "the student writer always toward the language that most nearly reproduces the immediate experience and away from language that might be used to understand it, transform it, and relate it to everything else." The "preferred style," he says, teaches students to value ahistoricism, empiricism, fragmentation, solipsism, and denial of conflict (396). Richard L. Graves, noting a different bias, suggests that many teachers believe that "style is like *class*, or *grace*, or even *sublimity* itself," that "style is something grand, something far beyond the ken of the unwashed adolescents one sees everyday" (186).

Nonetheless, Graves concludes, style has heuristic, meaning-making, epistemological force. Style, he says, is "a way of finding and explaining what is true. Its purpose is not to impress but to express" (190). One thing that style expresses, according to Jerome Thale, is a writer's "habits of mind." Thale contends that style "comes from, and therefore reveals something of, the writer's habitual way of seeing reality, and . . . is one of the ways in which a similar way of looking at the world is created for the reader" (286).

There have been repeated representations of style as either a dualistic or monistic entity. "There are only three real theories of style," Milic (1965) argues. The most familiar, "rhetorical dualism," implies "that ideas exist wordlessly and can be dressed in a variety of outfits, depending on the need for the occasion." The second theory, "individualist or psychological monism," maintains that "style is the man" (67), that "style is the expression of the student's mind and personality" (69). In other words, as Elizabeth D. Rankin puts it, "If the classicists view style as a conscious art to be mastered, the romantics see it as an unconscious voice to be discovered[,] . . . as a capacity to be realized" (307). Aesthetic monism, "the most modern theory of style," Milic (1965) contends, "denies the possibility of any separation between content and form[,] . . . [any] seam between meaning and style" (67).

While arguing for an inclusive view, John T. Gage nonetheless also contrasts dualistic and monistic theories of style, noting that in "the one case, the reality of the thing said and the way in which it is said are assumed to exist separately; in the other case they are not." In monistic theory, he says, we see "[s]tyle as the integration of personality[,] . . . as a process" which identifies "form and content[,] . . . content and person, and in some cases content and truth" (618). In dualistic theory, on the other hand, we see "[s]tyle as the application of conscious choice[,] . . . as a structure of elements" that "separate[s] form and content[,] . . . self from expression," and self "from the truth" (619). Thus, for Gage, "the problem of style is more than a linguistic or rhetorical problem. It is also an epistemological one." And thus, also, an ideological one: as Gage writes

> Ideology bears on our conception of style precisely at the point that we consider language as either adequate or inadequate to the task of depicting reality[,] . . . [which] depends on the sort of reality that is posited, and on the further question of the mind's ability to perceive it. (616)

But for Walker Gibson, style is at least one remove from reality. Style, he says, is how writers "present to us a *self*, the assumed author, not to be confused with that complex mass of chaotic experience making up the writer as human being" (13). Gibson contends that style is thus a means of "identifying ourselves and defining our relation with others," of "dramatizing a personality or voice," and that "[s]uch self-dramatizations in language are what I mean by style" (x).

We should acknowledge, as Rankin has, that style has been constructed in composition studies as one of the prominent features of the old paradigm (301); as something that exists in opposition to invention (302); as an amalgam of prescriptive "conventions" and "mechanics" (304); as a "low-level goal" in cognitive process models of writing (303); and as something that can "impede the composing process for many of our students" (305). Moreover, Rankin says, one pervasive result of the "paradigm shift" is that "style as a pedagogical concept . . . is out of style" (300). Style seems out of style as a theoretical concept as well. Since 1985, perhaps because of a burgeoning interest in discipline-specific, academic discourse conventions, style has been practically ignored in composition's scholarly journals and books.

These two developments notwithstanding, style continues to appear in writing textbooks, where it is frequently represented as a refined use of language which separates good writing from correct writing (e.g., Skwire and Wiener 474). Other times, style is invoked as one of the five canons of classical rhetoric, as a type of rhetorical appeal, and as consciously constructed tropes and schemes that make writing memorable (e.g., Crusius and Channell). The explicit definitions of style in textbooks range from the prosaic—style "as any use of words that sets itself apart from the most ordinary and predictable" (Rice 4)—to the poetic—style as "the ordinary materials of this world so poised and perfected as to stand out from the landscape and compel a second look" (Baker 13).

Paul Heilker
Virginia Tech

Works Cited

Baker, Sheridan. 1990. *The Practical Stylist*, 6th edition. New York: Harper & Row.

Chatman, Seymour. 1967. " 'Style': A Narrow View." *College Composition and Communication* 18: 72–76.

Crusius, Timothy, and Carolyn E. Channell. 1995. *The Aims of Argument*. Mountain View, CA: Mayfield.

D'Angelo, Frank. 1973. "Imitation and Style." *College Composition and Communication* 24: 283–290.

Gage, John T. 1980. "Philosophies of Style and Their Implications for Composition." *College English* 41: 615–622.

Gibson, Walker. 1966. *Tough, Sweet and Stuffy*. Bloomington: Indiana University Press.

Graves, Richard L. 1974. "A Primer for Teaching Style." *College Composition and Communication* 25: 186–190.

Lanham, Richard. 1974. *Style: An Anti-Textbook*. New Haven, CT: Yale University Press.

Milic, Louis T. 1965. "Theories of Style and Their Implications for the Teaching of Composition." *College Composition and Communication* 16: 66–69, 126.

———. 1966. "Metaphysics in the Criticism of Style." *College Composition and Communication* 17: 124–129.

Ohmann, Richard. 1979. "Use Definite, Specific, Concrete Language." *College English* 41: 390–397.

Rankin, Elizabeth D. 1985. "Revitalizing Style: Toward a New Theory and Pedagogy." *The Writing Teacher's Sourcebook*, 3rd edition. Ed. Edward P. J. Corbett, Gary Tate, and Nancy Myers. New York: Oxford University Press. 300–309.

Rice, Scott. 1993. *Right Words, Right Places*. Belmont, CA: Wadsworth.

Shopen, Tim. 1974. "Some Contributions from Grammar to the Theory of Style." *College English* 35: 775–798.

Skwire, David, and Harvey S. Wiener. 1993. *Student's Book of College English*, 6th edition. New York: Macmillan.

Sloan, Gary. 1981. "Mistaking Subject Matter for Style." *College English* 43: 502–507.

Thale, Jerome. 1968. "Style and Anti-Style: History and Anti-History." *College English* 29 (1968): 286–302.

Weathers, Winston. 1970. "Teaching Style: A Possible Anatomy." *College Composition and Communication* 21: 144–149.

White, E. B. 1979. "Introduction." *The Elements of Style*, 3rd edition, by William Strunk, Jr., and E. B. White. New York: Macmillan. xi–xvii.

Williams, Joseph M. 1981. *Style: Ten Lessons in Clarity and Grace*. Glenview, IL: Scott, Foresman.

teacher

The contested meanings of *teacher* represent important ways scholars and instructors have (re)positioned the role of writing teacher in its relations to academia and students; they represent who and what writing instructors have been, are, and want better to become.

The constructions of this keyword consistently begin by imagining a hyperbolically bad teacher of the past or present away from which the writer's contribution will help readers move. In 1969, Sidney P. Moss, for instance, portrayed composition teachers as "one of the most conservative bodies on campus," as people who, "in a kind of idiot repetition," resist innovation and "persist in their pedagogy in the face of failure remarkable only for its predictability" (215). Seven years later, Janice M. Lauer similarly represented composition teachers of the past as people who wrote and read journals full of gimmickry, operated by rules of thumb with no theoretical base, perpetuated the courses they had as freshman, were slaves to faddish textbooks, and who entered the classroom despairing that there was nothing they could teach (342). In 1978, Donald C. Stewart maintained that the typical writing teacher, in many cases, had no knowledge whatsoever of composition history and theory (175). Soon after, Maxine Hairston (1982) contended that "most teachers of writing" help "promote a static and unexamined approach to teaching writing" by defining "writing courses as service courses and skills courses." The "overwhelming majority" of composition instructors, she argued, were "not professional writing teachers" since they did not research or publish or know the scholarship or read the journals or attend the meetings in the field (78–79). Writing in 1986, Hairston likewise portrayed composition teachers as people who until very recently "have not known what they were doing," as overworked, exhausted, resentful "slaves" and disillusioned, self-pitying "faculty martyrs" (119).

The most influential demonized version of teacher, however, has been the teacher-as-authority: the teacher as "a storehouse and proctor of course-content knowledge, released in rationed doses" (Eulert 65) and poured into the empty vessels of students' skulls; the teacher as "the principal defender of good taste, an evangelist of tradition, an heroic voice speaking up for order" (Murray 118). Naturally, some writers have attempted to construe this version positively. In 1963, for instance, A. M. Tibbetts stated flatly, "the teacher is the authority. He is the boss, the expert, the editor, the one with experience, the one who knows. . . . He is full of judgments, and he is not afraid of using words like *good, bad, right, wrong*" (371). But these advocates lost out in the end to those who transformed the teacher-as-authority into someone who fettered students with a host of "counterproductive proscriptions, prescriptions, and pet peeves" (Adams 264).

This quintessential teacher of the "old paradigm" marked the far end of the pendulum's swing. But from here the pendulum began its sweep into "new paradigm" redefinitions of the teacher-as-*non*-authority as composition scholars began hyperbolically reconstructing this keyword in the opposite direction. As early as 1967, for instance, S. Leonard Rubenstein contended that the good composition teacher should be "not merely profoundly ignorant," but also "superficially ignorant." "He should not only lack wisdom," Rubenstein said, "he should lack information." Thus, a good composition teacher "needs his students' help. . . . The students he teaches teach him" (127). The teacher is, then, at best, "a fellow learner, a collaborator" (128). Two years later, Donald M. Murray explicitly articulated the political strand of the teacher-as-non-authority, arguing that "[e]very writing teacher should be a revolutionary, doubting, questioning, challenging," and thus creating a "constructive chaos" in which students can work (118–119). Teaching writing as a process likewise inspired versions of the teacher-as-non-authority, such as "the Delphic Oracle who does not give answers but riddles . . . to provoke the writer beyond his clichés" and the midwife who can only stand by "hoping for the birth of the insight" (Lauer 342).

Thus, writing instructors are typically offered two mutually exclusive definitions of teacher in composition scholarship—one bad, one good—from which to "choose." Composition scholarship still generally lacks a functional synthesis of these extreme, polarized portraits. In 1983, however, Peter Elbow offered one solution. He said that writing instructors embrace (rather than struggle with) the contrary, "conflicting mentalities" in *teacher*, only; becoming fiercely loyal to both halves of this keyword: to both teachers' "maternal" obligation to students *and* their "paternal" obligation to knowledge and society, to both their role as supportive and nurturing "allies and hosts" to students (327–329) *and* their role as "hawk-eyed, critical-minded bouncers at the bar of civilization" (339).

There are other important constructions of teacher beyond this fundamental antithesis which should be noted. First, there is the pervasive trope of the composition teacher as reader and teacher of reading (writ large), as interpreter and critic of texts (in an expansive sense). Lad Tobin, for example, redefines the teacher as a (mis)reader of students' texts, "students themselves, of [one's] own unconscious motivations and associations, and, finally, of the interactive and dialectical nature of the teacher-student relationship" (335). *Teacher* in composition studies has come to include the notion of someone who reads (and teaches students to read) writing, culture, and the world alike using the most advanced tools of rhetorical and/or literary criticism. Another important recent construction is teacher as a proselytizer for (and supplier of) a particular epistemology and ideology. James A. Berlin (1982, 1988), for instance, has argued for an understanding of the composition teacher as someone who is necessarily an ideologue, who unavoidably privileges one rhetorical/economic version of reality over others. Furthermore, Marguerite H. Helmers has documented how composition scholarship often self-servingly portrays the writing teacher as a powerfully creative hero who triumphs in the quest to discover the cure for his or her students' deficiencies. Sheryl I. Fontaine has also noted how the common representation of teachers as people who "reacculturate" students into academic discourse communities comes "dangerously close" to constructing teachers as " 'missionaries' who willingly share the Word with those whose words are less valuable" (92). Of late, *teacher* in composition studies has also come to mean theorist, researcher, and knowledge-maker, has come to signify someone whose epistemological work, moreover, "challenge[s] a number of assumptions underlying the traditional (positivist) paradigm in education" (Ray 175). Finally, composition teachers have been represented as exploited economic entities, as "slaves" and "serfs" (Kytle 339), as "pickers, piece-workers, [and] sharecroppers," as "an amorphous and transient labor force, demoralized by work loads and depressed returns" (Szilak 27). Invented by senior faculty and administrators as "an insulation against the ravages of retrenchment" according to Dennis Szilak, the "disposable composition teacher . . . [represents] the greatest labor-saving and money-saving device since the folding chair" (26).

In sum, the diverse range of meanings of *teacher* in composition studies reflect just how complex the job is, represent the many, often contesting roles writing teachers are called upon and/or forced to play.

Paul Heilker
Virginia Tech

Works Cited

Adams, Dale T. 1976. "Not Back to Pedagogic Basics." *College Composition and Communication* 27: 264–267.

Berlin, James A. 1982. "Contemporary Composition: The Major Pedagogical Theories." *College English* 44: 765–777.

———. 1988. "Rhetoric and Ideology in the Writing Class." *College English* 50: 477–494.

Eulert, Don. 1967. "The Relationship of Personality Factors to Learning in College Composition." *College Composition and Communication* 18: 62–66.

Elbow, Peter. 1983. "Embracing Contraries in the Teaching Process." *College English* 45: 327–339.

Fontaine, Sheryl I. 1988. "The Unfinished Story of the Interpretive Community." *Rhetoric Review* 7: 86–96.

Hairston, Maxine. 1982. "The Winds of Change: Thomas Kuhn and the Revolution in the Teaching of Writing." *College Composition and Communication* 33: 76–88.

———. 1986. "On Not Being a Composition Slave." *Training the New Teacher of Composition*. Ed. Charles W. Bridges. Urbana, IL: National Council of Teachers of English. 117–124.

Helmers, Marguerite H. 1994. *Writing Students: Composition Testimonials and Representations of Students*. Albany: State University of New York Press.

Kytle, Ray. 1971. "Slaves, Serfs, or Colleagues—Who Shall Teach College Composition?" *College Composition and Communication* 22: 339–341.

Lauer, Janice M. 1976. "The Teacher of Writing." *College Composition and Communication* 27: 341–343.

Moss, Sidney P. 1969. "Logic: A Plea for a New Methodology in Freshman Composition." *College Composition and Communication* 20: 215–222.

Murray, Donald M. 1969. "Finding Your Own Voice: Teaching Composition in an Age of Dissent." *College Composition and Communication* 20: 118–123.

Ray, Ruth. 1992. "Composition from the Teacher-Research Point of View." *Methods and Methodology in Composition Research*. Ed. Gesa Kirsch and Patricia A. Sullivan. Carbondale: Southern Illinois University Press. 172–189.

Rubenstein, S. Leonard. 1967. "From Need to Desire." *College English* 29: 126–128.

Stewart, Donald C. 1978. "Composition Textbooks and the Assault on Tradition." *College Composition and Communication* 29: 171–175.

Szilak, Dennis. 1977. "Teachers of Composition: A Re-Niggering." *College English* 39: 25–32.

Tibbetts, A. M. 1964. "Two Cheers for the Authoritarian." *College English* 25: 370–373.

Tobin, Lad. 1991. "Reading Students, Reading Ourselves: Revising the Teacher's Role in the Writing Class." *College English* 53: 333–348.

voice

The term *voice* in composition theory and pedagogy marks a profoundly wide intersection of meaning. It has been variously deployed as a rallying cry for expressivism (Stewart), a symbol for the stage of maturity in a schema of women's intellectual development (Belenky *et al.*), as a marker for resistance to political oppression (hooks), and as a metaphor or replacement term for style, naturalness, persona, authority, essence, and a variety of other abstractions. Its expansive scope as a signifier has prompted both a range of pedagogical applications and serious questions about its usefulness—even among those who use it (Elbow). As Darsie Bowden suggests, "voice is at the nexus of some of our most fundamental and overlapping concerns as teachers and theorists" (173–174).

Bowden locates a reliance on other "aural metaphors such as tone, rhythm, harmony, and euphony" in writing textbooks produced in the 1870s, near the very beginnings of organized, secondary-level American writing instruction. Although the concerted conflation of classical (oral) rhetoric and writing instruction would be in progress for nearly a century, according to Bowden the specific metaphor of *voice* didn't emerge until the 1960s. In 1962 Walker Gibson uses the term as a metaphor for persona, "an artificial product of the author's imagination" (11). Mixing both oral and literate examples, Gibson argues that "[w]e all employ different voices for different occasions," and that an effective writer "sees that he, too, must choose a voice, a role, a kind of personality as he expresses whatever it is he's got to say in language" (11). Gibson values a student "who is very aware all the time of the arbitrary man-made quality of his voice, the particular projection or personality he is putting before us," one who is "constantly conscious . . . [of] the gap between the blur of experience and the very artificial order of language" (13).

This sense of voice-as-construct would wait nearly thirty years for further articulation (Fulwiler). Use of the term in published articles through the rest of the sixties and seventies equated voice with what Donald Stewart called "a new philosophy, . . . a steadily increasing concern for the integrity of the written word. . . . [T]he words of the persuader must be true in the broadest and intensest meaning of that word" (224). Stewart declares that this "mood of progressive thinking about composition" is summed up in the introduction of Rohmann and Wlecke's *The Personal Voice*:

> "Voice," in good writing, is the liberated yet controlled expression of a human being deeply committed to what he is saying. A true voice will appear, if at all, when the writer ceases to evade or merely toy with his ideas and with his personal experience. . . . [By] merely permitting our students to echo the categories of their culture, they would never discover themselves within the writing process. (Qtd. in Stewart 226)

Likewise, finding a relationship between "natural voice," consistency, and confidence, Taylor Stoehr declared in 1968 that "[v]oice is the pervasive reflection, in written or spoken language, of an author's character" (150).

Bowden contends that advocates of personal voice during this period almost invariably equated "authenticity" with orality and declared students' attempts at "academic writing" counterfeit or clumsy. Stoehr asserts that "a writer has only one voice . . . his idiosyncratic way of talking" (150), but that "discovery" of it—even for a writer like Mark Twain—might occur only "gradually after many trials" (157). Robert Zoellner's "talk-write pedagogy," advanced in 1969, proposed "a vitalizing of the scribal mode, so that students' written 'voice' begins to take on some of the characteristics of the speaking 'voice' " (301). I. Hashimoto chronicles the use of voice as something of an umbrella term throughout the seventies and eighties for the pedagogical objectives of authenticity, honesty, and "self discovery" in the work of Ken Macrorie, Sheridan Baker, Donald Murray, Maxine Hairston, and Peter Elbow. According to Elbow, when writing in "real voice," "the words somehow issue from the writer's center—even if in a slippery way—and produce resonance which gets the words more powerfully to a reader's center" (qtd. in Hashimoto 73).

Yet according to Hashimoto, "the more [Elbow] writes, the more he fuzzes the issue up" (73). Declaring voice "non-rational," "mystical and abstract," and "anti-intellectual," Hashimoto maintains that it may be "nothing more than a vague phrase conjured up by English teachers to impress and motivate the masses to write more, confess more, and be happy" (76). Arguing that readers bring their particular matrices of values and concerns to any given text, and that each of us responds more favorably to given "content and context," Hashimoto suggests that voice is something constructed not by the writer but by the reader. — *interesting!*

Voice has also been a critical metaphor in two book-length social science studies that have powerfully influenced feminist theory and pedagogy in composition, Carol Gilligan's *In a Different Voice* and *Women's Ways of Knowing: The Development of Self, Voice, and Mind*, by Mary Belenky, Blythe Clinchy, Nancy Goldberger, and Jill Tarule.

Gilligan reports the results of three interview studies based on questions "about conceptions of self and morality, about experiences of conflict and choice." Gilligan is careful in her Introduction to make explicit the metaphorical use of voice to stand for the phrase "mode of thought," and she disavows any effort to generalize about "either sex," claiming that "the different voice . . . is characterized not by gender but theme" (2). In examining the interview data, however, Gilligan determined that "women's voices sounded distinct" (1). And it is through the lens of gendered difference rather than thematic difference that Gilligan's work continues to be read. Voice, for Olivia Frey, equates with a "feminine epistemic authority," a quality she locates in an essay by Jane Tompkins. "Me and My Shadow" is, Frey suggests, a

> brave experiment in writing literary criticism in her own personal voice . . . a new feminist language that is not derivative of male language, a new language that is accessible, concrete, real, an embodiment of the feminine. (507)

Her use of the term as both a representation of the personal and as a "language" notwithstanding, by characterizing Tompkins' achievement of voice as "a struggling to find," Frey uses the term as a sign of empowerment, a privileged position in a pattern of epistemological growth.

No text has been more influential in advancing this sense of voice than *Women's Ways of Knowing*. In "in-depth" interviews with 135 women, Belenky *et al.* "found that women repeatedly used the metaphor of voice to depict their intellectual and ethical development; and that the development of a sense of voice, mind, and self were intricately intertwined" (18). Elizabeth Flynn assents on both counts; suggesting that selflessness and voicelessness are isomorphic, Flynn articulates a writing pedagogy in which women students move "toward the development of an authentic voice and a way of knowing that integrates intuition with authoritative knowledge" (429). bell hooks—although warning against what she calls the "static notion" of authenticity and the "cliched . . . insistence that women share a common speech" (52–53)—uses voice in this developmental sense. "[C]oming to voice is an act of resistance," she writes. The evolution, for hooks, is from "object to subject"; "the liberatory voice" is "that way of speaking that is no longer determined by one's status as object—as oppressed being" (55).

It seems clear that one cannot employ the term *voice* without inviting controversy; when used in discussions about writing it is perhaps a too obvious trope, one that is often charged with invoking *dissimilarities* before it can achieve explanatory power. And use of the term quickly draws one into oppositional debates about self/community, orality/literacy. Yet judging by recent publications, voice shows no signs of falling out of the professional conversation any time soon. Essay collections edited by Peter Elbow—who promotes voice as a "practical critical tool" (*Voice and Writing* xlvii)—and Kathleen Yancy are recommended as entry points into the "discussion" about voice.

Peter Vandenberg
DePaul University, Chicago

Works Cited

Belenky, Mary Field, Blythe McVicker Clinchy, Nancy Rule Goldberger, and Jill Mattuck Tarule. 1986. *Women's Ways of Knowing: The Development of Self, Voice, and Mind.* New York: Basic.

Bowden, Darsie. 1995. "The Rise of a Metaphor: *Voice* in Composition Pedagogy." *Rhetoric Review* 14: 173–188.

Elbow, Peter, ed. 1994. *Voice and Writing.* Landmark Essays Series, Volume Four. Davis, CA: Hermagoras.

Flynn, Elizabeth. 1988. "Composing as a Woman." *CCC* 39: 423–435.

Frey, Olivia. 1990. "Beyond Literary Darwinism: Women's Voices and Critical Discourse." *College English* 52: 507–526.

Fulwiler, Toby. 1990. "Looking and Listening for My Voice." *College Composition and Communication* 41: 214–220.

Gibson, Walker. 1962. "The Voice of the Writer." *College Composition and Communication* 8: 10–13.

Gilligan, Carol. 1982. *In a Different Voice: Psychological Theory and Women's Development.* Cambridge: Harvard University Press.

Hashimoto, I. 1987. "Voice as Juice: Some Reservations about Evangelic Composition." *College Composition and Communication* 38: 70–80.

hooks, bell. 1994. " 'When I Was a Young Soldier for the Revolution': Coming to Voice." In Elbow, 51–58.

Stewart, Donald. 1969. "Prose with Integrity: A Primary Objective." *College Composition and Communication* 20: 223–227.

Stoehr, Taylor. 1968. "Tone and Voice." *College English* 30: 150–161.

Yancy, Kathleen Blake, ed. 1995. *Voices on Voice: A (Written) Discussion.* Urbana: NCTE.

writing center

Writing centers were originally called "writing laboratories," a term that reflects the influence of the Dalton Laboratory Plan that originated in England and was introduced to American education in the 1920s and 1930s. This plan called for extending the laboratory method of instruction in the sciences to all subjects within the curriculum (Durkin; Douglas). Writing students were to learn principles and theories of composition in the classroom and apply their knowledge in specialized classrooms, or laboratories, structured to encourage self-paced learning, individualized instruction, and collaborative group work (Sheridan).

The first writing laboratories assisted all students, but the focus of instruction rapidly shifted to aiding remedial students "whose writing skills are not sufficiently developed to permit them to enroll in the regular freshman course" (Reeve *et al.* 17). As a consequence, writing laboratories began to serve "as remedial agencies for removing students' deficiencies in composition" (Moore 388) and became more commonly known as "writing clinics," a term that embodied the idea of a site where individuals convened for supplemental or remedial instruction. This focus on remediation is not surprising since writing laboratories and clinics emerged historically under the paradigm of current-traditional rhetoric, with its emphasis upon diagnosing and correcting formal errors in students' writing. They also came to prominence at a time when the conservative view of the role of education in society was the dominant view. Consequently, writing laboratories and clinics developed from this perspective "served to foster the conservative agenda of having task-oriented students working to achieve the 'markers,' or measurable objectives, by which both intellectual progress and mastery of the techniques of literacy could be measured" (Murphy 277). Historically, the conservative agenda defined writing center practice throughout most of its early development and was given added potency by the introduction of computer technology into writing centers in the 1960s and 1970s. Computers allowed for rapid and quantifiable measurements of students' skill levels and also provided a means for instructing students on grammar, syntax, spelling, and punctuation through computerized drills, reviews, and tests.

The early history of writing centers problematized their role within the educational system by identifying writing centers almost exclusively with remediation, by separating writing center practice from classroom practice, and by placing writing centers at the margins of the academy as peripheral and supplemental forms of instruction. Peter Carino, for example, argues that the identification of writing centers with diagnosis, treatment, and cures and the use of descriptors like "clinic" and "laboratory" enclose writing centers in "a metaphor of illness" that "degrades" the students who seek assistance there (33), while Stephen M. North claims that the narrow focus on remediation of early writing centers forever defined the writing center as "the grammar and drill center, the fix-it shop, the first aid station" (437).

The paradigm shift in composition instruction from "product" to "process" that marked the decline of current-traditional rhetoric and the ascent of expressivism during the 1970s and 1980s generated a concomitant redefinition of writing center theory and practice. Particular attention was given to the purpose of writing centers and their role in the academy, with a heightened focus upon professionalism and defining the impact of writing center practice upon composition pedagogy (Simpson; Olson and Ashton-Jones). The term "writing center" replaced the earlier designations of "writing laboratories" and "writing clinics," which were abandoned for their scientific and impersonal connotations as well as for their imprecise descriptions of the work conducted in these sites. "Writing center" as a descriptor matched the philosophy to which writing centers aspired: to serve as the "centers of consciousness about writing on campus, a kind of physical locus for the idea and ideals of college or university or high school commitment to writing" (North 446). The focus upon the writing processes of individual students that characterized the expressivist movement prompted explorations of writing center pedagogy and reexaminations of the supposed differences between writing center practice and classroom practice (Healy). Research on the individualized instruction and peer mentoring developed in writing centers led to the identification of writing centers less with remediation and more with alternative forms of pedagogy—particularly those that embraced non-hegemonic collaboration and examinations of small-group dynamics (Clark; Lunsford). As the role of the writing teacher was called into question as a perhaps intrusive and unnecessary authority figure (Elbow), the non-hierarchical structure of writing center interactions between students and tutors offered options for investigating non-traditional pedagogical models.

An impetus for viewing writing centers as the "center" of writing concerns on a campus was also provided by the writing across the curriculum movement (WAC), with its centrifugal force of moving writing instruction out across the disciplines and its centripetal force of drawing concerns and explorations to a "center" or investigative base (Wallace). Theorists saw a similar pattern of centrifugal and centripetal forces in writing center efforts (Hughes), and, on a number of campuses, writing centers, and WAC programs joined forces to foster incorporating writing instruction into classroom pedagogy as a means for enhancing students' capacities for both self-discovery and critical thinking (Waldo). Ironically, the WAC movement also problematized both the role and the definition of the writing center as a "center" in that successful WAC programs prompted the development of satellite writing centers to meet the needs and address the rhetorical concerns of each discipline (Hughes). As colleges and departments within the university began to establish writing centers of their own, the concept of a "center" as a central site serving an entire campus was replaced by multiple sites of writing instruction that addressed local and specific issues within disciplines and divisions of the university (Waldo).

Contemporary writing centers continue to deal with the issues that surround the concept of a "center." The introduction of sophisticated computer technology has further contributed to the "de-centering" of the writing center through electronic networks that allow individuals to access the writing center from virtually any location in the world. OWLs, or online writing centers, have called into question traditional notions of the writing center as a physical place or location on a campus and have generated a need to reconsider face-to-face conferencing and "teaching one-to-one" (Harris) as the defining feature of writing center pedagogy.

Philosophical challenges to what the purpose and role of a writing center should be have matched the "de-centering" of writing centers physically. While writing centers traditionally have been understood in terms of their service function to the academy, advocates of social constructionism, feminism, and cultural studies have urged reconceptualizing the writing center in terms of social agency. These theorists view the writing center as a language community, a "Burkean parlor," concerned with investigating how knowledge is socially constructed by discourse communities (Lunsford) and argue that the writing center is in a good position "to serve as a site of critique of the institutionalized structure of writing instruction in college" (Cooper 98). They also value the writing center's capacity to foster the values of "community and equality" within institutions as a means of reducing patriarchal hegemony (Woolbright 228).

Murphy and Law speculate that "as writing centers advance toward the next century, their scholarship and practice will continue to respond to the ways in which knowledge is created, assessed, and implemented within a culture" (xv). Both enterprises will emphasize "the writing center's role within society rather than solely its place within the academy" (xv). This focus represents an important philosophical shift in defining writing centers, a progression from instructional sites for remediation to epsitemological sites for investigating and critiquing "the social influences upon knowledge production within a culture" (Murphy and Law xv).

Christina Murphy
Texas Christian University

Works Cited

Carino, Peter. 1992. "What Do We Talk about When We Talk about Our Metaphors: A Cultural Critique of Clinic, Lab, and Center." *The Writing Center Journal* 13: 31–42.

Clark, Irene Lurkis. 1985. *Writing in the Center: Teaching in a Writing Center.* Dubuque: Kendall/Hunt.

Cooper, Marilyn. 1994. "Really Useful Knowledge: A Cultural Studies Agenda for Writing Centers." *The Writing Center Journal* 14: 97–111.

Douglas, Lucile. 1924. "Teaching English on the Dalton Plan." *English Journal* 13: 335–340.

Durkin, Margaret. 1926. "The Teaching of English in England under the Dalton Plan." *English Journal* 15: 256–266.

Elbow, Peter. 1973. *Writing without Teachers.* London: Oxford University Press.

Harris, Muriel. 1986. *Teaching One-to-One: The Writing Conference.* Urbana: National Council of Teachers of English.

Healy, Dave. 1993. "A Defense of Dualism: The Writing Center and the Classroom." *The Writing Center Journal* 14: 16–29.

Hughes, Bradley T. 1991. "Writing Center Outreach: Sharing Knowledge and Influencing Attitudes about Writing." *The Writing Center: New Directions.* Ed. Ray Wallace and Jeanne Simpson. New York: Garland. 39–55.

Lunsford, Andrea. 1991. "Collaboration, Control, and the Idea of a Writing Center." *The Writing Center Journal* 12: 3–10.

Moore, Robert H. 1950. "The Writing Clinic and the Writing Laboratory." *College English* 11: 388–393.

Murphy, Christina. 1991. "Writing Centers in Context: Responding to Current Educational Theory." *The Writing Center: New Directions.* Ed. Ray Wallace and Jeanne Simpson. New York: Garland. 276–288.

Murphy, Christina, and Joe Law. 1995. "Introduction." *Landmark Essays on Writing Centers.* Ed. Christina Murphy and Joe Law. Davis: Hermagoras Press. xi–xv.

North, Stephen M. 1984. "The Idea of a Writing Center." *College English* 46: 433–446.

Olson, Gary A., and Evelyn Ashton-Jones. 1988. "Writing Center Directors: The Search for Professional Status." *WPA: Writing Program Administration* 12: 19–28.

Reeve, Frederic E. *et al.* 1951. "Organization and Use of a Writing Laboratory." The Report of Workshop No. 9. *College Composition and Communication* 2: 17–19.

Sheridan, Marion C. 1926. "An Evaluation of the Dalton Plan." *English Journal* 15.7: 507–514.

Simpson, Jeanne H. 1985. "What Lies Ahead for Writing Centers: Position Statement on Professional Concerns." *The Writing Center Journal* 5/6: 35–39.

Waldo, Mark. 1993. "The Last Best Place for WAC: The Writing Center." *WPA: Writing Program Administration* 16: 15–26.

Wallace, Ray. 1988. "The Writing Center's Role in the Writing across the Curriculum Program." *The Writing Center Journal* 8: 43–48.

Woolbright, Meg. 1992. "The Politics of Tutoring: Feminism within the Patriarchy." *The Writing Center Journal* 13: 16–30.